IMAGES
of America

SUNCOOK VILLAGE

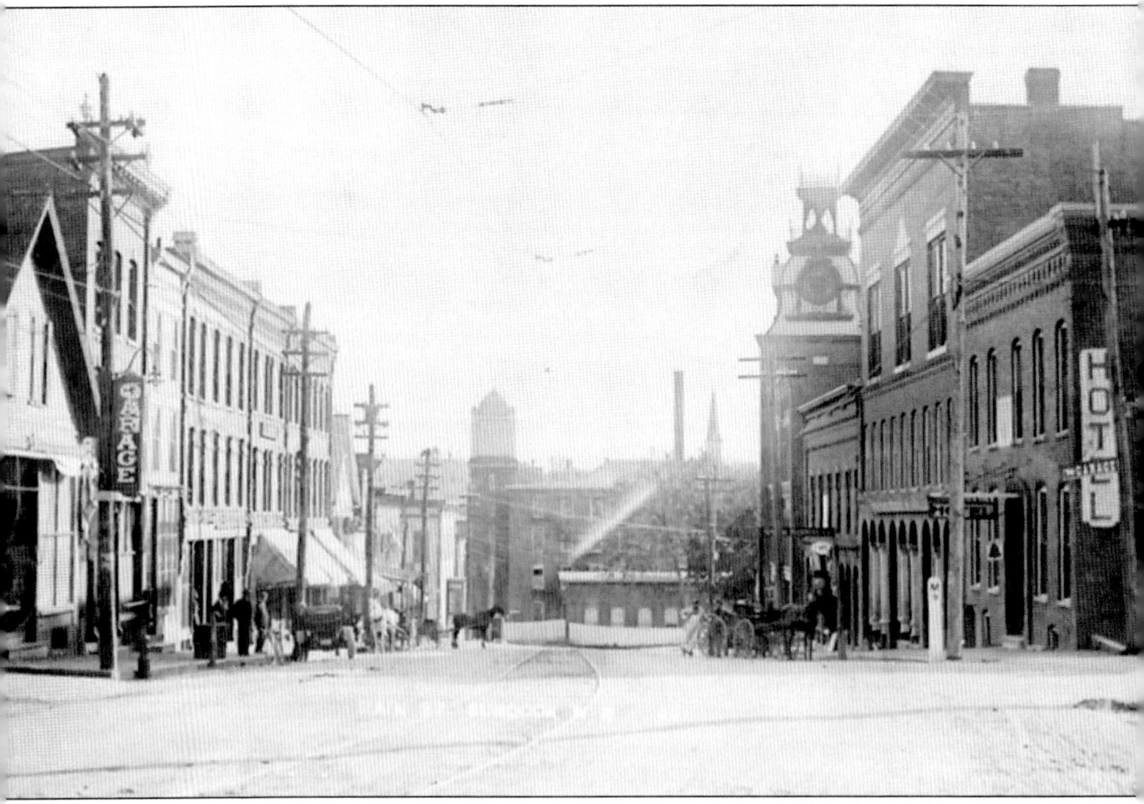

Main Street in Suncook Village is shown in this view looking south. The Webster Mill tower and the Boston and Maine (B&M) trolley tracks are in the center of the photograph. Although the horses and buggies outnumber the one automobile, the garage sign indicates the beginning of the transition. (Courtesy of Allenstown, New Hampshire, Historical Society.)

On the cover: The second National Association of Railroad Enthusiasts (NARE) Suncook Valley excursion pauses at the Suncook Railroad station with Suncook Valley No. 1 waiting for fans on November 4, 1934. This fan trip was sponsored by NARE. The group went from Hooksett to Center Barnstead. The man holding the flag in front of the engine is William (Bill) Moneypeny. The Suncook station was located on Exchange Street in the village. A second set of tracks leading to Fowler Brothers Grains was located directly behind the station. (Brent Michiels collection courtesy of Brent Michiels and Larry Perron.)

IMAGES
of America

SUNCOOK VILLAGE

Carol A. Martel

ARCADIA
PUBLISHING

ISBN 978-0-7385-5752-6

Published by Arcadia Publishing
Charleston SC, Chicago IL, Portsmouth NH, San Francisco CA

Printed in the United States of America

Library of Congress Catalog Card Number: 2007934558

For all general information contact Arcadia Publishing at:
Telephone 843-853-2070
Fax 843-853-0044
E-mail sales@arcadiapublishing.com
For customer service and orders:
Toll-Free 1-888-313-2665

Visit us on the Internet at www.arcadiapublishing.com

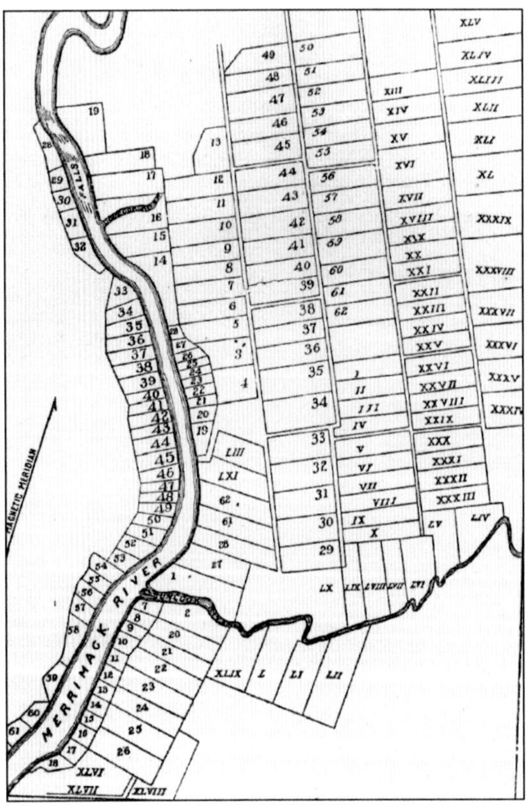

This Suncook Township, or Lovewells Township, map was drawn by N. F. Carter for the book *History of Pembroke, N.H. 1730–1895*. This map shows the first and second division of lots. The first division was listed numerically and the second division was listed alphabetically. Settlement in this township began between 1727 and 1730.

Contents

ACKNOWLEDGMENTS

While selecting the images for this pictorial history of Suncook Village, I examined over 1,000 photographs from numerous collections. The images chosen for this book were taken by hobbyists, historians, and professionals. They illustrate the landscape, development, growth, and cultural and social nucleus of Suncook Village. Joseph Wilkins, a local early-20th-century photographer, captured scenes around town. Railroad enthusiasts, now past, who recorded the last days of the railroad lines through photography were Howard T. Moulton, E. Harold Young, Albert G. Hale, Donald S. Robinson, William Moneypeny, Peter Cornwall, and Norton D. Clark. Railroad historian and author Brent Michiels has collected and preserved their work and many facets of local history through his vast photographic collection. I thank him for sharing his collection, his knowledge of the railroad and local history, and his time.

I am eternally grateful to Connie French for sharing her postcard collection and to Allenstown, New Hampshire, Historical Society archivist Claudette Verville, Pembroke Historical Society president Charlie Mitchell, George Rainville, and Larry Perron, for recording, collecting, and caring for photographic collections. Their work ensures the preservation of local history for future generations.

I would like to thank the many people and agencies who supplied documentation and photographs for this publication. Brent Michiels; Larry Perron; Charlie Mitchell; Connie French; Joyce McKay; George Rainville; Arlene and Victor Fleury; Bob St. Germaine; Jim and Jackie Lane; Armand and Claudette Verville; Roland Martel; Carol and Richard Merrill; Leandre Desrochers; James Garvin; Joan Bailey; Gloria Reeves; New Hampshire Division of Historical Resources; Allenstown, New Hampshire, Historical Society; Allenstown Library; Pembroke Historical Society; Pembroke Library; Meet Me In Suncook; Beverly Historical Society and Museum, Beverly, Massachusetts; and New Hampshire Historical Society.

For editing this publication, a special thank you to Pastor Dan Stauffacher, Brent Michiels, and Joyce Mc Kay.

My gratitude and love to my husband, Roland Martel, and to family members Sylvianne Martel and Rolande Duford, who answered my never-ending questions about the village they grew up in.

This publication is dedicated to the residents of Allenstown, Pembroke, and Suncook Village.

My Sincere Gratitude,
Carol A. Martel

INTRODUCTION

In August 1728, a tract of land known as Suncook Township was granted by the Province of Massachusetts Bay to Capt. John Lovewell's men who fought at Pigwacket. The first band of men visited the area in 1729 and shortly thereafter laid claim to the land and settled upon it. Early boundary disputes between the Province of New Hampshire and the Province of Massachusetts Bay resulted in the territory of Suncook being incorporated within two towns, northwestern Allenstown and southwestern Pembroke. Despite early controversies and boundary adjustments, Suncook Village maintains a strong sense of identity that continues into the present day.

Suncook Village is situated between the Suncook River Valley and Merrimack River Valley. The area is bounded by the Merrimack River to the west, Turnpike Road to the east (today known as Route 3), Broadway to the north, and the Allenstown and Hooksett town lines to the south. Suncook has often been an illusive name applied to places extending far beyond its true geographic boundaries. The name Suncook originated from a Native American term meaning "rocky river, place of the loon or goose." This term accurately described the Suncook riverbed and the Merrimack riverbed, which provided a natural habitat for ducks and geese. At their confluence, these two rivers created a more than adequate source for natural waterpower. This factor greatly contributed to the development of large mills and, in turn, a densely populated village.

As in all new colonies, life was riddled with the continuous uncertainty of Native American raids. The Buntins, Gaults, and Guays resided along the banks of the Merrimack and Suncook Rivers. In May 1747, James Carr, Robert Buntin, and Buntin's 10-year-old son Andrew crossed the Merrimack River opposite the mouth of the Suncook River. While working, they were surprised by Native Americans. Carr was shot and Robert and Andrew were captured and taken to Canada. They were sold to a French trader from Montreal, and 11 months later, they were ransomed and returned from Louisburg, Nova Scotia, to New England in the schooner *Brittania*. Andrew later served in the Revolutionary War.

American life changed dramatically during the Industrial Revolution. In Suncook, the opening of the Middlesex Canal system from Manchester to Concord in 1815 helped merchants to receive and ship more goods via river barges and boats. In 1812, Gen. John Stark's eldest son, Caleb, owned a cotton mill in Suncook. When Caleb escorted Gen. Marquis de Lafayette on a tour through New Hampshire in 1825, he stopped at his home in the Suncook Village business district.

The canal system was soon followed by the building of the Concord and Portsmouth Railroad line and the Suncook Valley Railroad, nicknamed the Blueberry Express. The scene was set at the confluence of the Suncook and Merrimack Rivers. The force of these rivers provided an adequate water source for powering large industrialized mills. By 1860, a plan for three large textile mills at Suncook was drawn. The village was about to become a part of the great mechanized and industrialized America connected to people and commerce on a national and international level.

The Pembroke Mill was constructed in 1860, the Webster Manufacturing Company was built in 1865, and the largest of all, the China Manufacturing Company, was built in 1868. All three mills were managed by the Suncook Mills Company. New railroads provided transportation for shipping and receiving large amounts of goods. Immigrants from many ethnic backgrounds were recruited in large numbers, particularly the French Canadians. The Suncook Mills built tenements to house the influx of new employees and boardinghouses were opened. The landscape of the once predominantly English village began to change as well as its culture. By the late 1800s, residents were predominantly French Canadian and the language most commonly spoken was French. Suncook Village became known as "Le Petite Canada."

As the village grew so did opportunities for employment. Many residents worked for the railroad, brickyards, sawmills, glassworks, or the granite quarry. The Main Street business district bustled and offered every provision or service needed. Trolleys traveled from Concord to Manchester and the Boston and Maine Railroad connected with Manchester, Concord, and Portsmouth. Hotels were built on Main Street to accommodate visitors or travelers. The Bartlett Hotel and Opera House stood five stories tall and was the largest hotel. Hayes Hall and Opera House offered entertainment from local performers, traveling shows, and concerts. There were ice cream parlors, billiard halls, bowling alleys, saloons, barrooms, and a Chinese laundry. Numerous social and cultural organizations were established, meeting at any one of several halls. With all it had to offer, Suncook Village was considered to be one of the most culturally desirable places to live in New England.

In the early 20th century, Suncook began to change. The New England textile industry was adversely affected by the depression. In September 1934, employees of the Suncook Mills went on strike. This dealt a final blow to the Boston-based textile conglomerate. On June 5, 1937, the Suncook Mills sold all of its residential holdings at public auction and placed the mills on the real estate market. Emerson Manufacturing Company of Hooksett purchased the Webster Mill and moved its furniture factory to Suncook. Textron Manufacturing Company purchased the China and Pembroke Mills. Textron produced synthetic fabrics and a product called Flight Tech. During World War II, Textron manufactured parachute cloth and fabric used to cover the fuselage of planes. The mills at Suncook became a high security area, and a fire hose house at the China Mill was converted to a police station for security guards. On December 16, 1942, the Suncook Mills received the Army-Navy Production Award. A ceremony was held at the China Mill, where an E flag was presented for the mills efforts and contributions during the war.

The mid-20th century brought dramatic changes to Suncook. Textile mills throughout New England were closing and it was necessary for residents to seek employment in other places; automobiles allowed them do so. In 1951, Textron sold Pembroke Mill to Emerson Lounge Company, who expanded operations utilizing the mill. The China Mill was leased and later purchased by Dole Suncook in 1968. Simultaneously, shopping centers began to open in the area. Most Main Street businesses moved or closed their doors, changing Suncook forever.

Given the extensive amount of research information and documentation, it would be impossible to completely convey in this condensed history what it was like to live in Suncook Village more than 100 years ago. It is hoped that through the photographic collections contained within this book, the reader may catch a glimpse of what it was like to be part of a community that lived in and loved their surroundings and their lifestyle. Despite disputes over land grants or boundaries and diversity, the name remains defended and most affectionately the same Suncook Village.

A considerable portion of Suncook Village has been determined to be eligible for the National Register of Historic Places. Only a small part of the business district is listed at this time. The remainder awaits the final application process.

One

Rivers, Water Transportation, Canals, and Dams

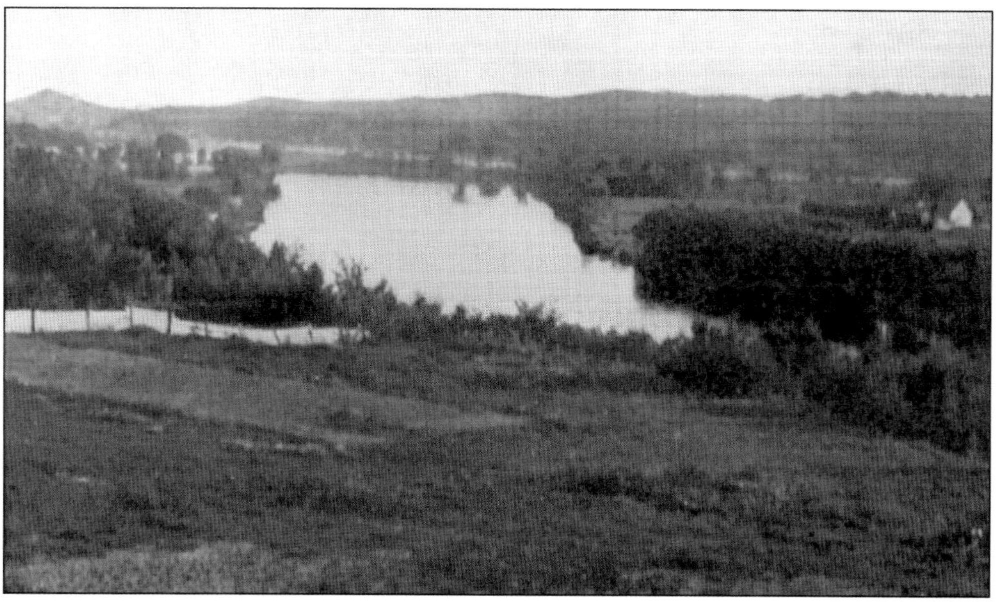

The Merrimack River and Suncook Village are picturesque in this view from Pembroke Hill. After the Middlesex Canal was opened for travel in 1803, a plan was formulated to make the Merrimack River navigable from Chelmsford, Massachusetts, to Concord through a series of canals and locks. The canal system continued to do well until the railroad was extended to Concord on September 6, 1842. The last canal toll was logged in 1851. (Courtesy of Connie French.)

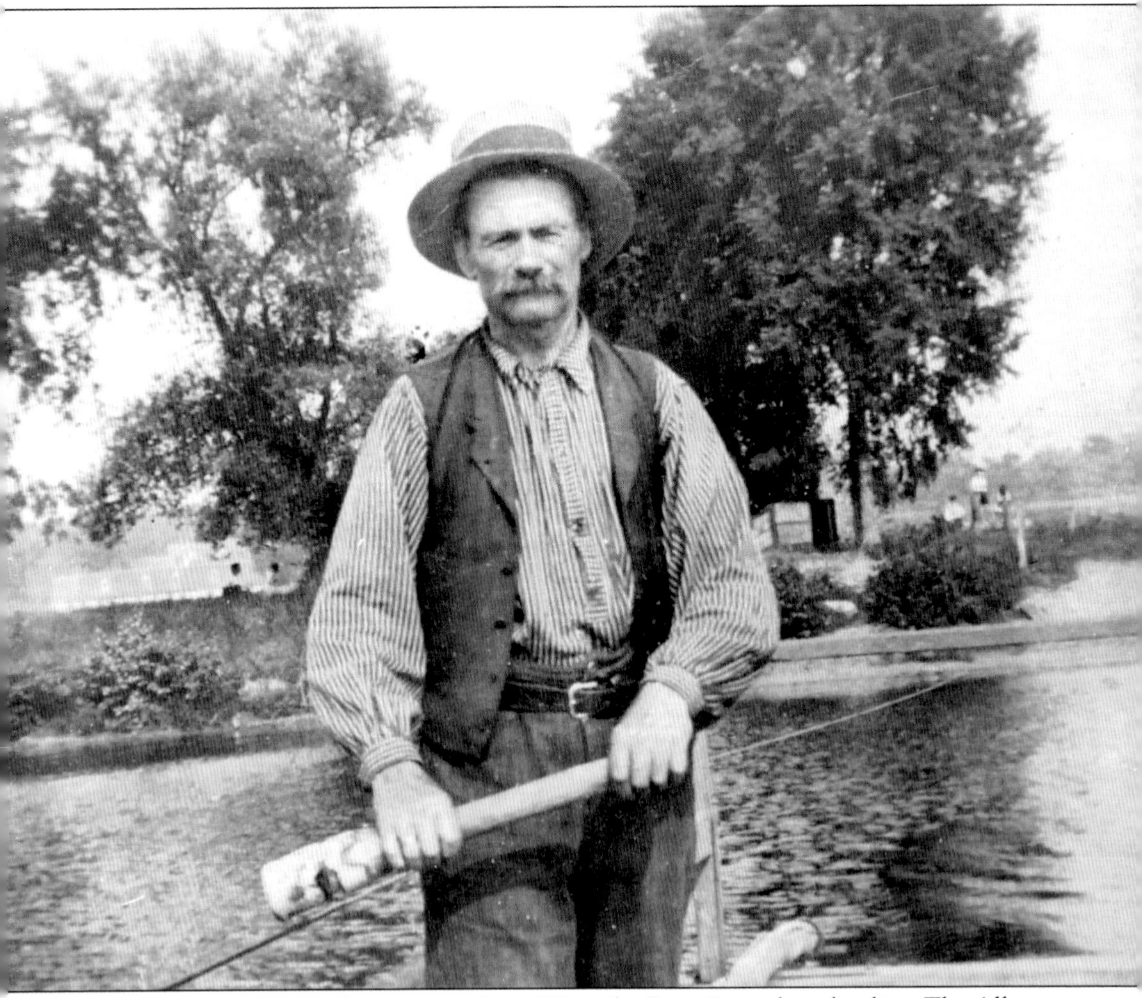

Ferry operator Jean Leduc is pictured in 1911 at the Ferry Street boat landing. The Allenstown and Bow ferry operated on the Merrimack River with landings on both sides of the river. This rope ferry carried passengers, animals, and goods. In 1809 the Amoskeag Canal at Amoskeag Falls opened with nine locks. The Hooksett Falls Canal was next in 1811 with two lift locks. The Bow Canal at Garvin's Falls was completed in 1812, consisting of a guard lock and three lift locks. Suncook's location connected it to the Merrimack River water transportation system. A store house for the Boston and Concord Boat Company was built close to the Merrimack River. Local manufacturers contracted shipment for their goods or owned canal boats or barges. Despite the decline of water transportation with the arrival of the railroad, ferries remained part of Suncook's transportation system into the early 20th century. (Courtesy of Allenstown, New Hampshire, Historical Society.)

This photograph of a young lady seated in a rowboat was taken on the Merrimack River close to the China Mill and ferry landing. During the 19th and early 20th century a variety of boats traveled the Merrimack River and its canals. Canal boats, river boats, and barges transported goods through the extended water ways. A steamboat called the *Favorita*, was owned by mill agent David Lymen Jewell who used it for hauling cotton waste and for social excursions with visiting dignitaries. (Courtesy of Roland Martel.)

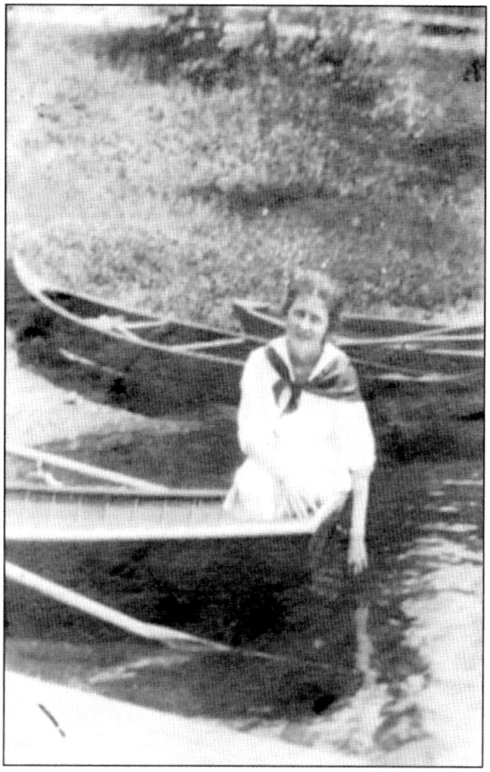

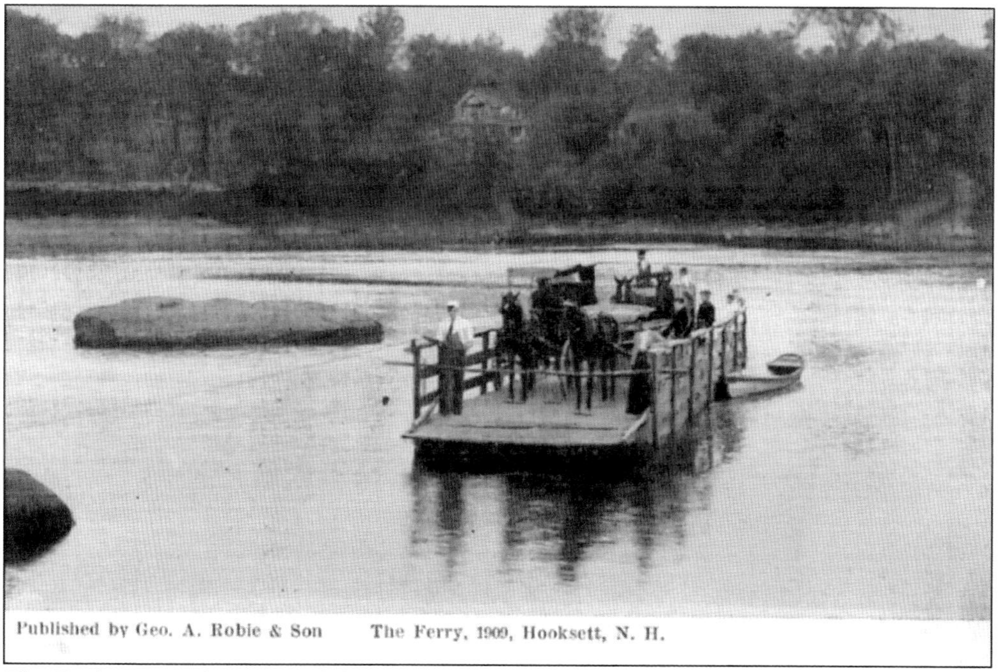

The Hooksett rope ferry crossed the Merrimack River at Martin's Ferry landing in south Hooksett not far from Suncook. This large ferry was probably similar to the Allenstown and Bow ferry of the early 1900s. (Photograph by Frank Swallow; courtesy of Brent Michiels.)

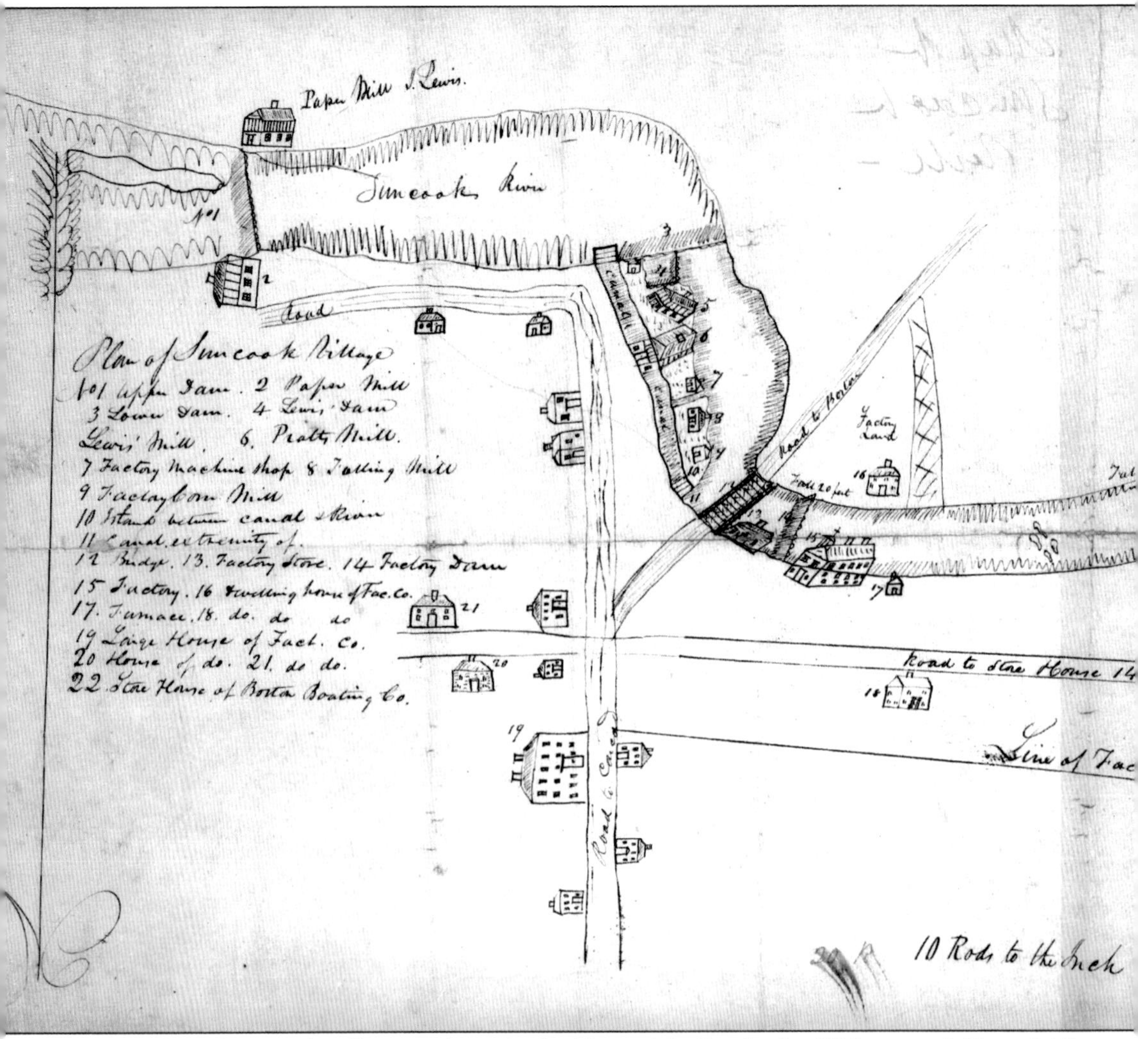

The plan of Suncook Village predates the building of the Pembroke, Webster, and China Mills. A few factory dwelling houses were in existence to house mill workers. The furnace may have been a retort used to generate gas for lighting the mills. John Cochran created the island by cutting the canal for the purpose of water or mill privileges. The Boston Boating Company owned a storehouse located on the Merrimack River. This storehouse was used to receive goods, such as cotton, and to ship locally-made goods by the Merrimack River and the canal system.

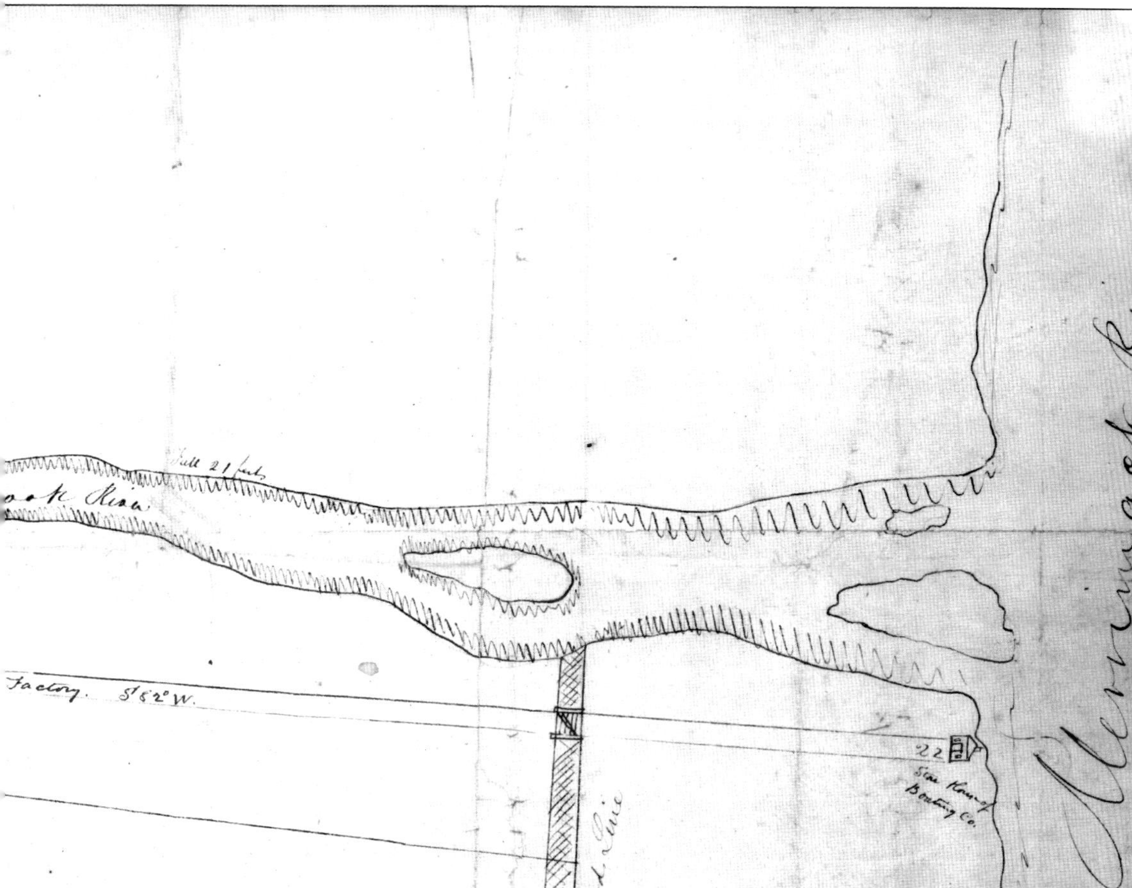

The plan's key lists the following: Upper Dam (1); Paper Mill (2); Lower Dam (3); Lewis Dam (4); Lewis Mill (5); Pratt's Mill (6); Factory machine shop (7); Fulling Mill (8); Factory Mill (9); Intake between canal and river (10); Canal extremity of (11); Bridge (12); Factory store (13); Factory Dam (14); Factory (15); Dwelling House of factory company (16); Furnace (17); Do, do, do (18); Large House of factory company (19); House of do (20); do do (21); and Store House of Boston Boating Company (22). (Courtesy of New Hampshire Historical Society.)

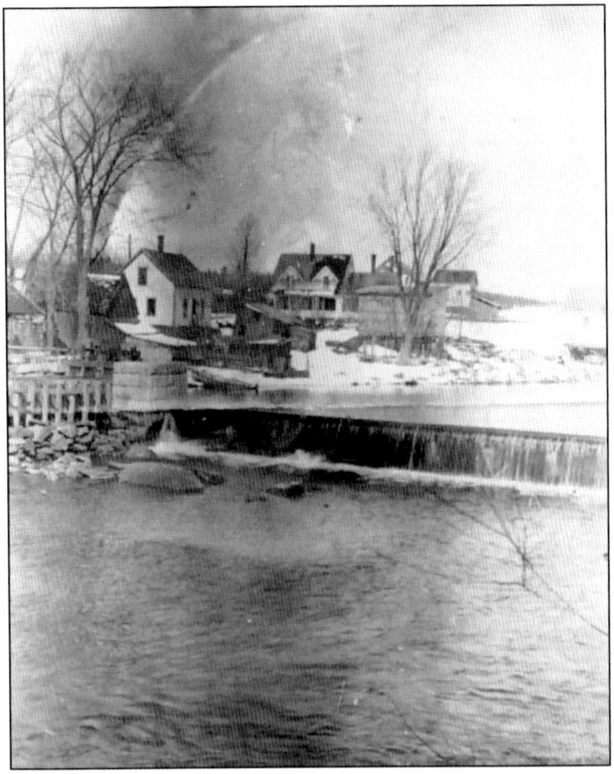

Osgood's Dam, located at Glass Street and Turnpike Street, was one of many early dams along the Suncook River. Further upstream at the Buck Street Island, several mills were powered by two dams. Downstream, the Suncook River flowage supplied the most abundant water source for powering mills before its confluence with the Merrimack River. (Courtesy of Roland Martel.)

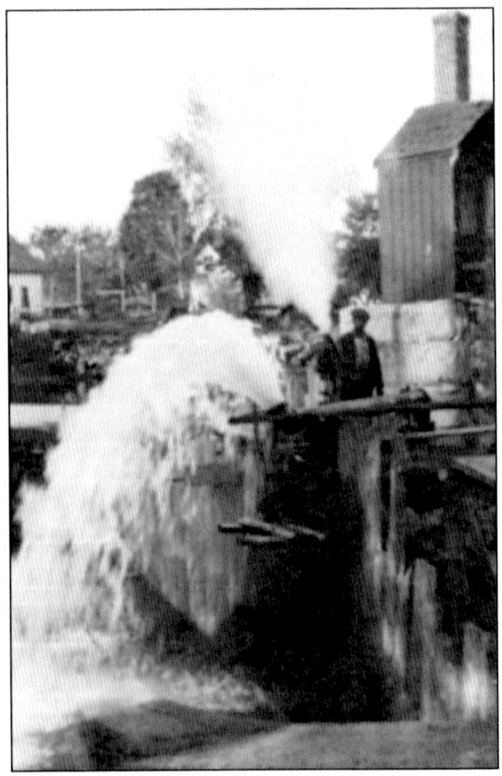

The Osgood Dam supplied water to power Osgood's Sawmill. In this photograph, a worker can be seen releasing water from the dam, possibly during a spring thaw or at the beginning of a workday. (Photograph by Ernest McNeal; courtesy of Brent Michiels.)

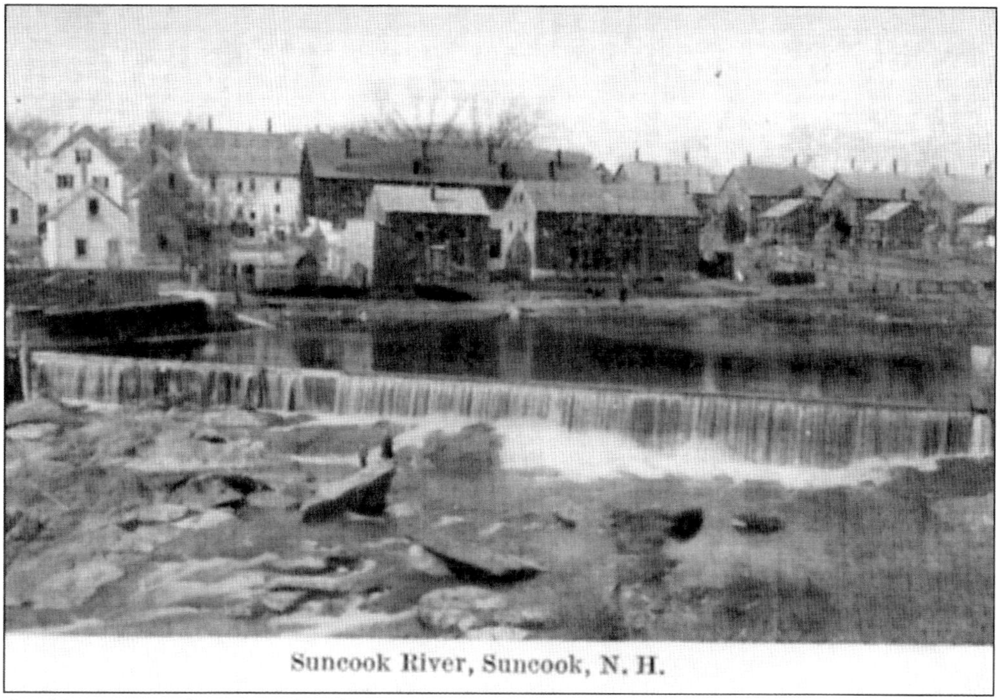

On Glass Street, the original Webster Dam on the Suncook River is pictured. In the background are the company houses and tenements. (Courtesy of Connie French.)

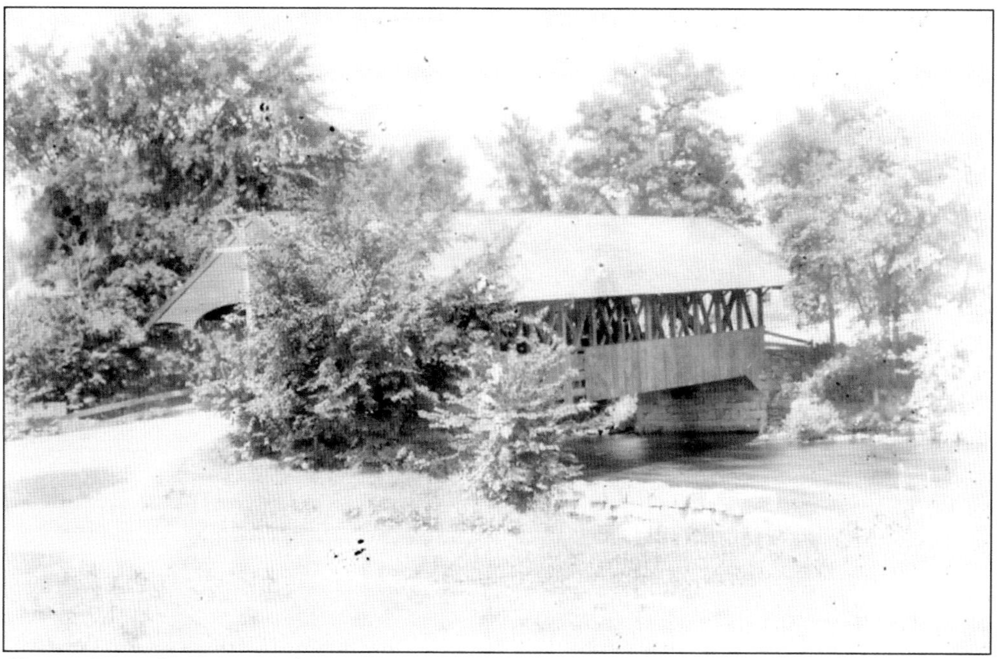

Chester Turnpike was one of two primary roads through Suncook. The Turnpike bridge over the Suncook River was located close to Osgood's Dam and Mill. The alternate route was known as the "Road to Boston." (Photograph by Joseph Wilkins; courtesy of Brent Michiels.)

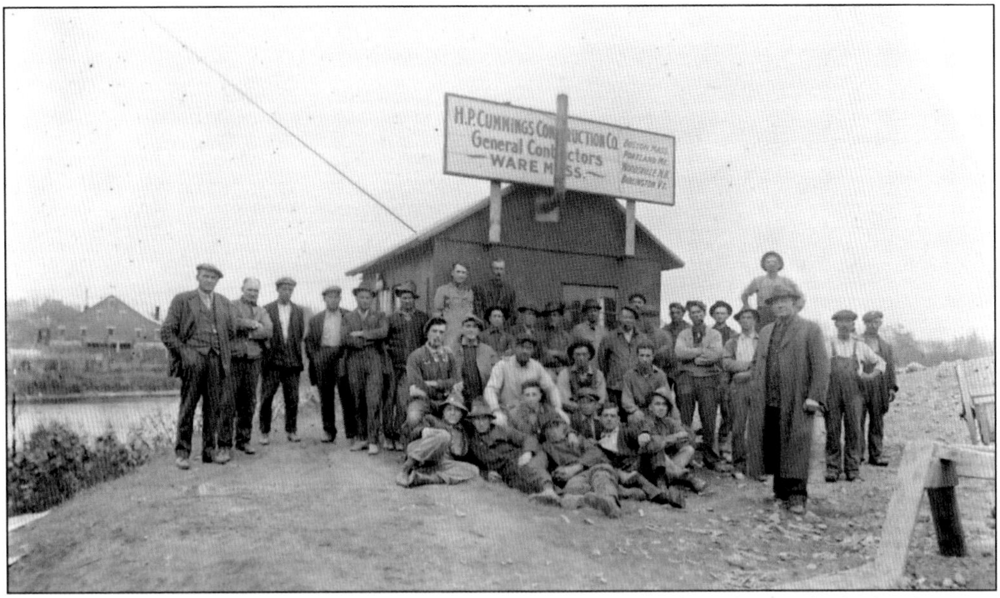

H. P. Cummings Construction Company crew is photographed at the work shed. The crew replaced the old Webster Mill Dam in 1916. The Suncook River had three areas well suited for dams, including upstream east of Main Street, west of Main Street, and further downstream before the Suncook River's confluence with the Merrimack River. The glassworks building that was converted to apartments is to the left. (Photograph by Joseph Wilkins; courtesy of Brent Michiels.)

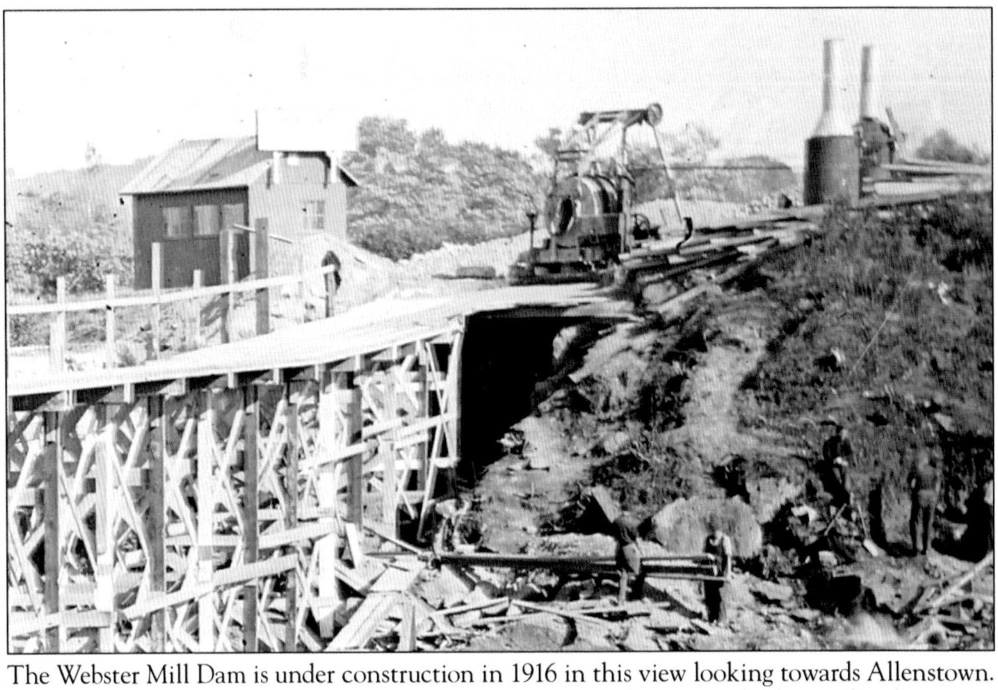

The Webster Mill Dam is under construction in 1916 in this view looking towards Allenstown. In the background, construction equipment is visible, including steam boilers and early cement mixers. The Webster Dam and its head race are in the same location as the early dam and canal system. (Photograph by Joseph Wilkins; courtesy of Brent Michiels.)

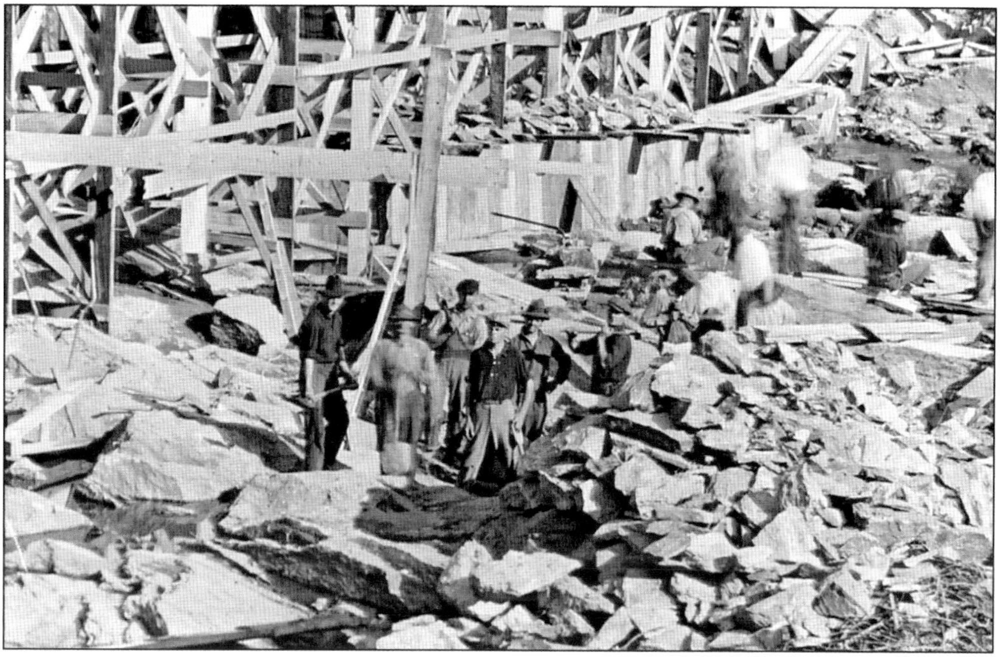

H. P. Cummings workers are pictured at the base of the Webster Mill Dam in 1916. Notice the height of the dam in comparison to the men. The sharp drop of the dam increased the velocity of the water when it passed through the mill's turbines and therefore powered the Webster Mill's machinery. (Photograph by Joseph Wilkins; courtesy of Brent Michiels.)

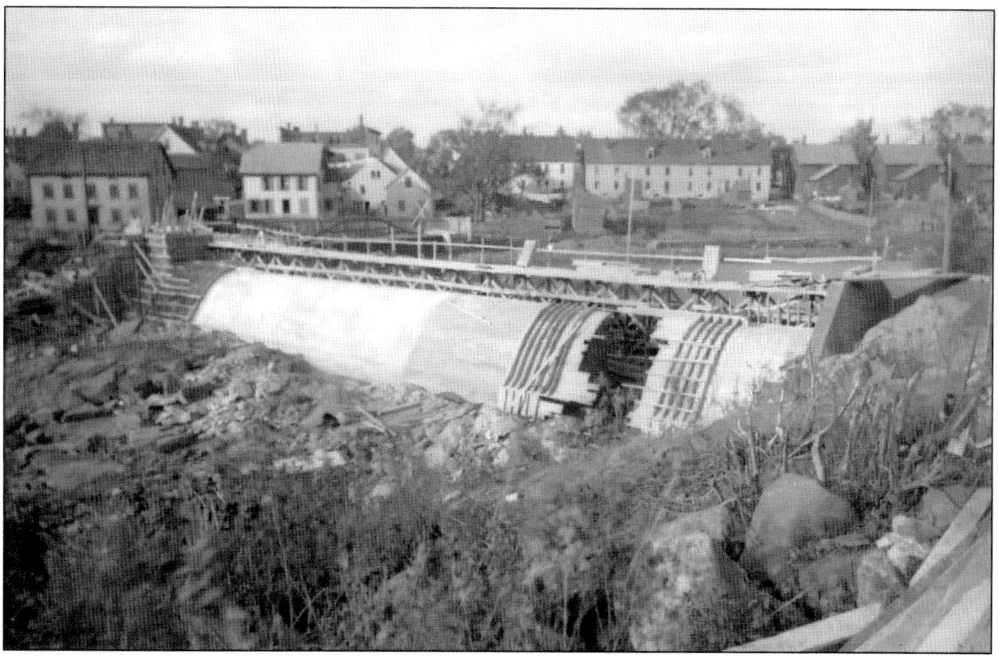

The Webster Mill Dam is nearly completed in this 1916 view looking northeast towards Pembroke, with Glass Street in the background. After powering the mills machinery, excess water was returned to the river through the earlier canal's tailrace. (Photograph by Joseph Wilkins; courtesy of Brent Michiels.)

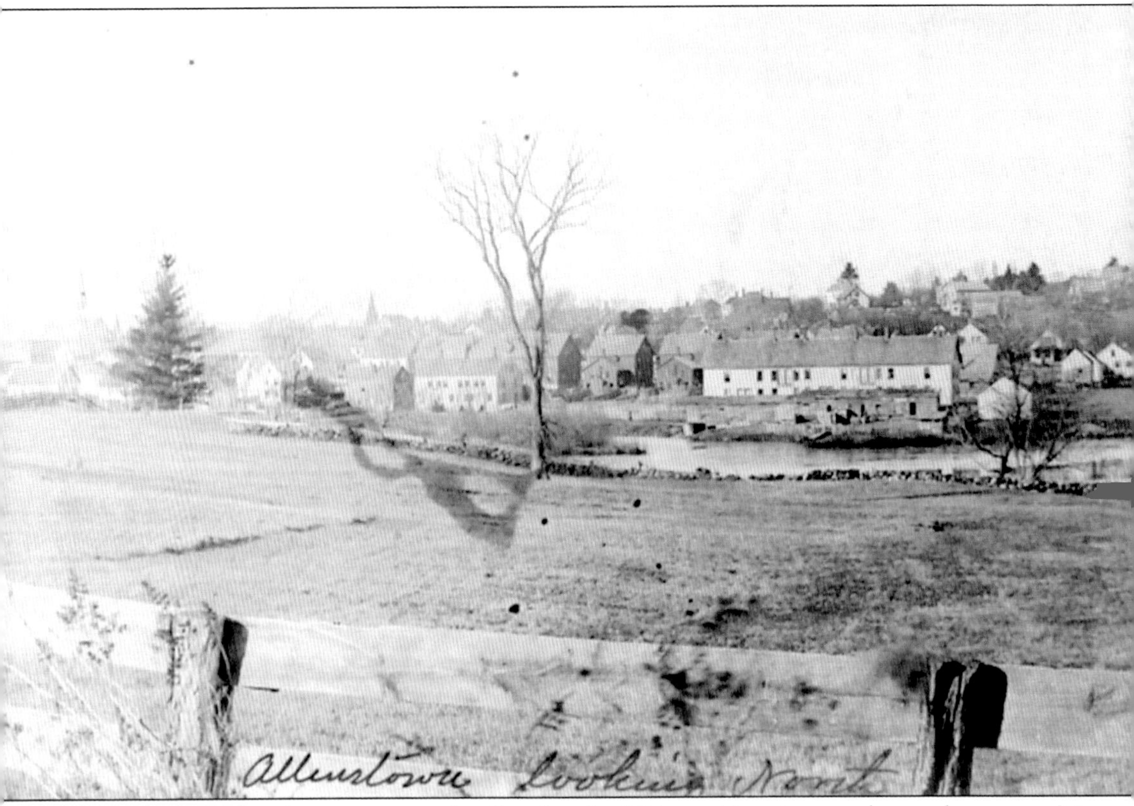

Osgood's field is shown prior to flooding for the Webster Dam impoundment, known as Iris Pond. This photograph was taken looking north from Osgood's field. The Osgood homestead was located beyond the scope of this image to the far right. After the flooding of the field, the homestead was located on a peninsula between Iris Pond and the Suncook River that was known as Osgood's Island. (Courtesy of Brent Michiels.)

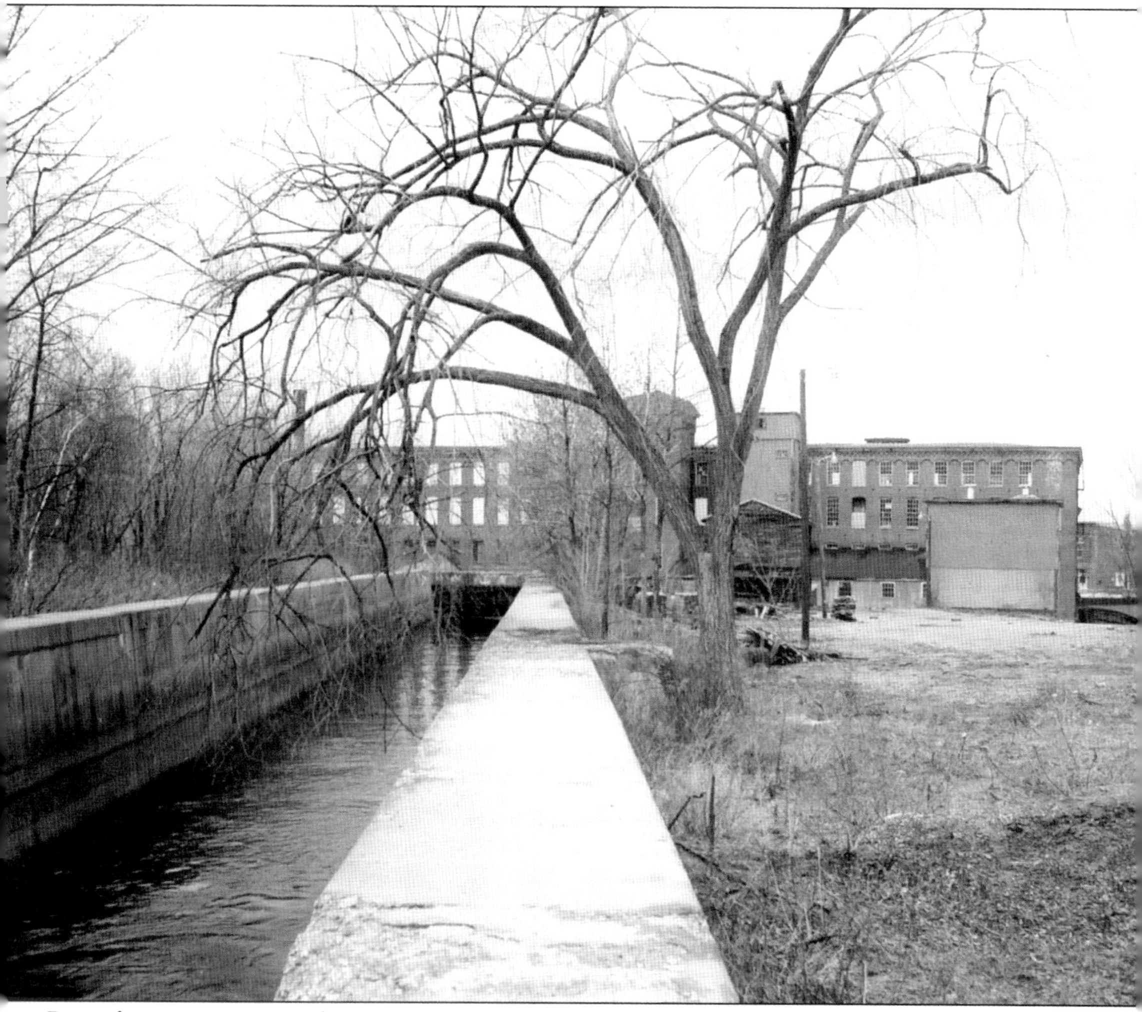

Part of an extensive canal system in Suncook, the Webster Mill Canal was a 450-foot power canal that channeled the water under the mill through penstocks, then dropping it through the turbines The drop promoted water velocity when it reached the turbines. The turbines would then spin, operating the mechanical belt system that powered machinery in the mill. Next the water went through a tailrace back into the Suncook River. (Photograph by Brent Michiels.)

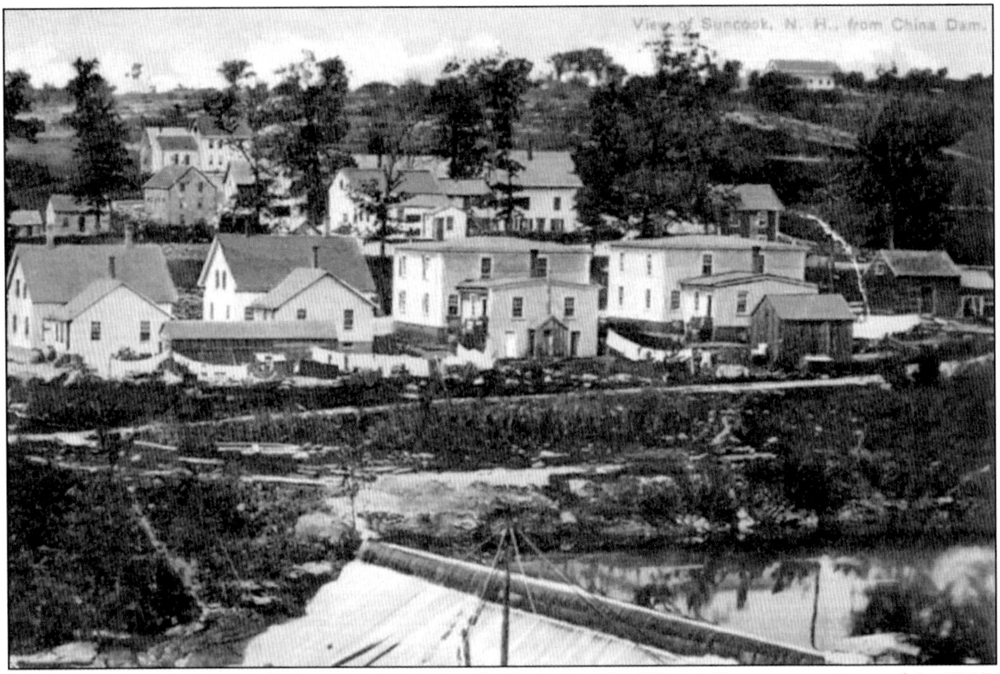

The China Mill Dam and the tenements on the lower end of Front Street are pictured in 1907. Railroad tracks ran behind these buildings from the depot on Exchange Street to both the Pembroke and Webster mills. (Courtesy of Connie French.)

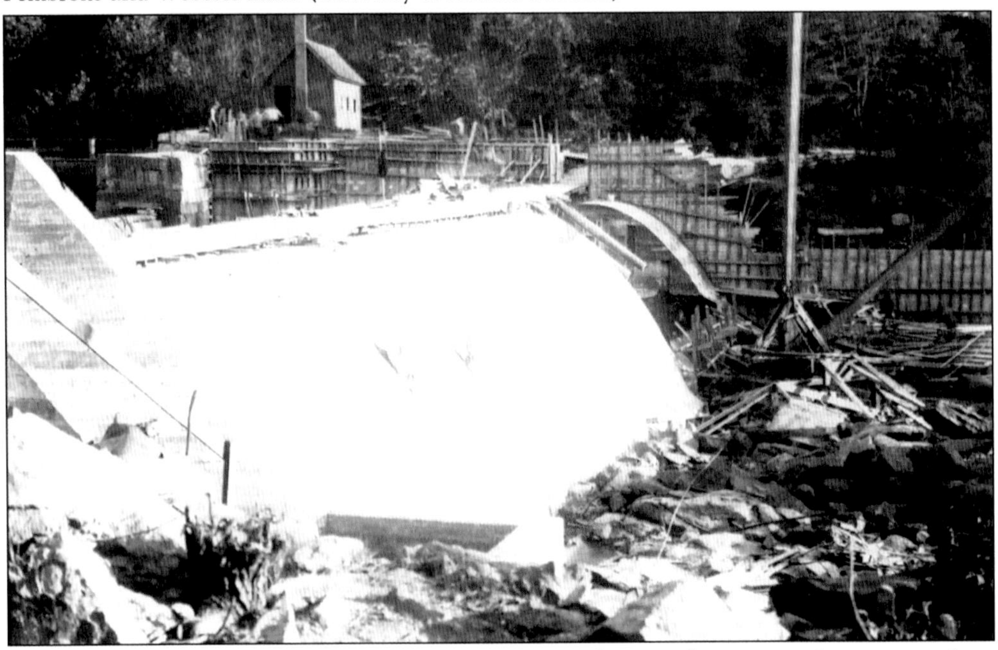
The China Mill Dam, under construction in 1926, is in the same location as the previous dam. The gatehouse is dated September 1922. The China Mill was converted from hydromechanical power to hydroelectric power in 1899. The impoundment for this dam lies between the China Dam and the Pembroke Dam. It encompasses 1.5 acres. (Photograph by Joseph Wilkins; courtesy of Brent Michiels.)

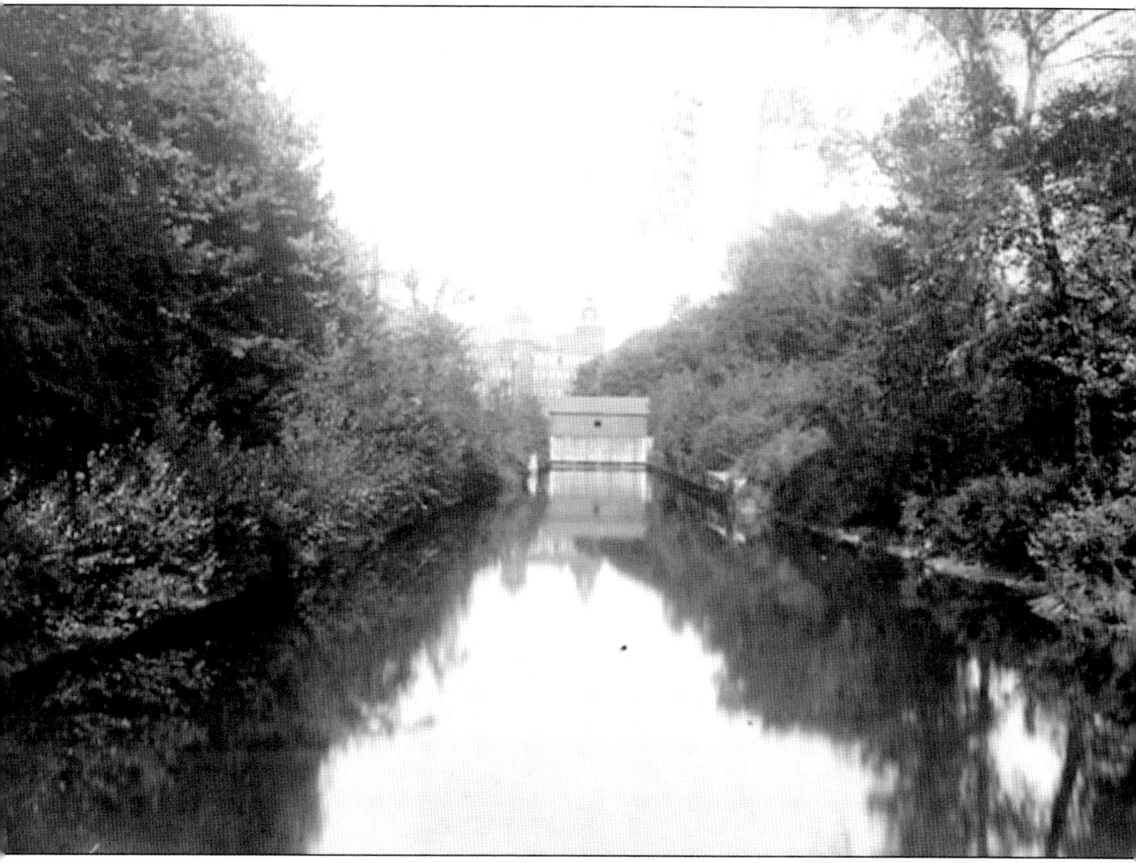

The China Mill Canal with a scenic view of the village is seen looking east towards Suncook Village. The China Mill was originally operated by hydromechanical power and later converted to hydroelectric power. The mill is still operated by hydroelectric power in the present day. The generator is vintage, patented in 1900 and 1901, and came from the Alabama Power company in 1927. (Courtesy of Pembroke Historical Society.)

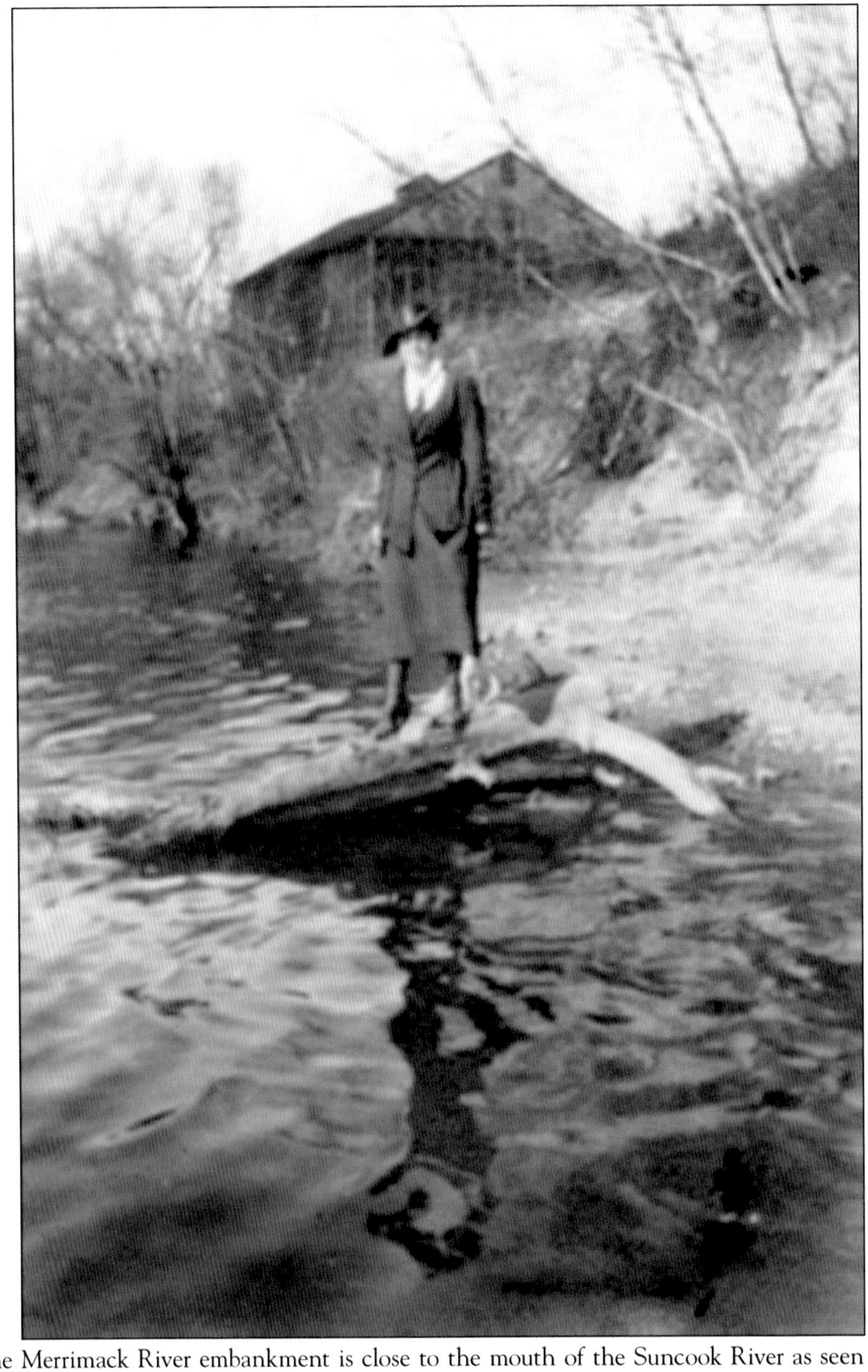

The Merrimack River embankment is close to the mouth of the Suncook River as seen here around 1915. The building directly behind the woman was located very close to the river. The structure may have previously been the Boston Boat Company Storehouse. A close up view reveals that it was built into the embankment along the river. This suggests that it was used as a storehouse during the time of river transportation. (Courtesy of Roland Martel.)

Two

THE RISE OF SUNCOOK'S TEXTILE INDUSTRY

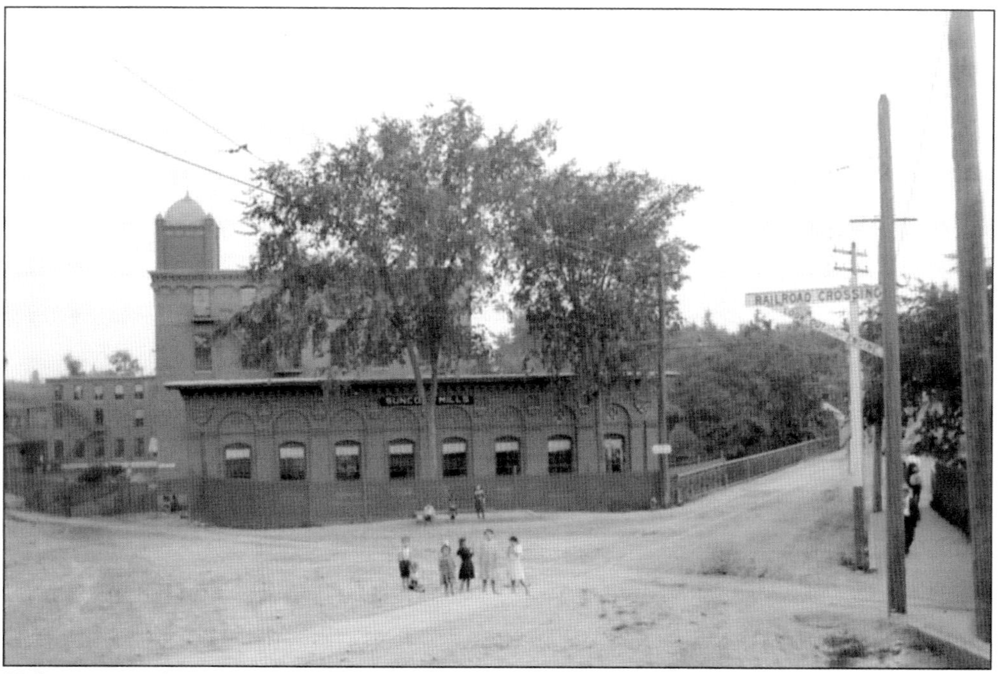

Webster Manufacturing Company, seen here, was the gateway to the Suncook Mills. Between 1790 and 1860, mechanized and industrial production changed American life. The Suncook River falls and confluence with the Merrimack River was a tremendous resource for powering large, modern, industrialized mills. In 1847, the Suncook Manufacturing Company was incorporated. By 1860, a plan was drawn for the Pembroke, Webster, and China Mills. (Courtesy of Brent Michiels and Larry Perron.)

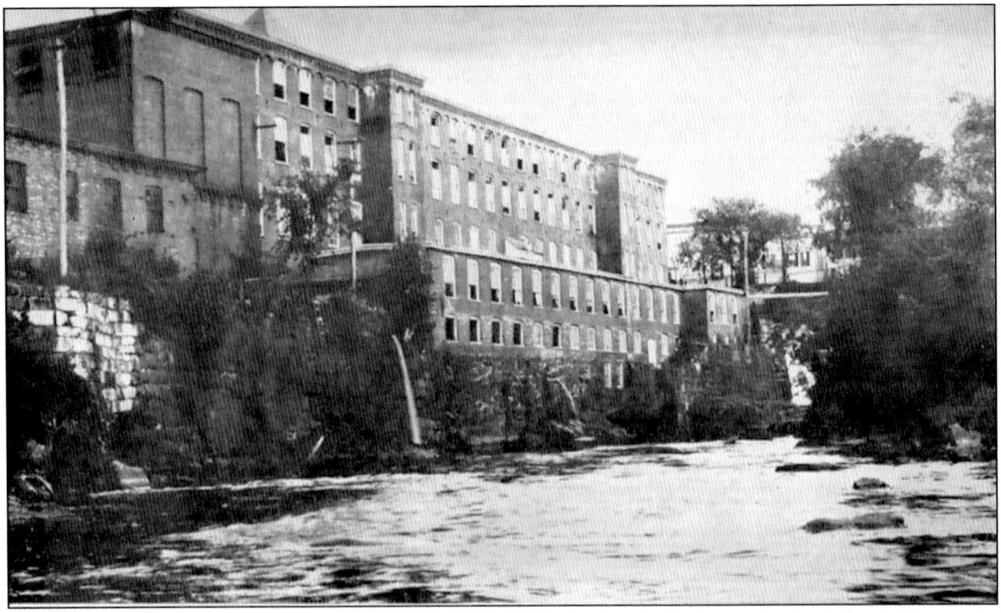

Pembroke Mill, built around 1860, was brick Italianate in design, four stories tall, 72 feet wide, and 273 feet long. Two turbine waterwheels that generated 440 horsepower and two Corliss steam engines that provided a 400 horsepower backup powered the hydromechanical operation. In full operation, it turned 20,000 spindles and 422 looms, with 255 employees producing 110,000 yards of cotton cloth per week. (Courtesy of Connie French.)

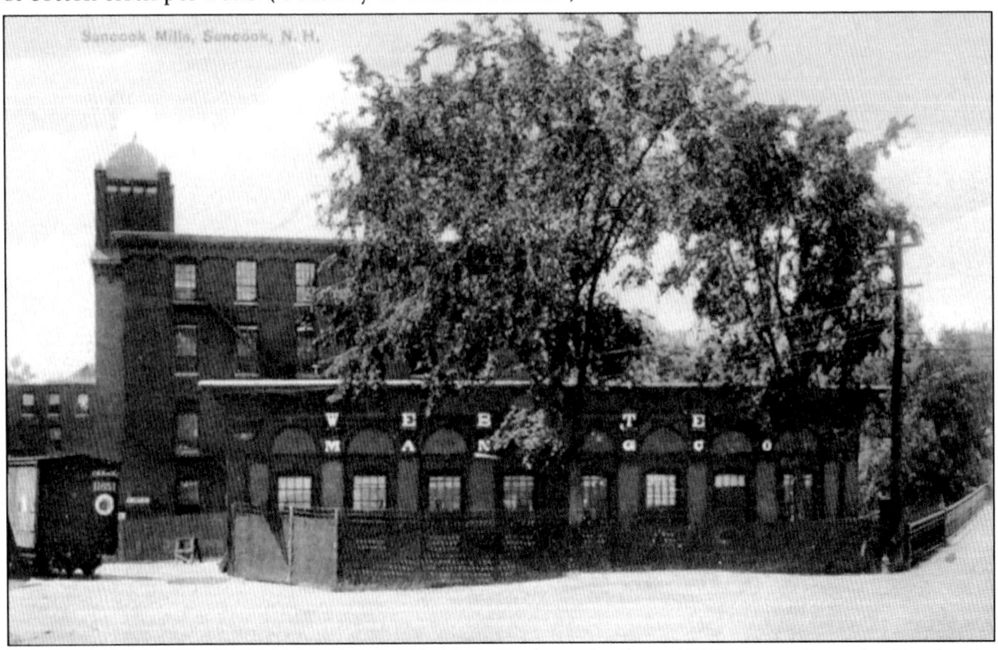

Webster Mill (or Webster Manufacturing Company) was built in 1865. Located on the Pembroke side of Suncook Village, this mill was four stories, 72 feet wide, and 310 feet long. It had two turbine waterwheels generating 800 horsepower and two Corliss steam engines for back up that also generated 800 horsepower. This textile mill employed 500 operatives and produced 225,000 yards of cloth per week. (Courtesy of Connie French.)

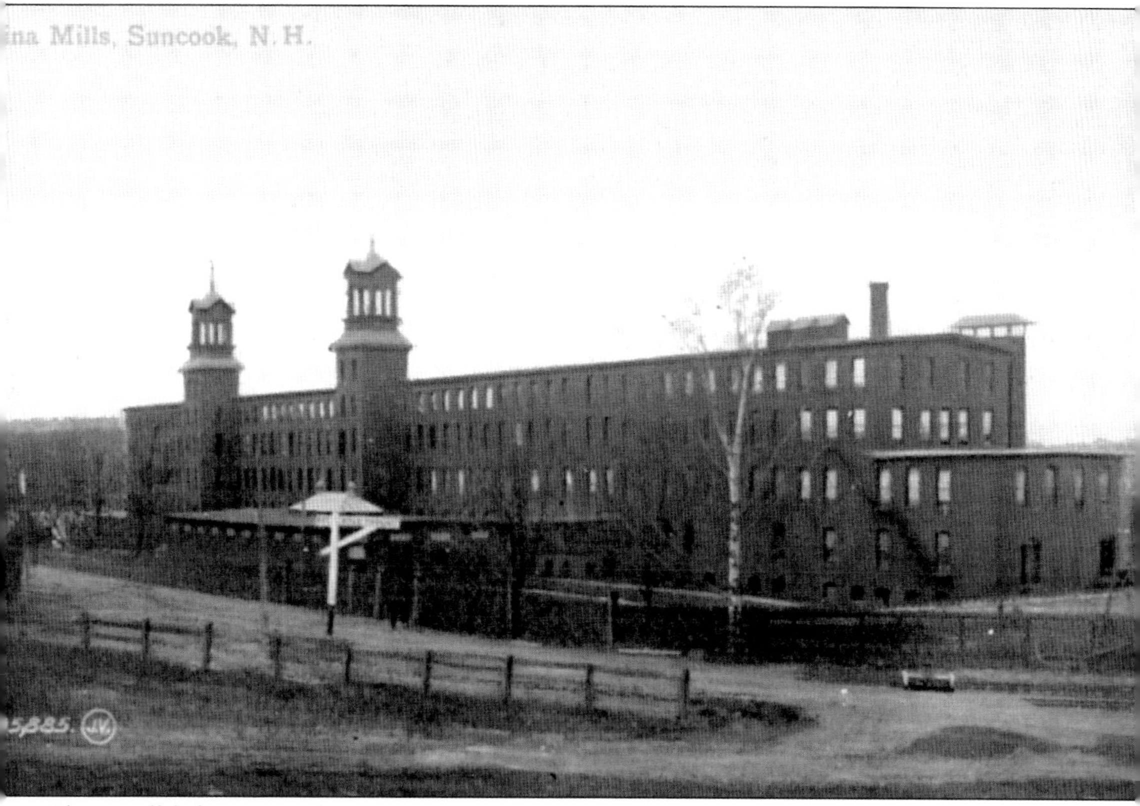

China Mill (China Manufacturing Company) was incorporated in 1867 and built in 1868 at the confluence of the Suncook River with the Merrimack River, on the Allenstown side of Suncook Village. The structure was the largest of the three Suncook mills. The building was Italianate in style, displaying two cupola towers and a large, brick smokestack. It was 58 bays long and five stories high, measuring 510 feet long by 72 feet wide. It had 230 arched windows with 12 over 12 glass that provided light supplemented by gaslights. Gas from retorts was made 1,000 feet from the mill. The mill was powered by two turbine water wheels generating 1,000 horsepower and two Corliss steam engines generating 800 horsepower. The 1875 Barlow Insurance Survey recorded a number four fire pump run by steam or water tied into the systems of the other mills. Water tanks at the top of the rear towers supplied the fire hydrants and Grinnell automatic sprinklers. In 1895, the China Mill employed 800 operatives and produced 330,000 yards of cloth per week. (Courtesy of Connie French.)

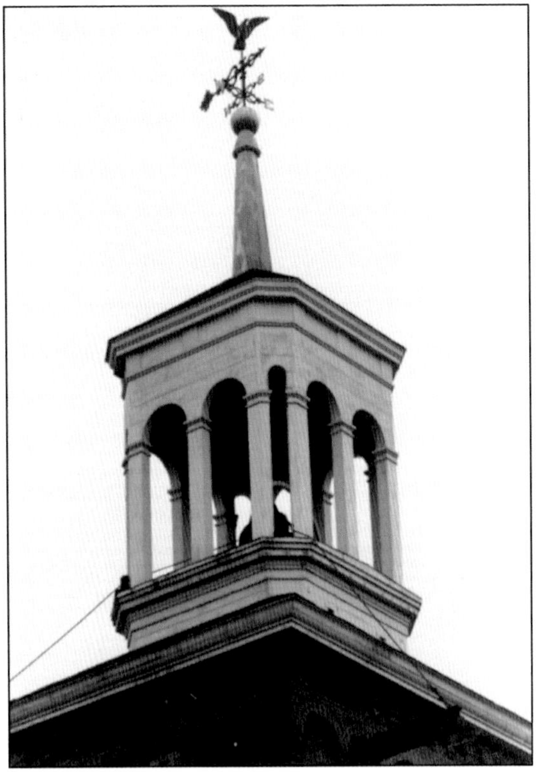

The China Mill bell tower seen in this photograph is one of two matching cupola towers. The towers are identical but only one tower contained a bell and was adorned with a gold leaf ball and eagle weathervane, as seen here. In 1870 the bell rang at 6:30 a.m. beginning a 12-hour day that included a one hour lunch break. Mill operatives worked a 60-hour week. The tolling bell called employees to work, let them know when it was time for lunch, and dismissed them at the end of the day. The twin cupola towers on the China Mill underwent repairs during the 1930s. Sometime after 1981 the bell and weathervane were removed from the tower. (Photograph by Dan Chase; courtesy of Roland Martel.)

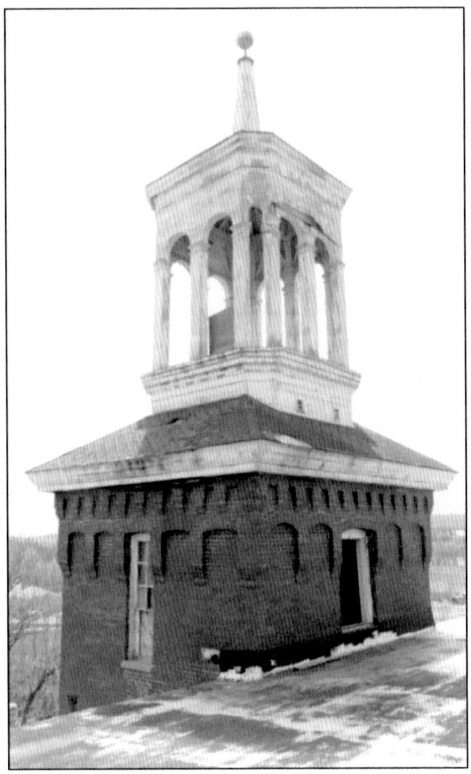

Seen here is the second cupola tower as it appears today. Both towers contain staircases that rise four stories but one tower has a spiral staircase. David Lymen Jewell was the engineer and draughtsman who designed the Pembroke, Webster, and China Mills. The towers can be seen at most viewpoints in the village and across the Merrimack River and greatly contribute to the visual landscape of Suncook Village.(Courtesy of Joyce McKay.)

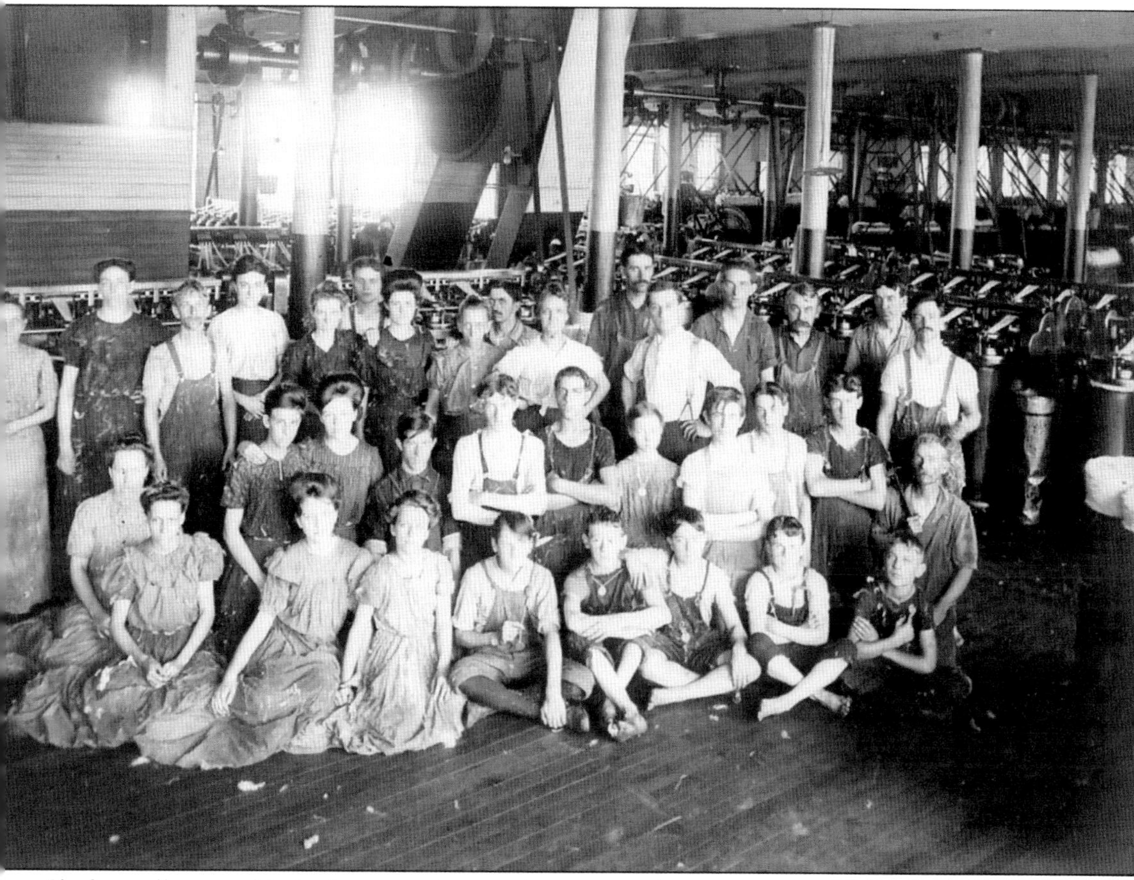

Shafts, pulleys, and belts for operating machinery can be seen in the background of this photograph of China Mill workers. It is believed a conversion from hydromechanical to hydroelectric power took place in 1899. This image most likely predates the time of conversion. There are 14 children seated or kneeling in the center of the group. The Child Labor Act was passed in 1916. (Courtesy of Allenstown, New Hampshire, Historical Society.)

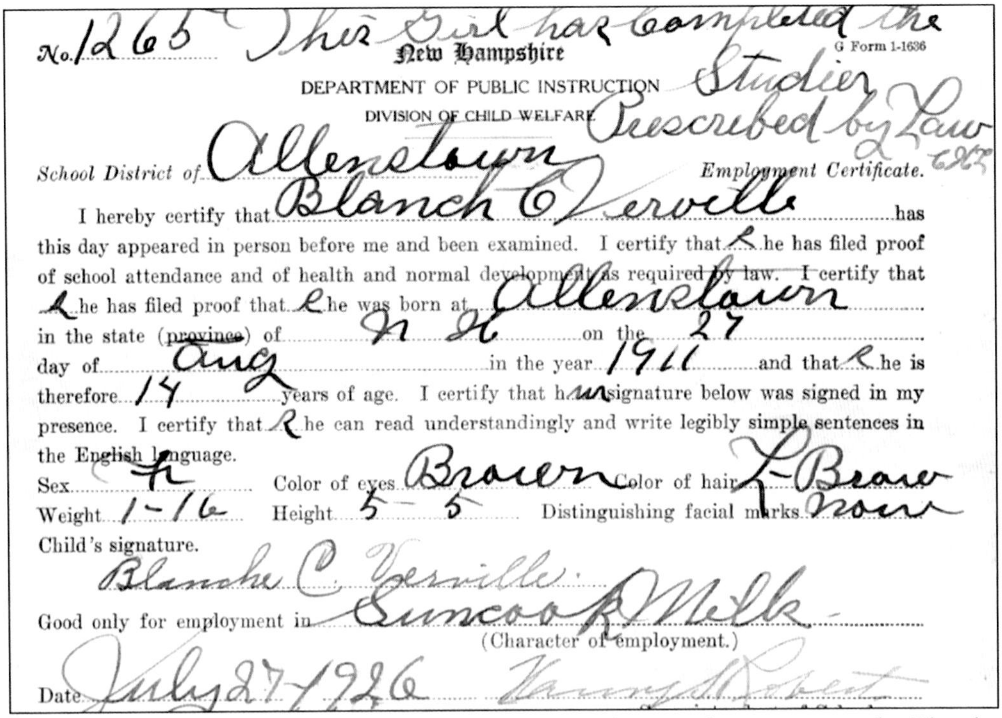

No. 1265 This Girl has completed the Studies Prescribed by Law

New Hampshire

G Form 1-1636

DEPARTMENT OF PUBLIC INSTRUCTION

DIVISION OF CHILD WELFARE

School District of Allenstown *Employment Certificate.*

I hereby certify that Blanch C Verville has this day appeared in person before me and been examined. I certify that she has filed proof of school attendance and of health and normal development as required by law. I certify that she has filed proof that she was born at Allenstown in the state (~~province~~) of N H on the 27 day of Aug in the year 1911 and that she is therefore 14 years of age. I certify that her signature below was signed in my presence. I certify that she can read understandingly and write legibly simple sentences in the English language.

Sex F Color of eyes Brown Color of hair L-Brown

Weight 1-16 Height 5 5 Distinguishing facial marks None

Child's signature.

Blanche C. Verville

Good only for employment in Suncook Mills

(Character of employment.)

Date July 27 1926 Henry [illegible]

State of New Hampshire child labor papers confirm educational requirements for Blanche Verville, age 14, on July 27, 1926. (Courtesy of Armand and Claudette Verville.)

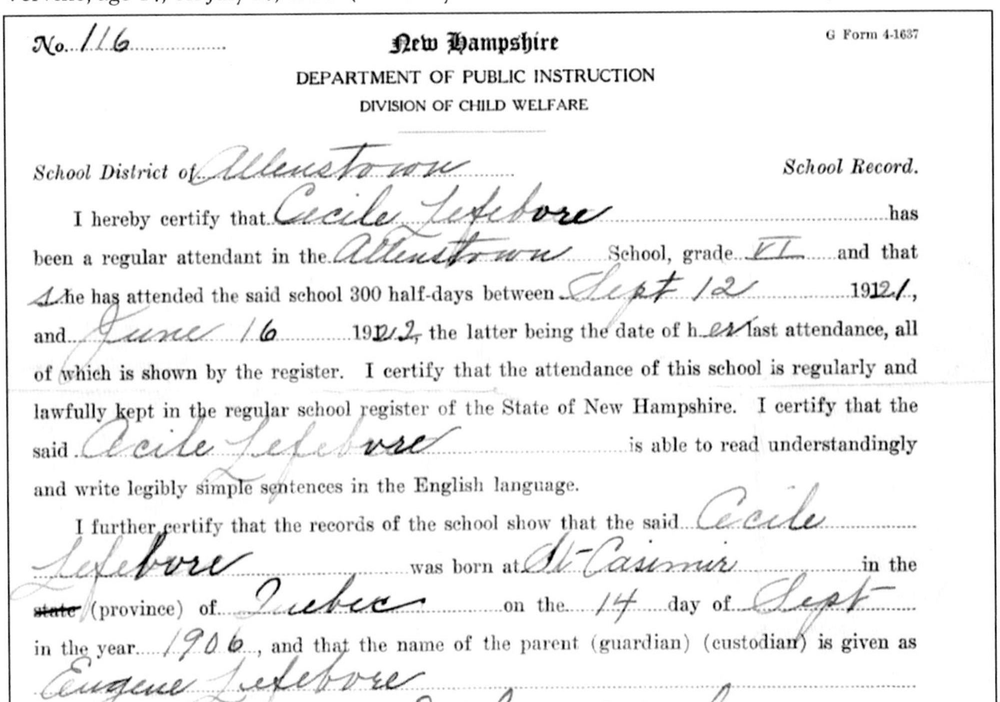

No. 116

New Hampshire

G Form 4-1637

DEPARTMENT OF PUBLIC INSTRUCTION

DIVISION OF CHILD WELFARE

School District of Allenstown *School Record.*

I hereby certify that Cecile Lefebvre has been a regular attendant in the Allenstown School, grade VI and that she has attended the said school 300 half-days between Sept 12 1921, and June 16 1922, the latter being the date of her last attendance, all of which is shown by the register. I certify that the attendance of this school is regularly and lawfully kept in the regular school register of the State of New Hampshire. I certify that the said Cecile Lefebvre is able to read understandingly and write legibly simple sentences in the English language.

I further certify that the records of the school show that the said Cecile Lefebvre was born at St-Casimir in the ~~state~~ (province) of Quebec on the 14 day of Sept in the year 1906, and that the name of the parent (guardian) (custodian) is given as Eugene Lefebvre

This child labor work permit from the State of New Hampshire, dated June 16, 1922, is for Cecile Lefevre, age 15. (Courtesy of Armand and Claudette Verville.)

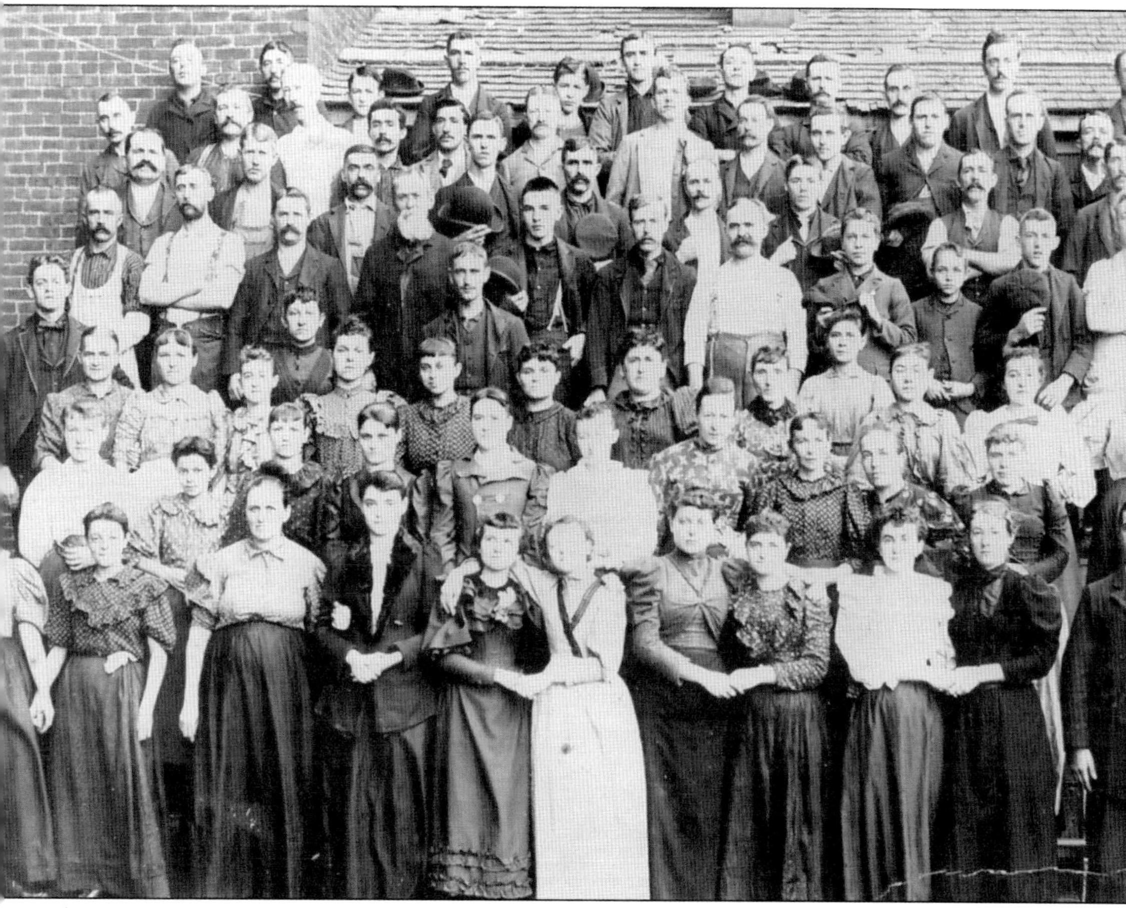

China Mill employees are photographed in front of the mill. Prior to the building of the Suncook Mills, the population on both sides of the village was English, Scottish, and Irish. Local residents viewed the new mills as an opportunity for employment and prosperity. Many young women living on area farms became the first wave of employees in the Suncook Mills. Additional workers were brought in from England and Ireland. The Pembroke, Webster, and China Mills were independent companies managed by the Suncook Mills Company, located at 30 State Street in Boston, Massachusetts. Francis M. Weld was treasurer, David Lymen Jewell was agent, and Edmund Truesdell was superintendent and paymaster. At the height of operation the Suncook Mills used 119,000 pounds of cotton to make 34,580,000 yards of cloth per week. In 1937, the depression, strikes, and the decline of the textile industry led to a series of changes in ownership. Today, only one mill remains in operation—the China Mill is possibly the longest continuously operating textile mill in New England. (Courtesy of Allenstown Library.)

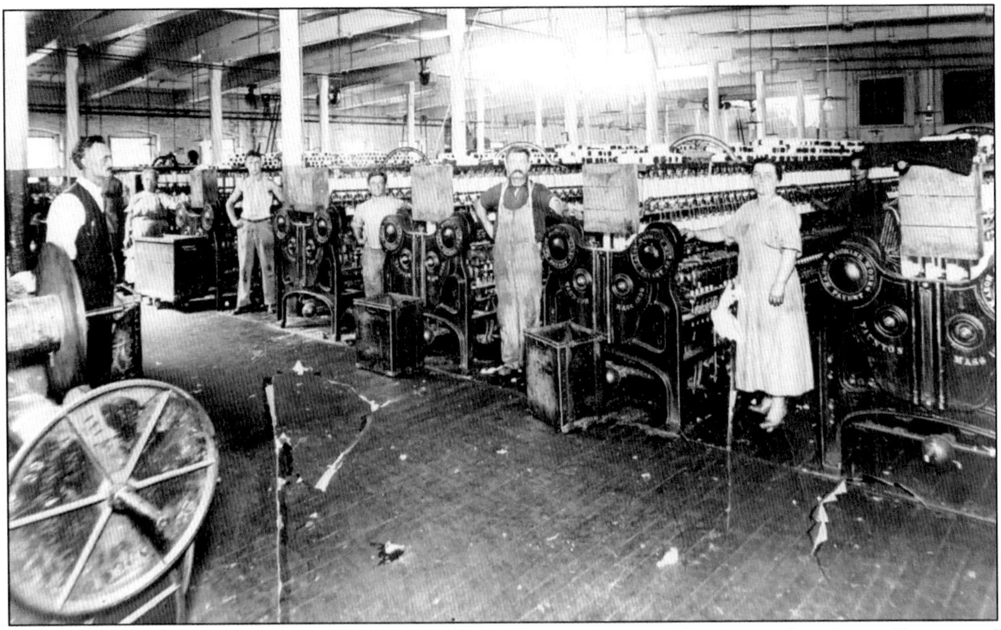

China Mill spinning room operatives are seen with an overseer. Not long after the mills opened in Suncook, an agricultural depression in Canada created a new labor force. The French Canadians began emigrating in unbelievable numbers to work in the Suncook Mills. Between 1860 and 1870, the population of Allenstown and Pembroke nearly doubled. (Courtesy of Allenstown Library.)

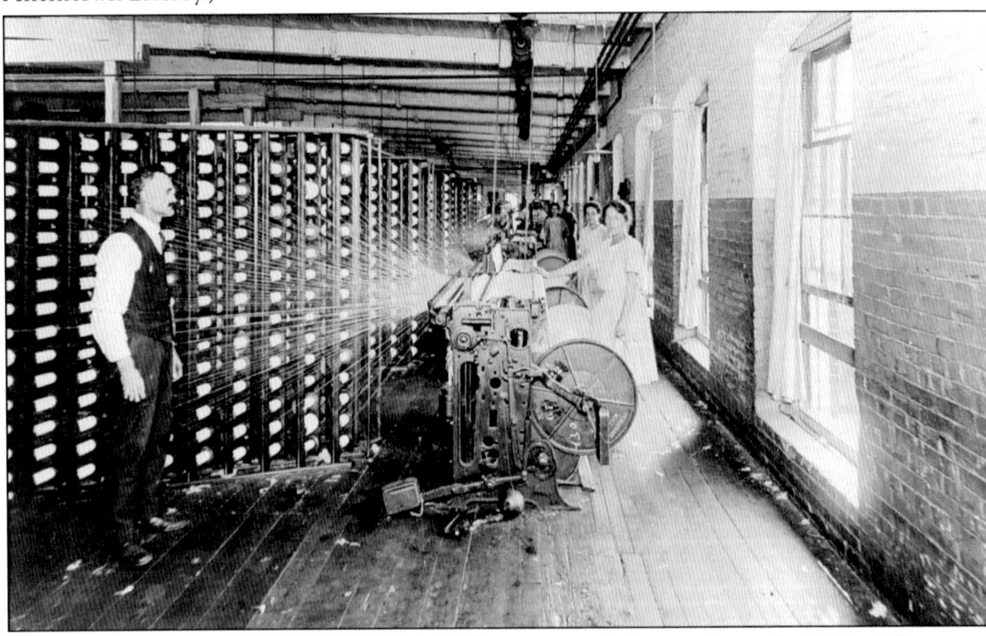

Spinning room operatives in the China Mill are at work during the early 1900s. The young woman to the right appears to be standing on a stool or bench in order to gain height to operate the machinery. The girls are wearing caps to prevent their hair from accidentally becoming tangled. A machinist or supervisor stands around the corner observing the operation. (Courtesy of Allenstown Library.)

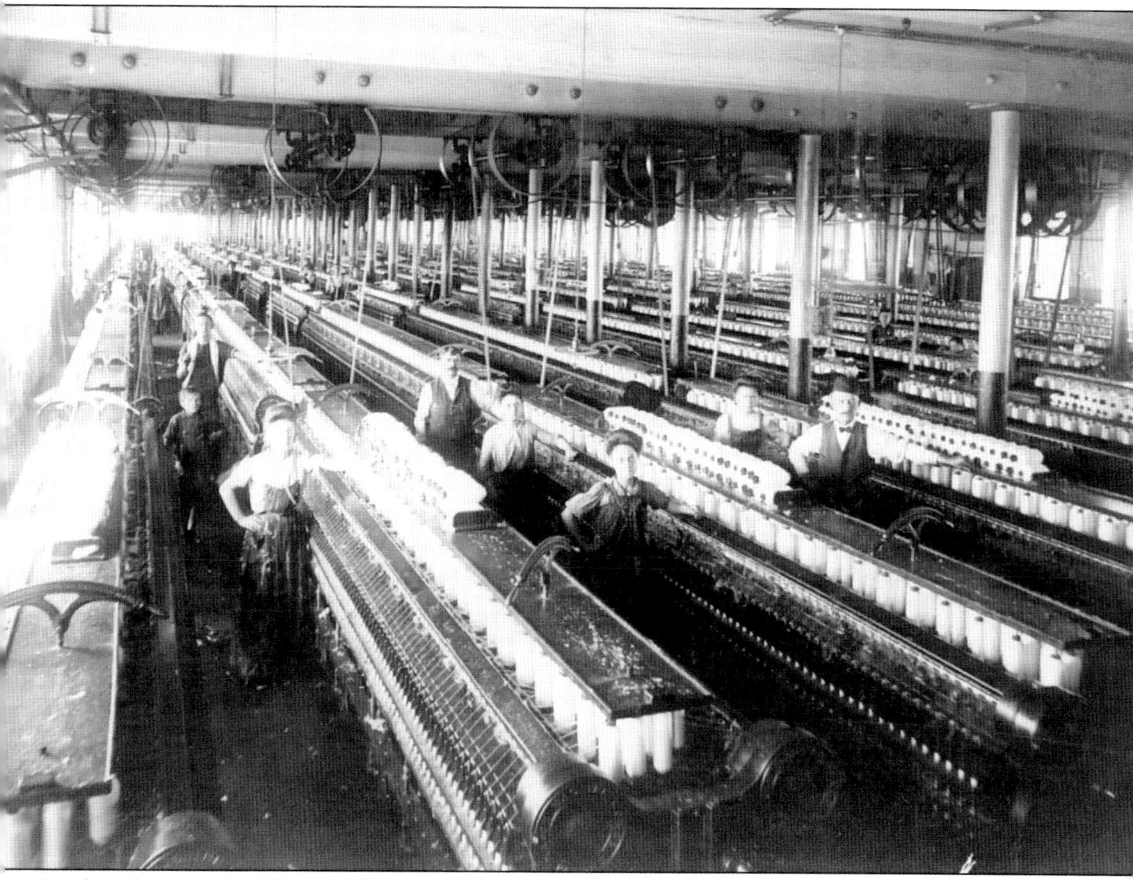

In this photograph, China Mill spinning room operatives include a young boy. Workdays were long and difficult for mill operatives. Children worked with or without parents. Most of the people who immigrated to the area did not find the adjustment to mill life easy. (Courtesy of Allenstown, New Hampshire, Historical Society.)

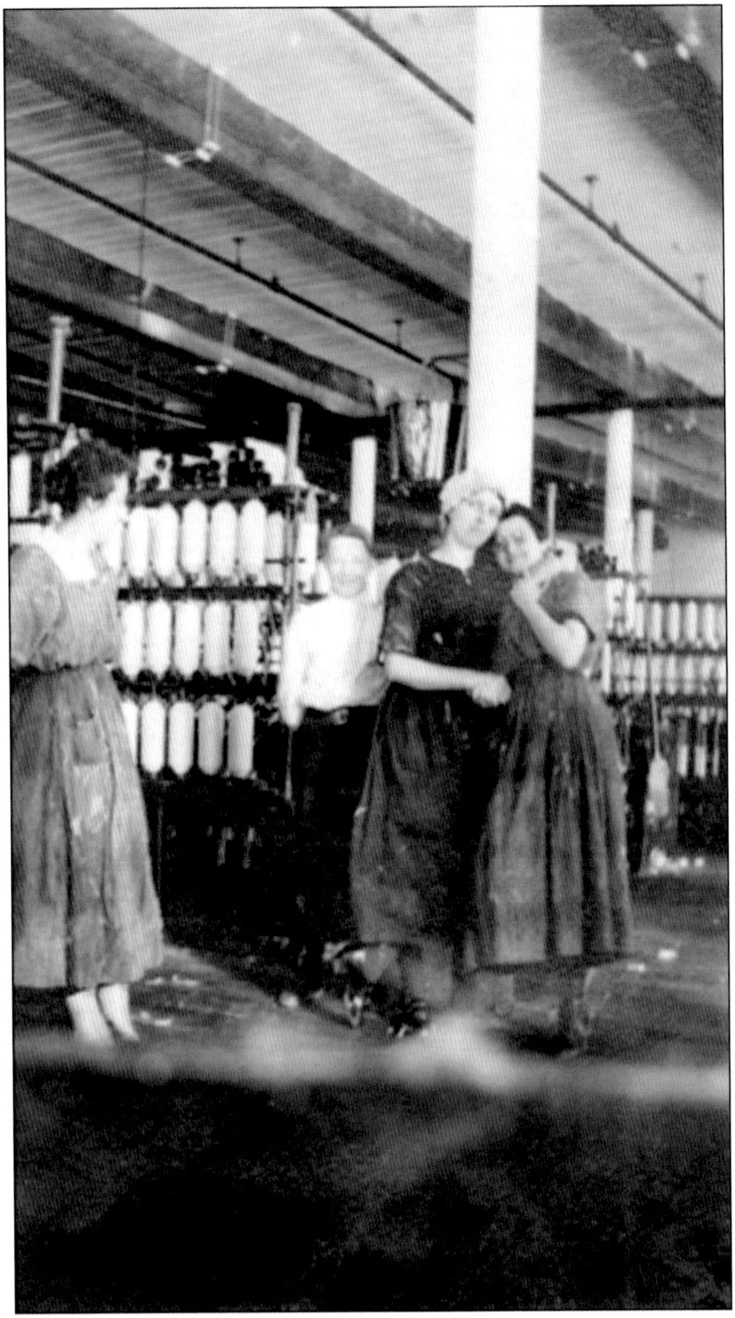

This photograph of the spinning room around 1910 is the first of a series of images that began inside the China Mill. Alice Roy (far right) is with a young boy and two friends. As a baby, Roy came from St. Norbert, Quebec, with her parents, Gustave and Roseanna Roy. Most of Suncook's textile operatives were French Canadians. Many hoped to return to their homeland after earning enough money to do so. It was not unusual to see entire families come to America and settle in areas close enough to visit each other. There was a strong French Canadian connection between the textile families in Suncook, Manchester, Lowell, and Lawrence. (Courtesy of Roland Martel.)

An unidentified photographer captured the end of the workday for these China Mill cotton girls around 1910. Cotton remnants can be seen clinging to their heavy dresses and two girls were wearing caps that prevented their hair from getting tangled in the mill machinery. Roy is at the top right of this image. (Courtesy of Roland Martel.)

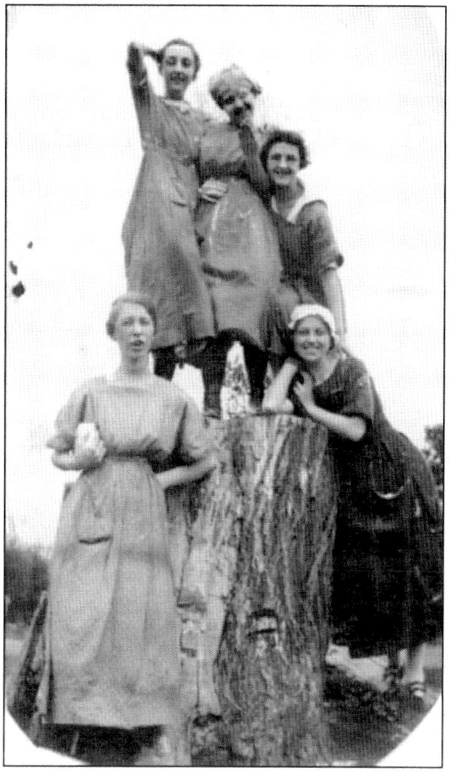

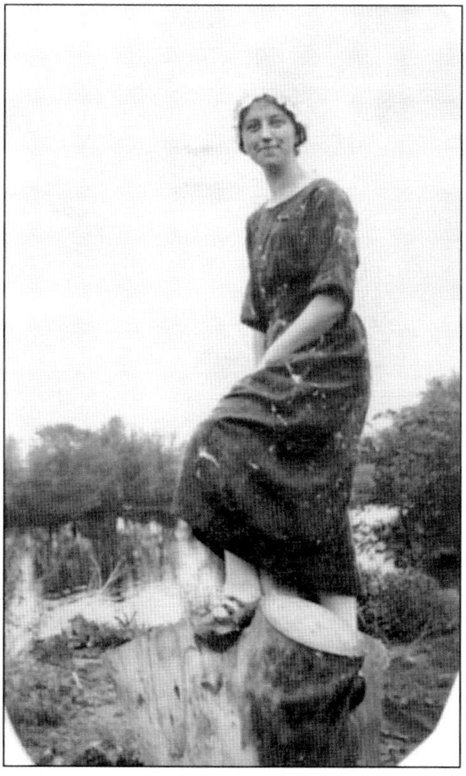

One cotton girl posed for the camera on the top of a tree stump with the river behind her. The image was taken in the vicinity of where Memorial Field is located today. The group of girls most likely took a dangerous and disapproved shortcut across the railroad trestle over the Suncook River. Many China Mill employees took this route to save time. (Courtesy of Roland Martel.)

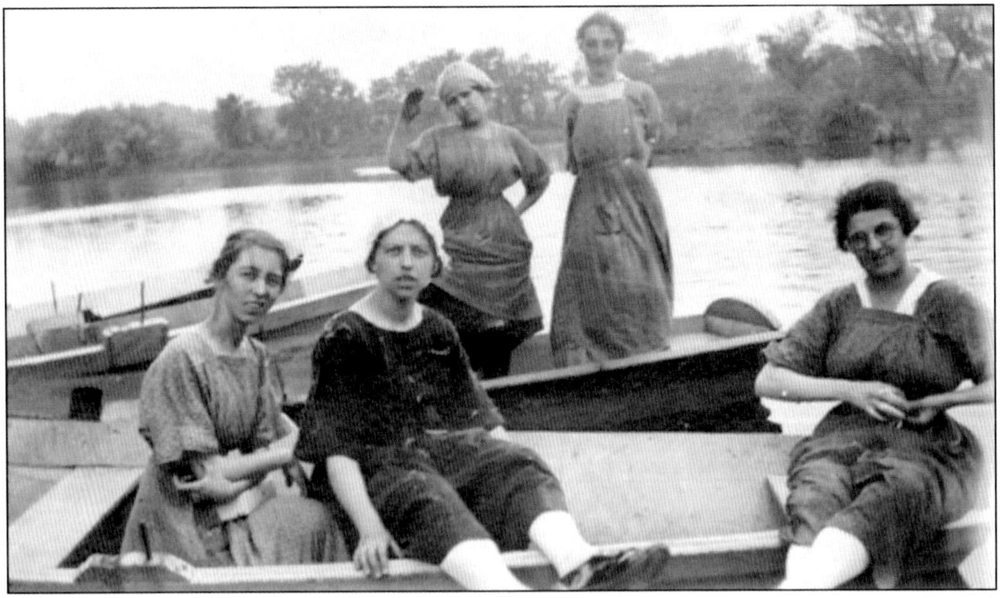

Cotton girls, pictured at their destination on the Merrimack River, are boating at the Roy camp. Larger rowboats on the Merrimack River sometimes had cloth overhead canopies to shield passengers from the sun. The Bow riverbank is in the background. (Courtesy of Roland Martel.)

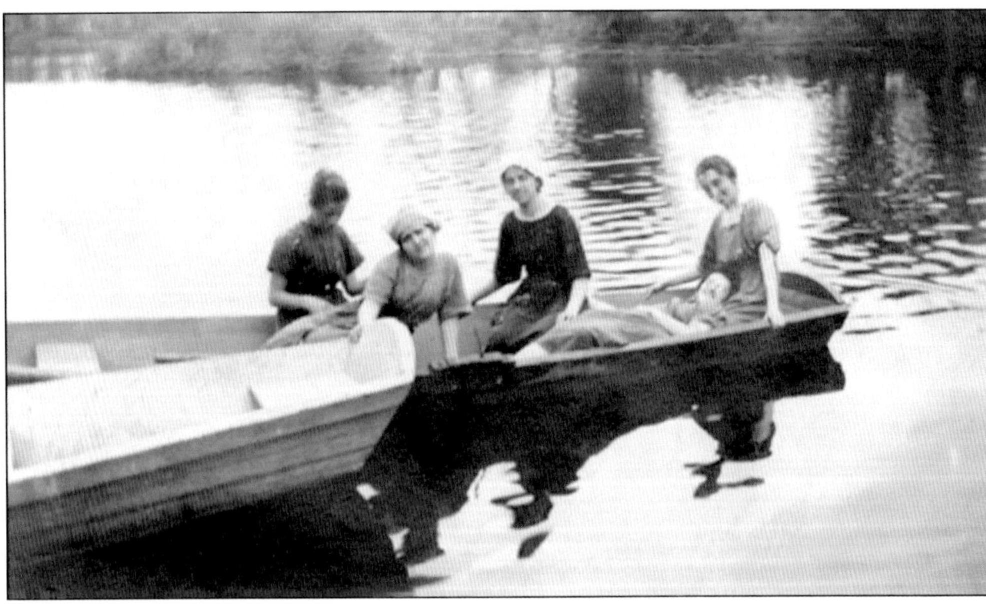

The cool water of the Merrimack River was a refreshing reward at the end of a hot, summer day spent in the mills. During the summer months, many Suncook residents enjoyed pleasure boating on the Merrimack and Suncook Rivers, often taking their boats to baseball games and other activities at the ball field. (Courtesy of Roland Martel.)

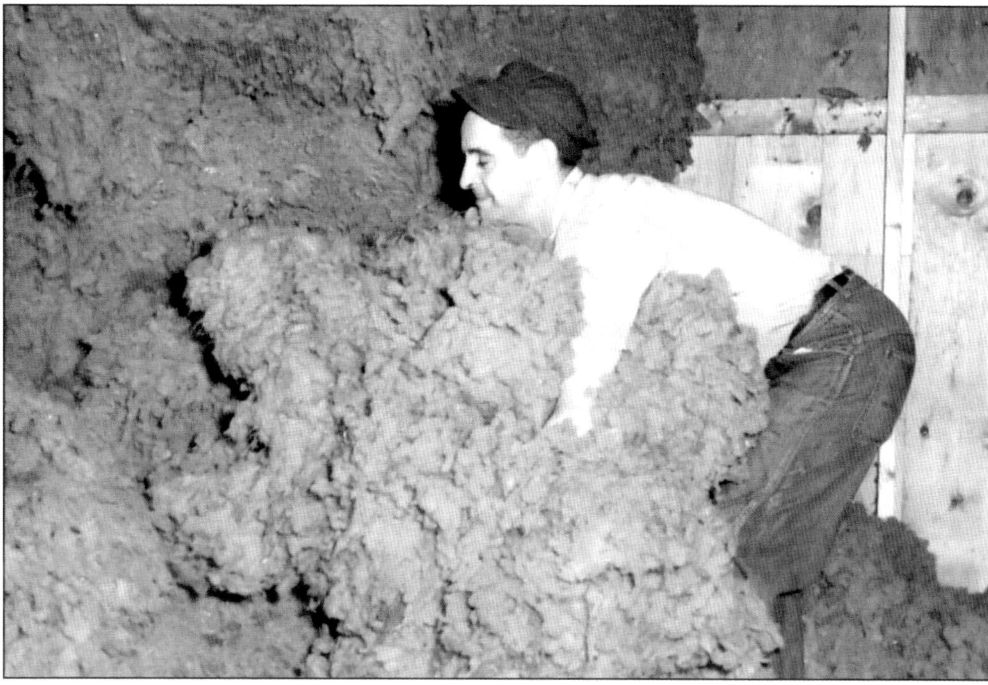

Rene Beauchesne feeds the picker at the Dole-Suncook Mill (originally called the China Mill) in the 1960s. The picker had a vacuum system sending the fiber into a room in the basement of the mill. (Courtesy of Pembroke Historical Society.)

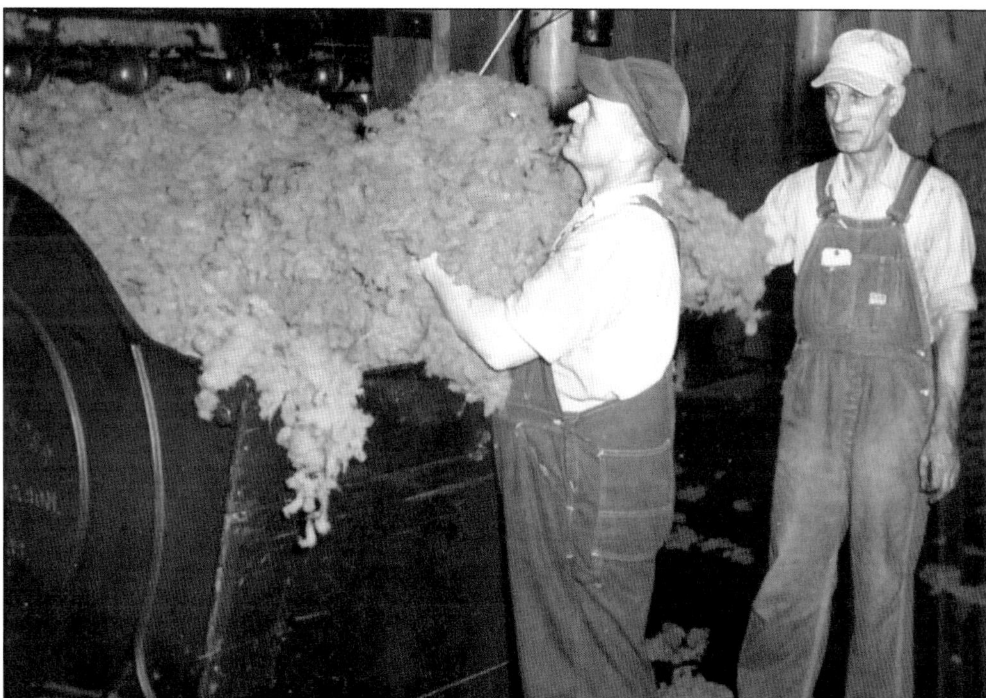

Joseph Fanny and Albert Labrie feed the picker at the Dole-Suncook Mill in the 1960s. The fiber processed by the picker was fed into a card hopper. (Courtesy of Pembroke Historical Society.)

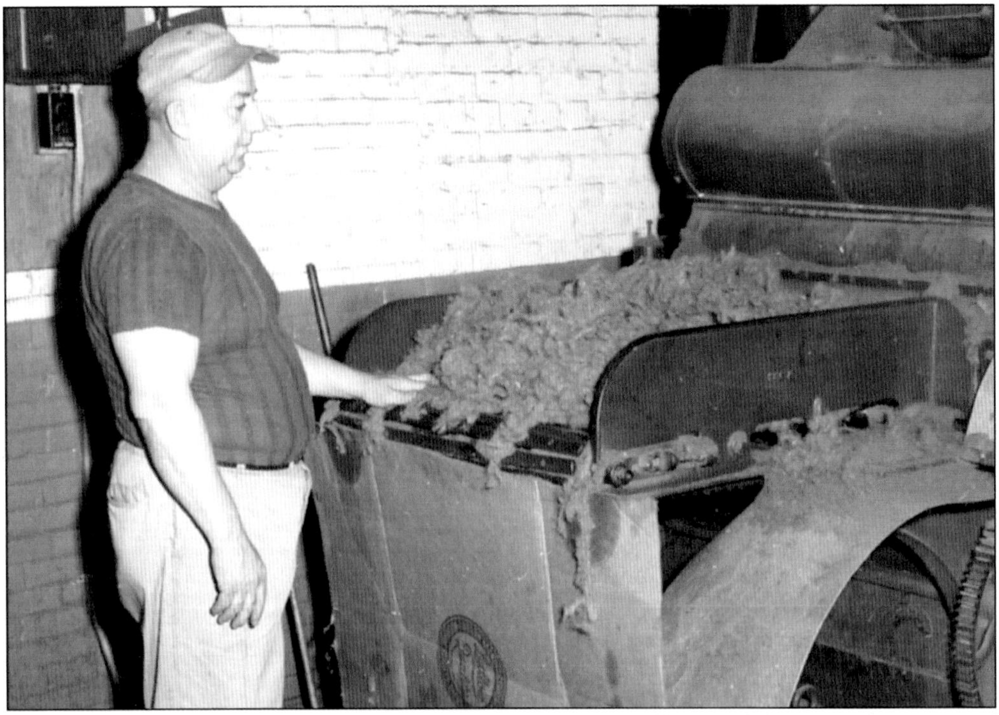

Roland Grandmaison feeds the duster at the Dole-Suncook Mill around the 1960s. (Courtesy of Pembroke Historical Society.)

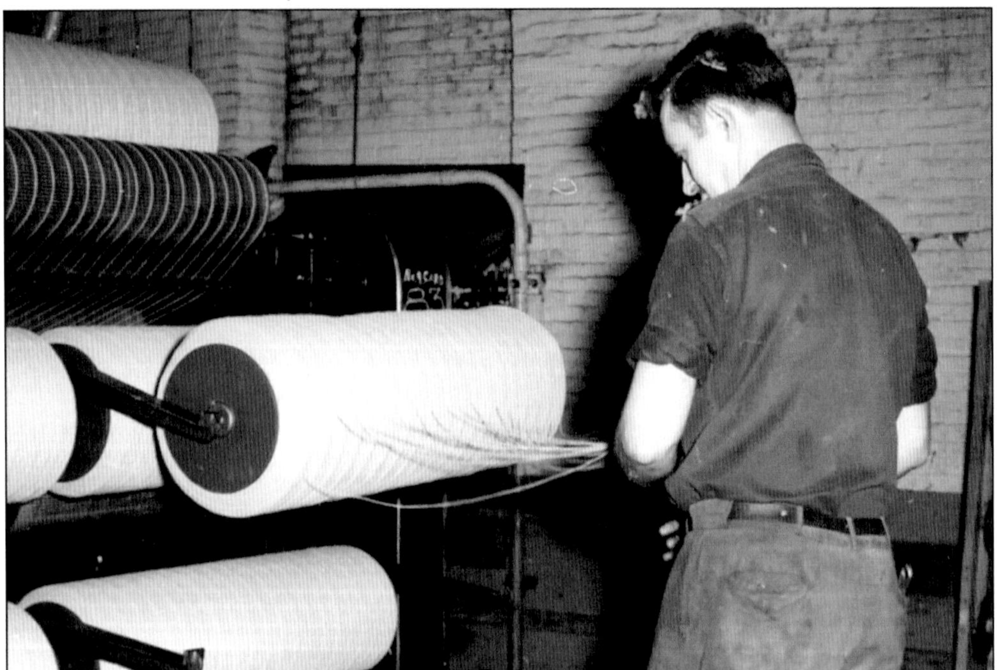

Rudolph Duford is operating a carding machine. The carding process cleaned the fiber and produce strands, as shown in this picture at the Dole-Suncook Mill in the 1960s. A small card had four spools and a large card had eight. (Courtesy of Pembroke Historical Society.)

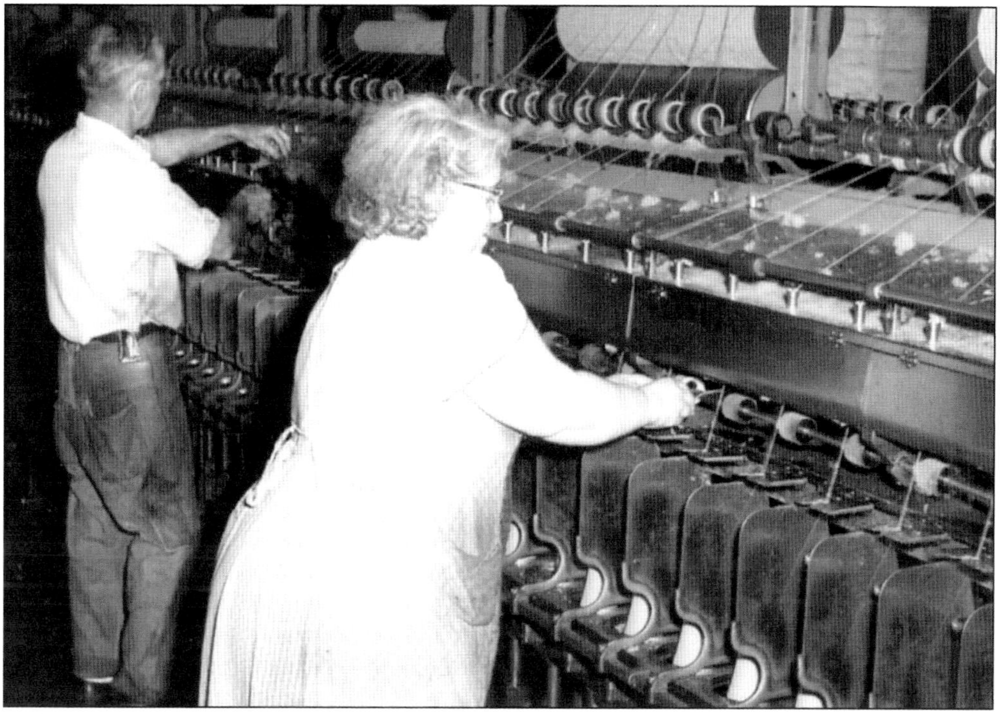

Dolores Martel and Alcide Saucier spin at the Dole-Suncook Mill in the 1960s. After carding, the strands were sent to spinning. (Courtesy of Pembroke Historical Society.)

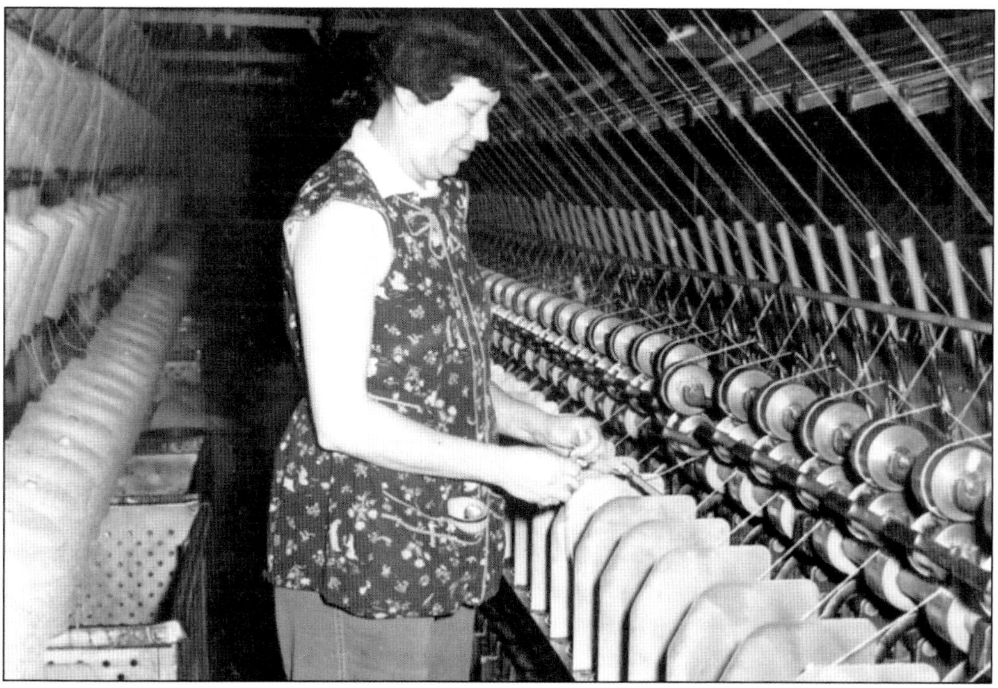

Cecile Brisbois twists fibers at the Dole-Suncook Mill in the 1960s. The twisting process combined different types of fibers, such as wool, with synthetic fiber. (Courtesy of Pembroke Historical Society.)

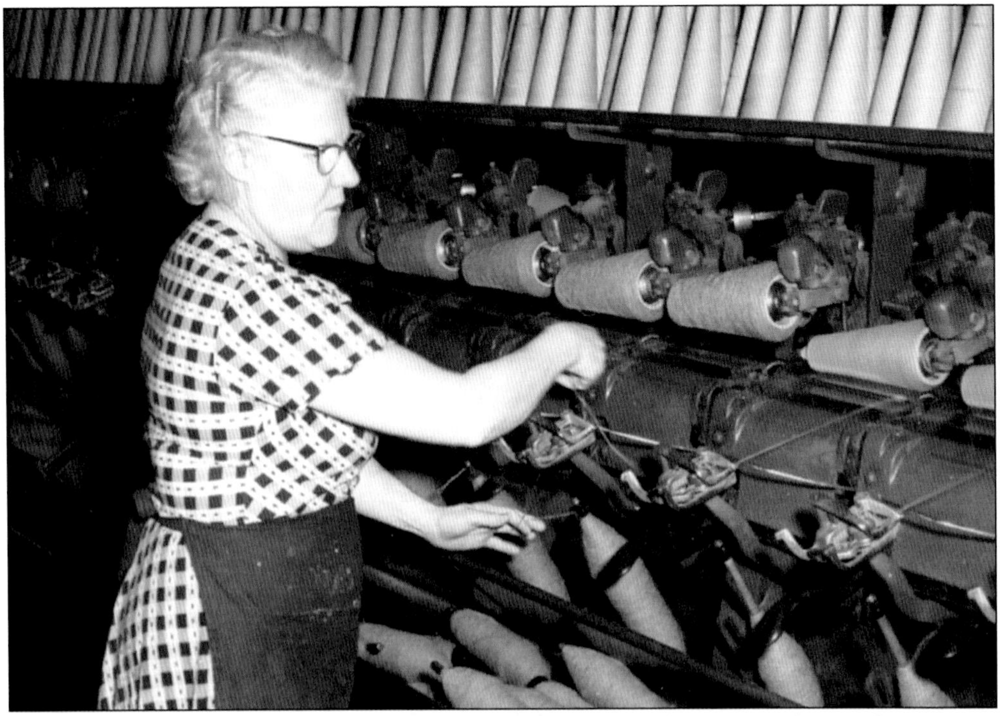

Laura Beaudoin winds strands at the Dole-Suncook Mill in the 1960s. The winding process combined multicolor strands. (Courtesy of Pembroke Historical Society.)

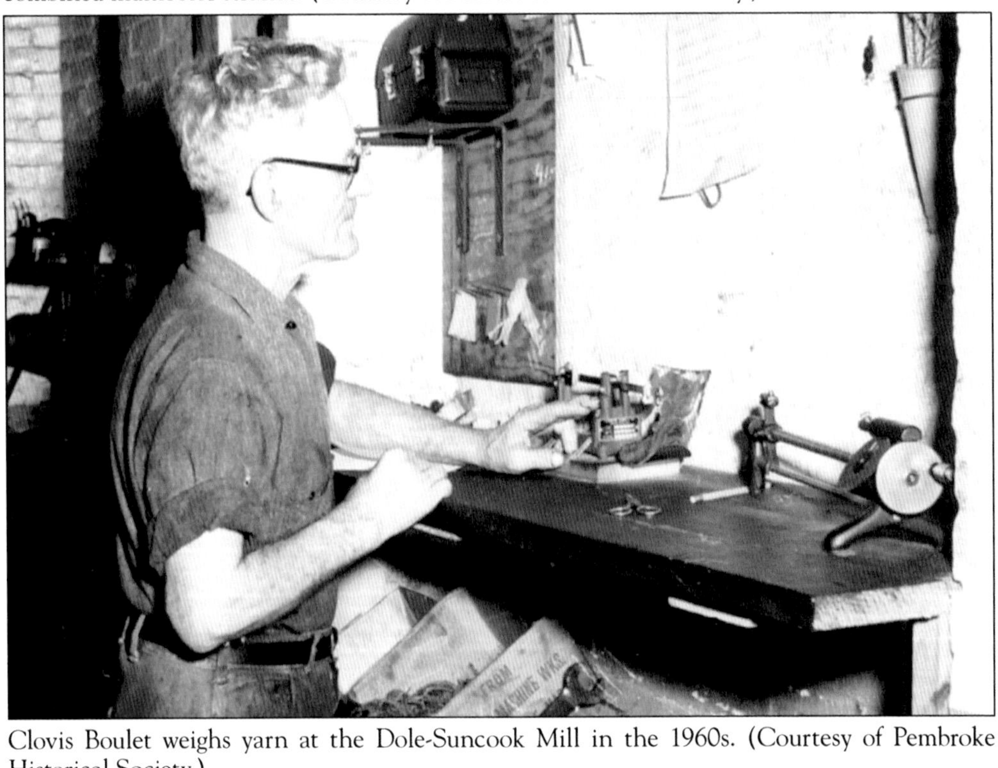

Clovis Boulet weighs yarn at the Dole-Suncook Mill in the 1960s. (Courtesy of Pembroke Historical Society.)

Three

The Whistle of the Locomotive

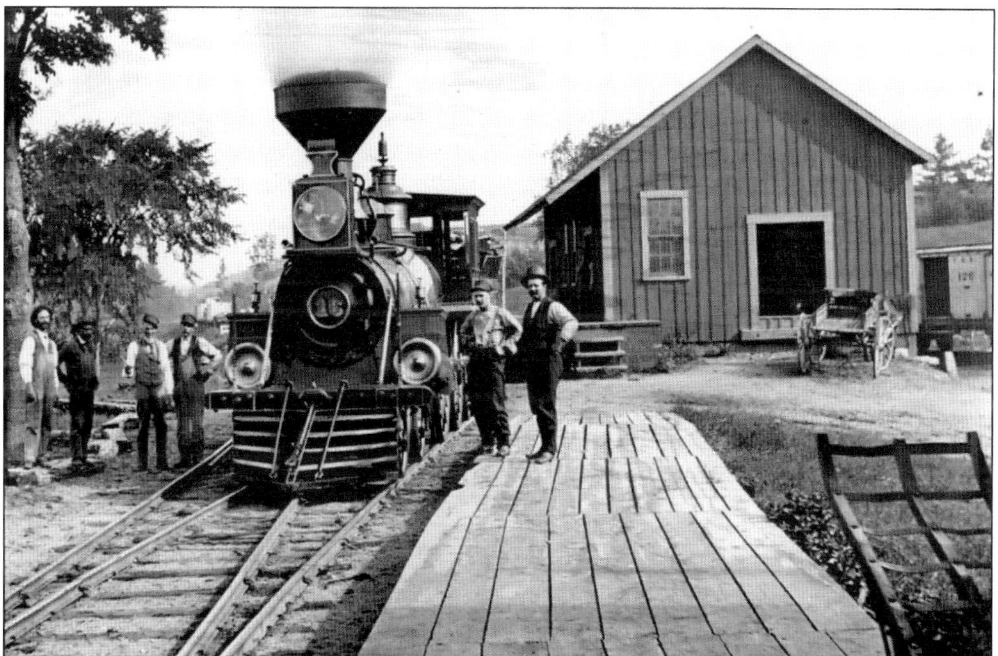

The balloon stacked Concord and Portsmouth Railroad engine, American Standard No. 16 "IXION," is paused on the tracks next to the original freight station in Suncook around 1860. As the 19th century progressed, railroad transportation became essential for shipping and receiving large amounts of goods. The railroad system played a significant role in the development of Suncook Village and its mills. Railroading lasted in the valley for 100 years. (Courtesy of the Beverly Historical Society and Museum, Beverly, Massachusetts.)

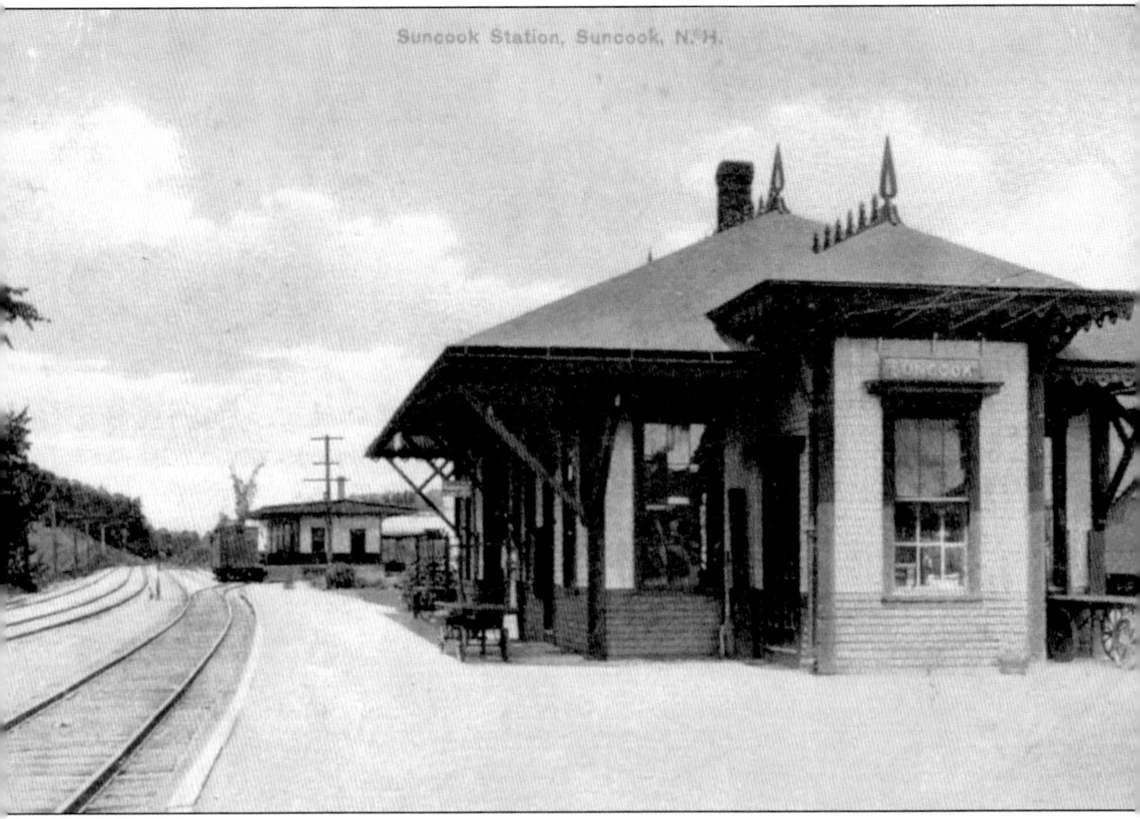

The Suncook station and freight depot were located on Exchange Street. The first Suncook station built in 1852 was a small and less elaborate building than the one above. The structure was replaced in 1887 after the original was destroyed by fire. The Suncook freight depot can be seen to the left of the photograph. In 1852 the Portsmouth and Concord Railroad line was established in Suncook. By 1869 the Suncook Valley Railroad, also known as the Blueberry Express, opened a line from Pittsfield through Allenstown connecting at the Concord Portsmouth junction. In 1890, the Concord Railroad and Boston, Concord and Montreal Railroad merged as the Concord and Montreal Railroad. The Boston and Maine (B&M) leased the Concord and Montreal Railroad in 1895. This lease continued for 91 years. These railroad lines opened Suncook to a national and international market. Within a few years Suncook Village grew and changed dramatically. Suncook became one of the most desirable locations to live in New England. (Courtesy of Brent Michiels and Larry Perron.)

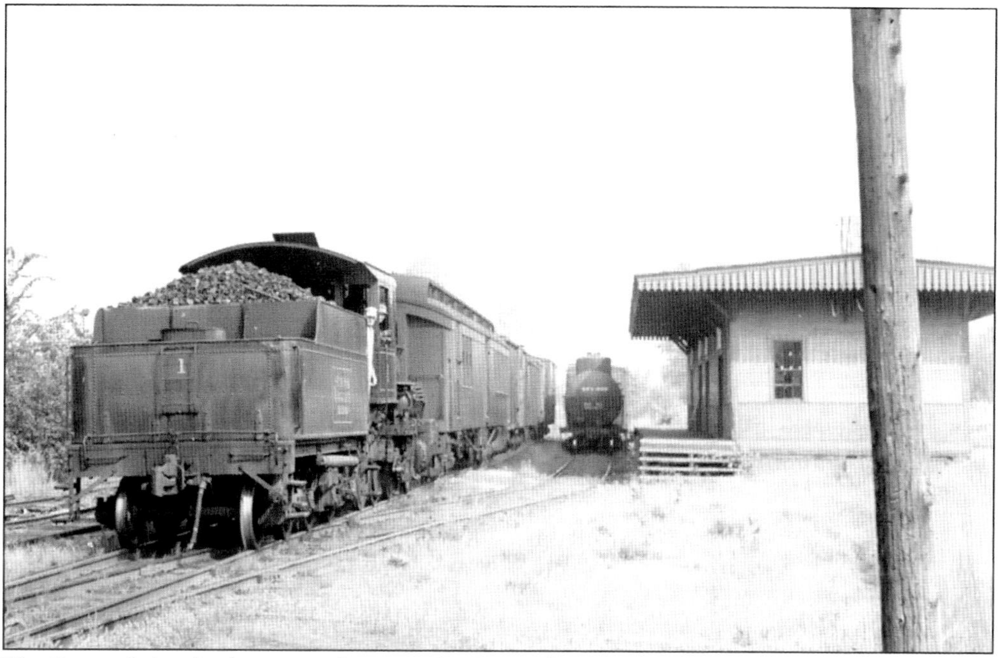

The Suncook freight depot stood next to the Suncook station, as shown in this August 23, 1940, photograph. A residential area was across the street from the station and depot, and a brickyard and grain mill were located behind the station and depot. The station was destroyed by fire in 1957 during efforts to convert it to a private home. (Photograph by Harold W. Boothroyd; courtesy of Brent Michiels.)

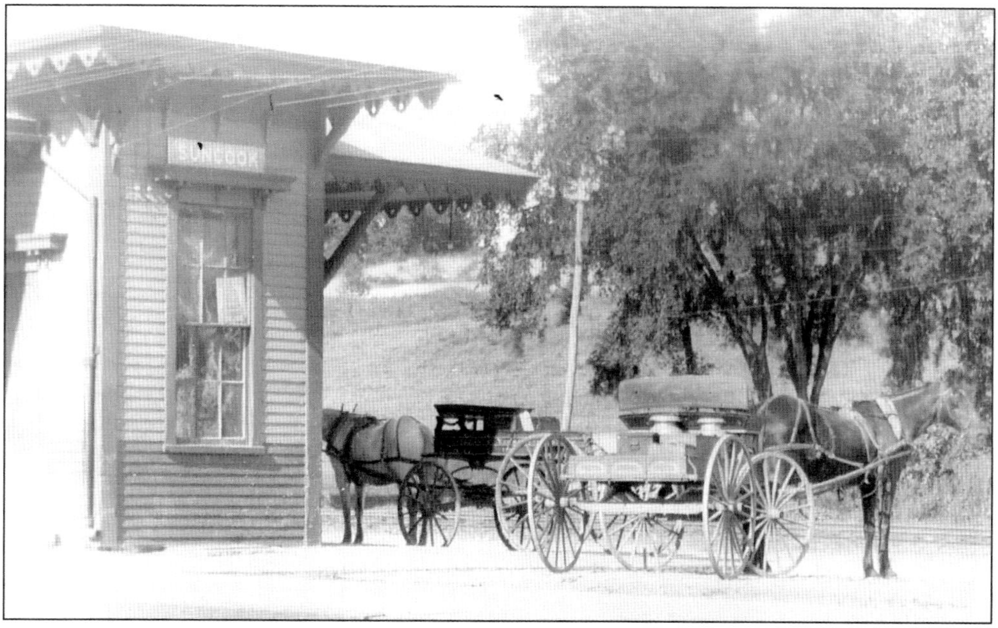

Suncook Station is shown in this view looking east. Waiting for the train to arrive are a passenger wagon and an American Express delivery wagon. Milk, produce, and large quantities of freight, including lumber and bricks, were shipped via the Suncook depot. The sign in the window advises that the station has a public telephone available. (Courtesy of Brent Michiels.)

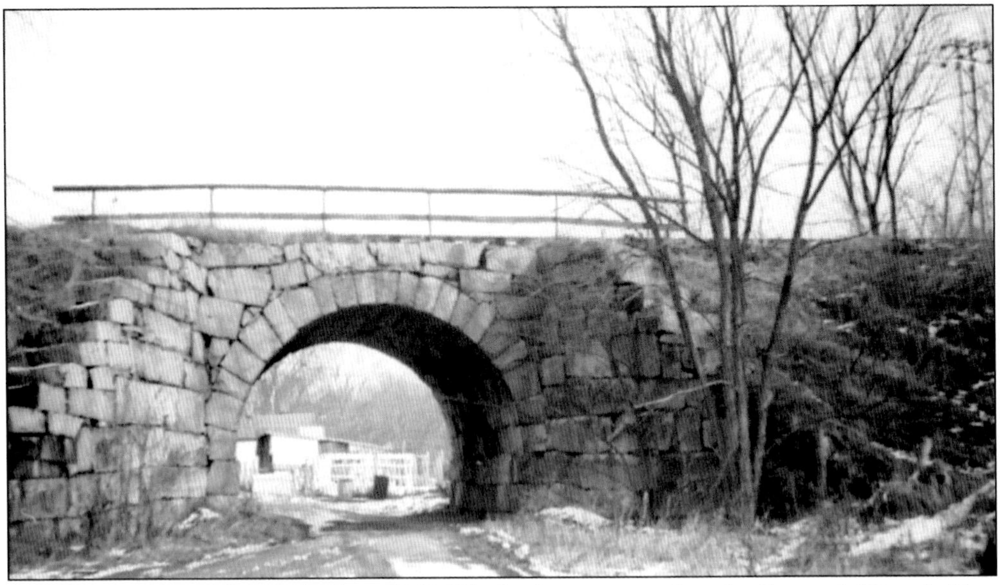

The Stone Arch Bridge was built in 1852. The bridge connected to the Suncook River Bridge. The Boston and Maine Railroad and the Suncook Valley Railroad used the overpass. The road under the Stone Arch Bridge led to the Boston Boat Company storehouse on the bank of the Merrimack River. This photograph was taken on December 1, 1951. (Photograph by Norton D. Clark; courtesy of Brent Michiels.)

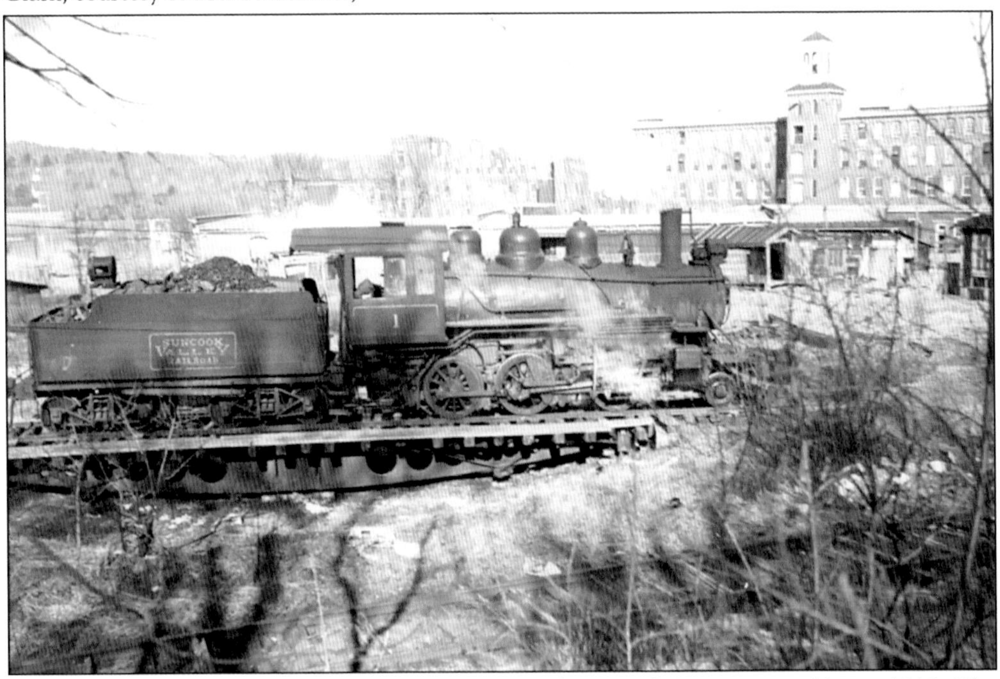

The Suncook Valley Railroad No. 1 is shown at the Canal Street turntable in 1946. The Suncook Valley Railroad transported freight, mail, and passengers between Pittsfield and Suncook. The line became known as the Blueberry Express because it carried fresh blueberries to surrounding communities when in season. (Photograph by Howard T. Moulton; courtesy of Brent Michiels.)

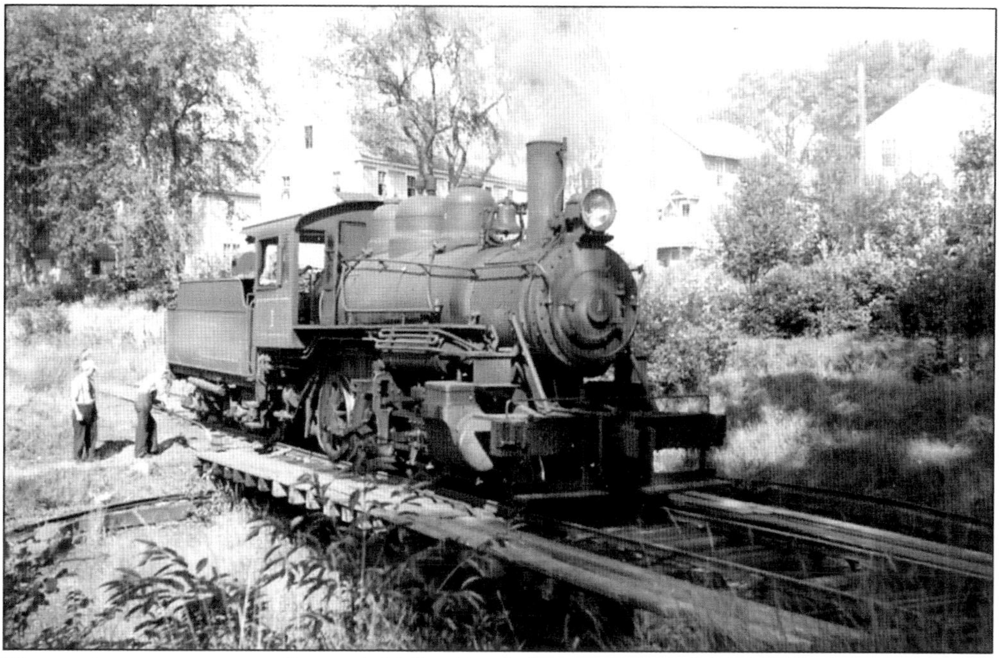

The engineer is preparing Suncook Valley No. 1 for turning on the Canal Street turntable in 1946. After being turned around on the turntable, the engine sometimes pushed the train across the Stone Arch Bridge located nearby. The engine then changed its position to the head of the train at the Suncook depot. (Photograph by Howard T. Moulton; courtesy of Brent Michiels.)

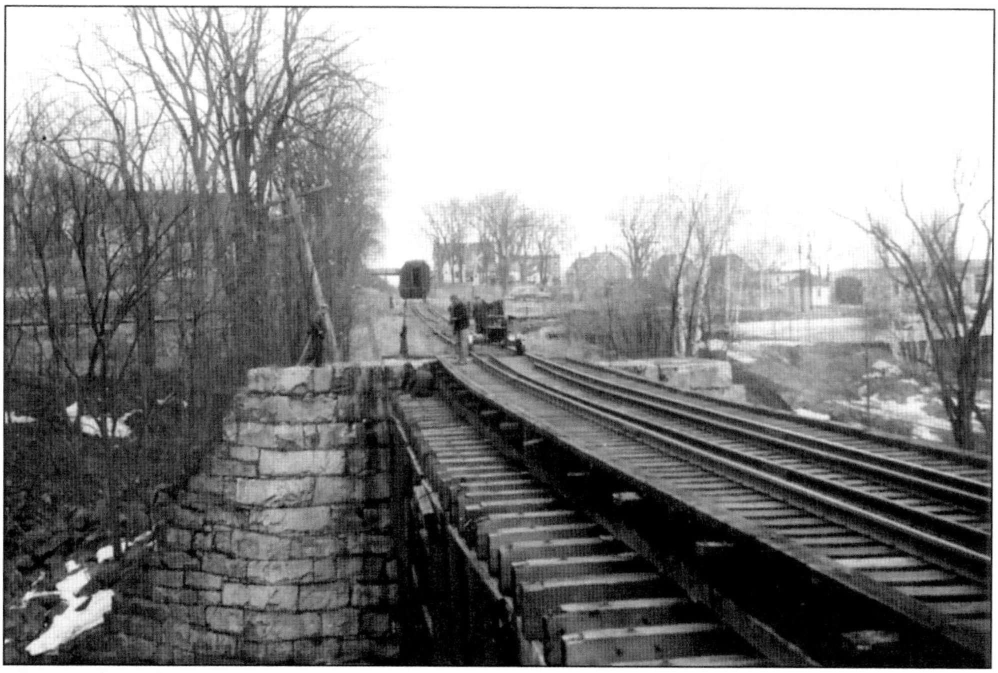

This is the China Mill Canal overpass, embargoed bridge, and tracks at Canal Street in Allenstown on April 8, 1952. The Suncook River Bridge was deemed unsafe and closed for repairs several times. (Photograph by Howard T. Moulton; courtesy of Brent Michiels.)

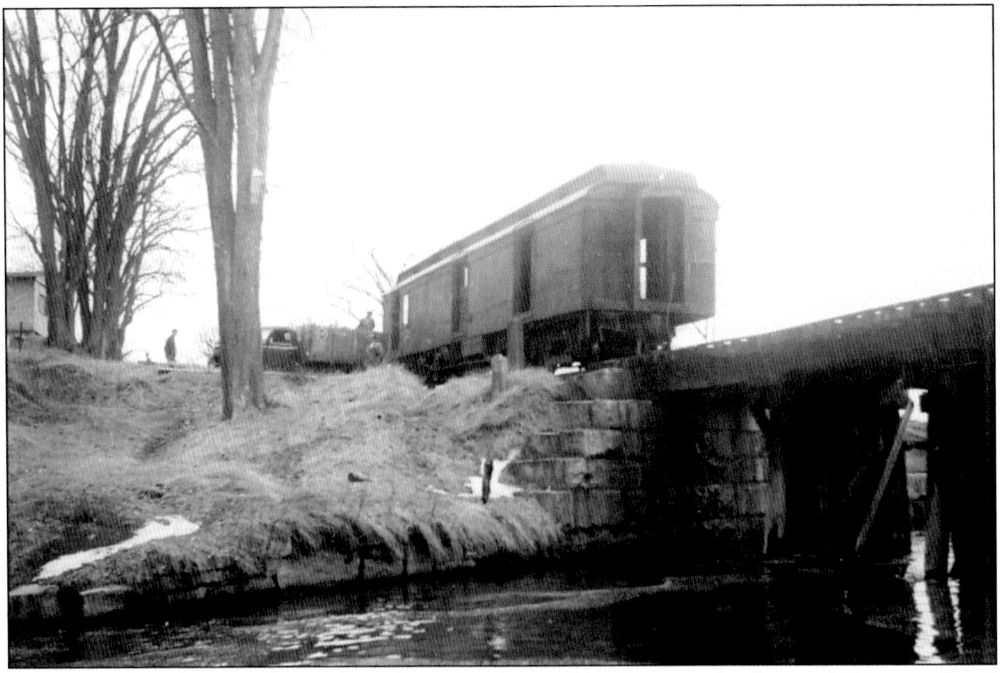

Pictured is the China Mill Canal trestle and embargoed bridge over the Suncook River at Canal Street in Allenstown on April 8, 1952. The men are unloading mail into a truck destined for Pittsfield. (Photograph by Howard T. Moulton; courtesy of Brent Michiels.)

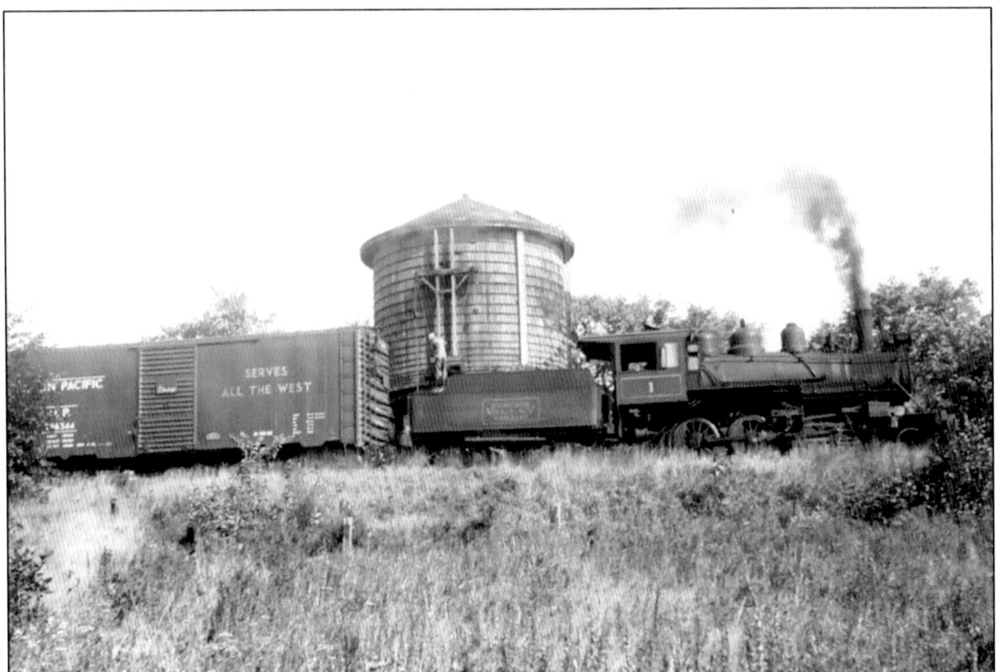

The Ferry Street water tower is shown with Suncook Valley No. 1 taking on water in 1946. The tower was located close to a running brook on Ferry Street and located on the line to Hooksett Village. (Photograph by Howard T. Moulton; courtesy of Brent Michiels.)

Filling up at the Ferry Street water tower is fireman George Becker. The chain shown in this photograph controlled the spout of the water tower. The spout was maneuvered to fill the tank. Becker was a railroad enthusiast from Cambridge, Massachusetts. While vacationing in New Hampshire, he enjoyed playing the role of fireman for the day. (Photograph by William Moneypeny; courtesy of Brent Michiels.)

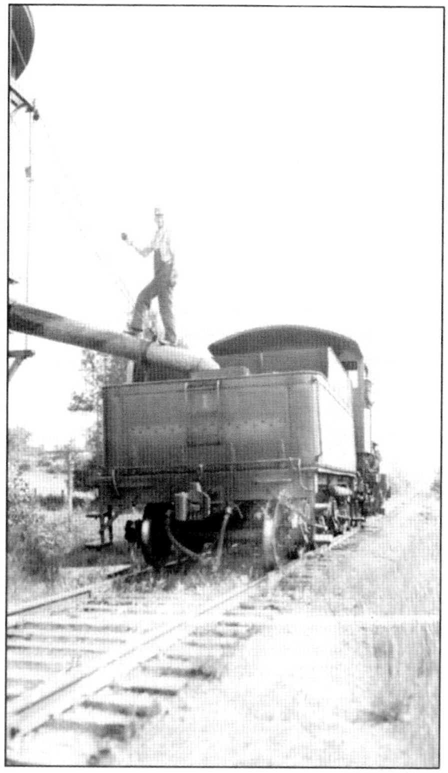

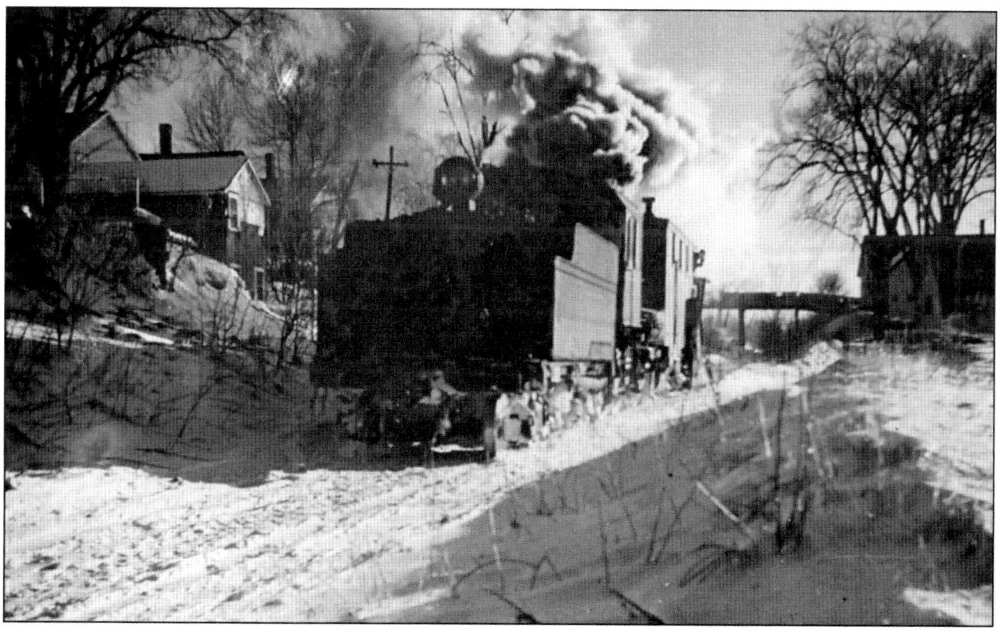

The Suncook Valley No. 502 snowplow backs up towards Suncook on tracks leading to Suncook Village in the winter of 1947–1948. Prior to 1861, this was a mainline railroad between Concord and Portsmouth. The Ferry Street overpass is to the right. Today the overpass has been removed and the area is completely filled in. (Photograph by Howard T. Moulton; courtesy of Brent Michiels.)

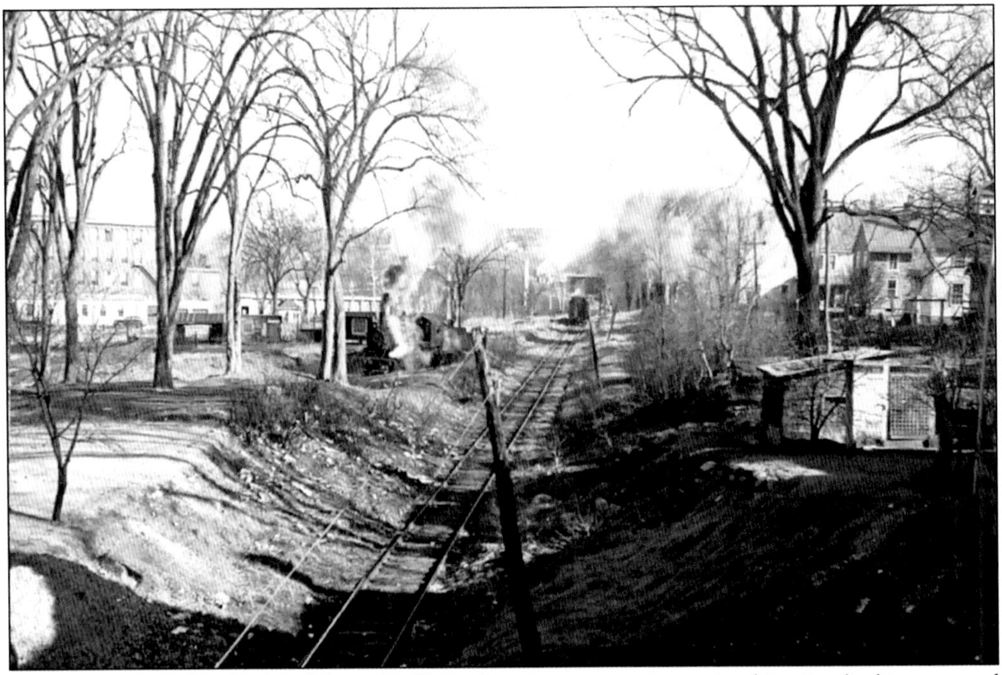

The Suncook Valley Railroad from the Ferry Street overpass is seen in this view looking toward Suncook depot in 1946. The China Mill is to the left of the train and turntable. (Photograph by Howard T. Moulton; courtesy of Brent Michiels.)

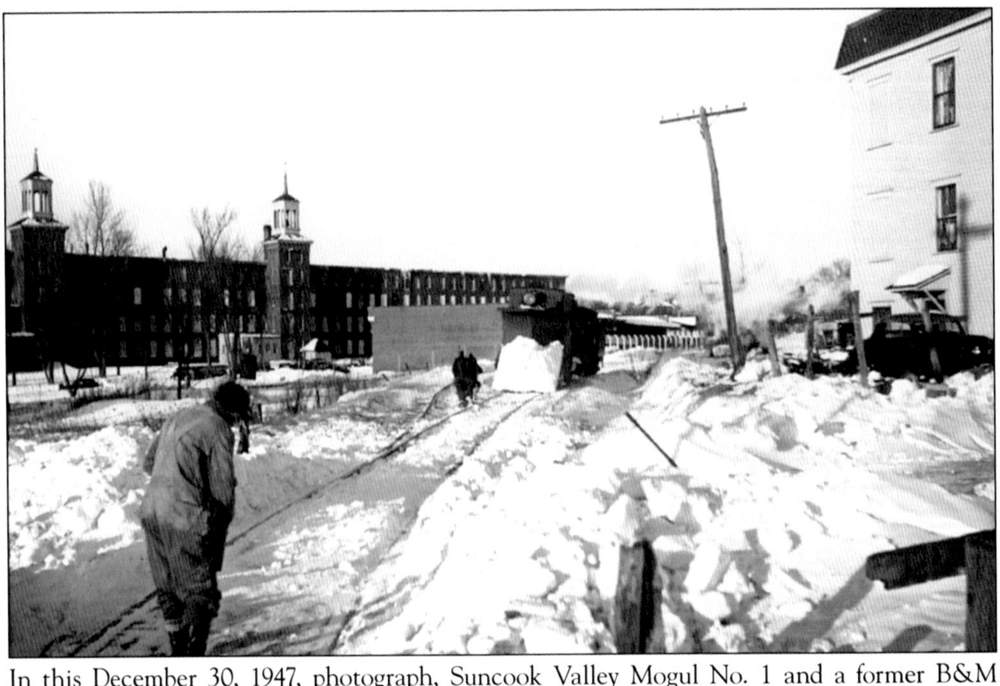

In this December 30, 1947, photograph, Suncook Valley Mogul No. 1 and a former B&M snowplow are pictured at the China Mill approaching Ferry Street on the tracks that lead to the water tank and Hooksett. Today this area is a road between Ferry and Canal Streets. (Photograph by Howard T. Moulton; courtesy of Brent Michiels.)

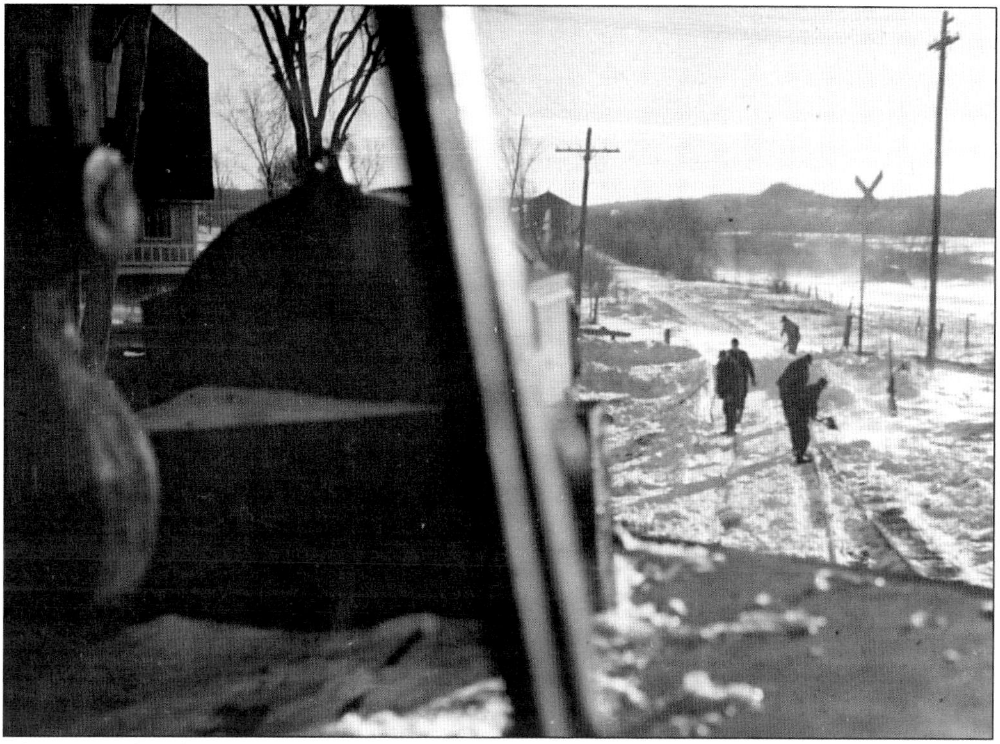

The Suncook Valley Mogul No. 1 and the Suncook Valley No. 502 plow snow at the corner of Ferry Street on December 30, 1947. The maintenance of way workmen are clearing the railroad switch into the China Mill. (Photograph by Howard T. Moulton; courtesy of Brent Michiels.)

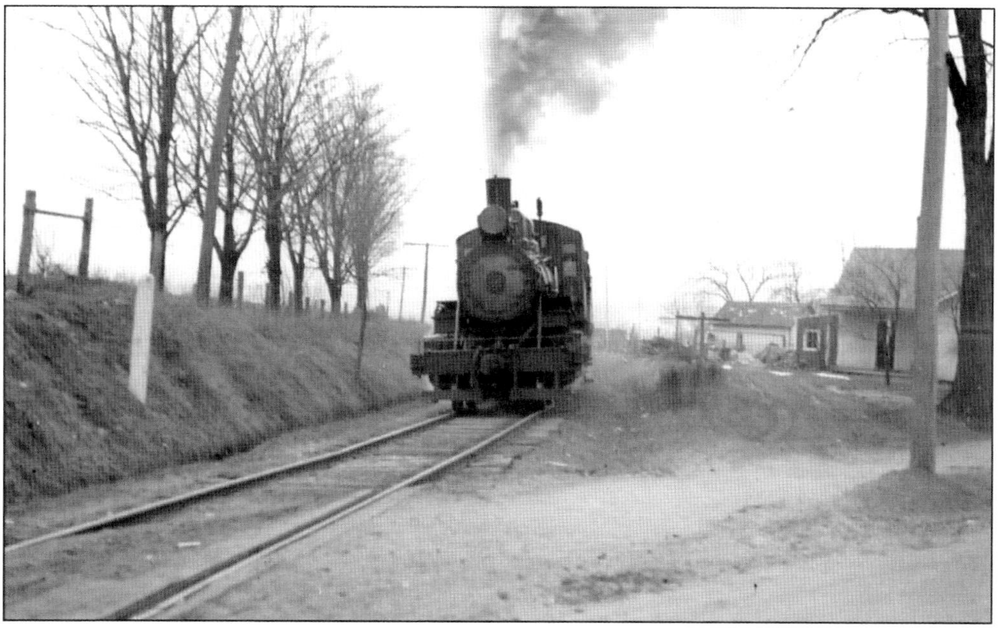

The Suncook Valley No. 1 at Ferry Street near the Allenstown Fire Station leaves the switchback heading towards Blodgett station en route to Center Barnstead in 1932. (Photograph by Albert G. Hale; courtesy of Brent Michiels.)

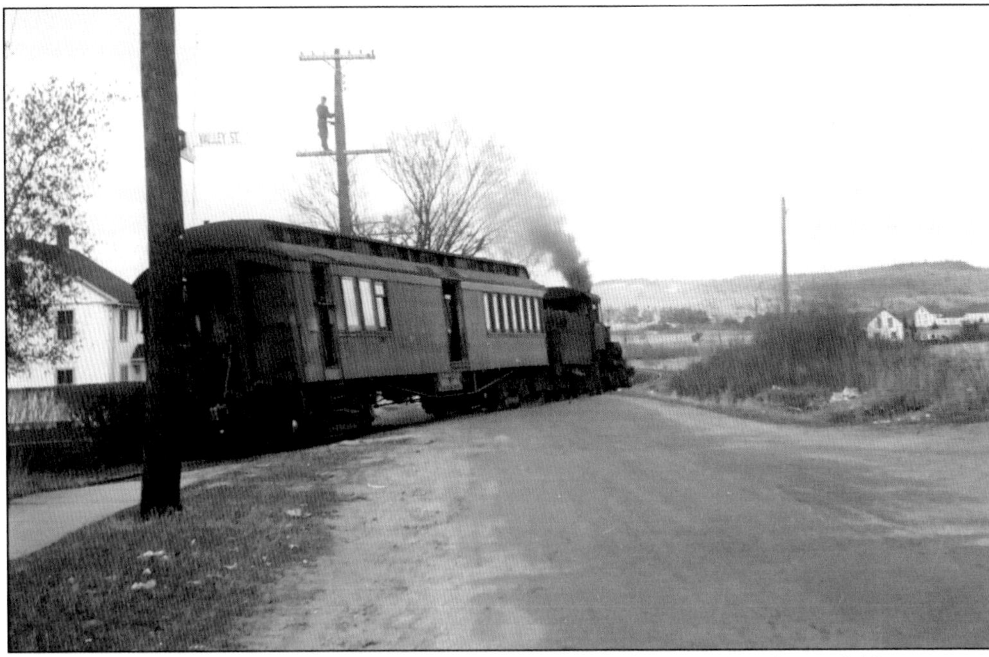

The School Street crossing at Valley Street heading towards Route 3 and Pittsfield is pictured on April 2, 1949. George Michiels from Public Service Company of New Hampshire is standing on the utility pole above the train while installing the first Allenstown Fire Department alarm system. (Photograph by Howard T. Moulton; courtesy of Brent Michiels.)

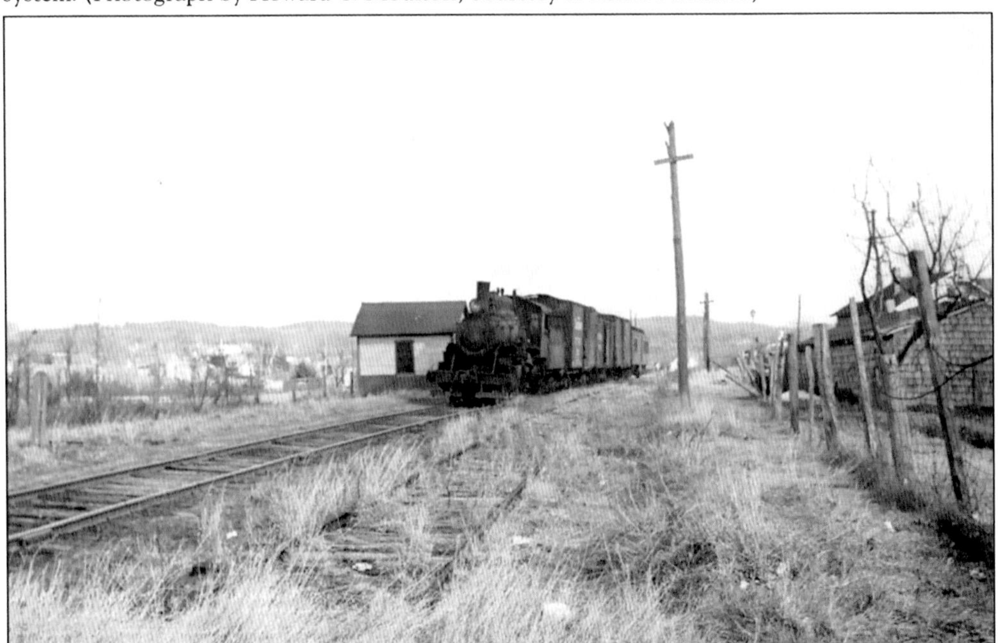
School House Siding east of the Allenstown Grammar School is seen in this photograph taken in 1946. Engineer Oscar Brian tooted the whistle when he passed the Allenstown grammar school and St. Jean the Baptist grammar school. (Photograph by Howard T. Moulton; courtesy of Brent Michiels.)

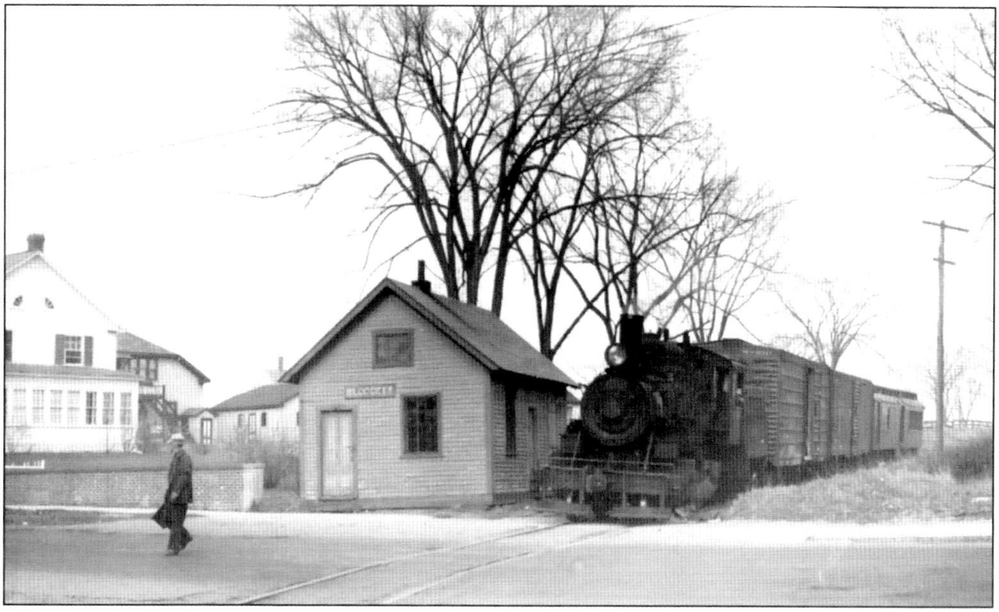

At Blodgett station, Suncook Valley No. 1 heads towards the China Mill. Blodgett station was located next to St. Jean the Baptist Catholic church. This run, on April 22, 1949, was the last for Suncook Valley No. 1. The Blodgett station was also used as a trolley stop. (Photograph by Donald S. Robinson; courtesy of Brent Michiels.)

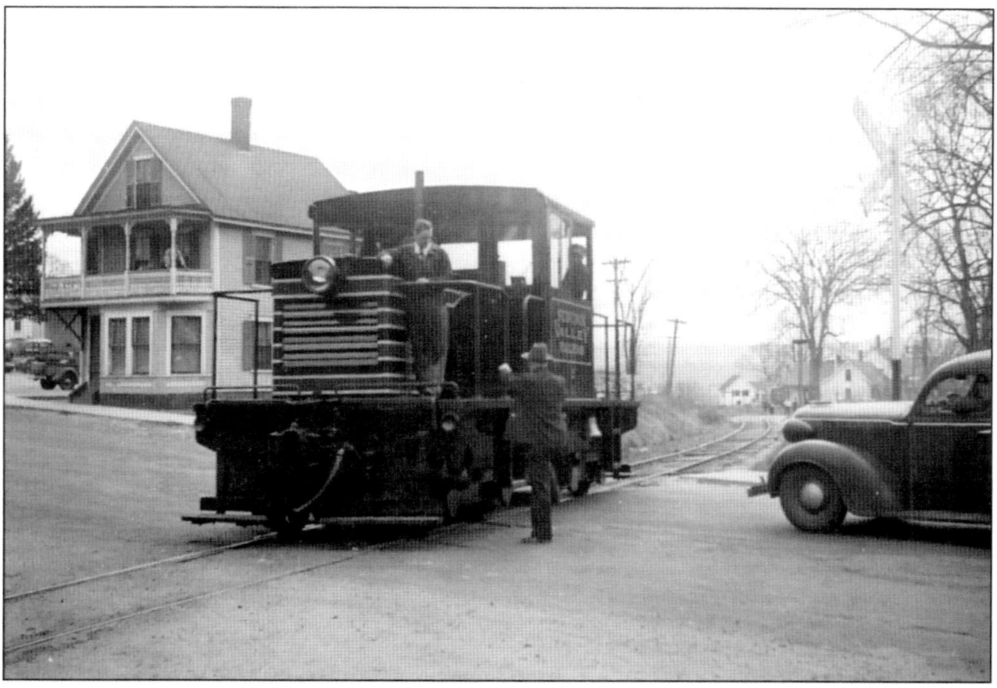

Suncook Valley No. 2, at the Ferry and Main Streets crossing, heads towards Pittsfield at Blodgett station on April 22, 1949, the day of its first run. Today this corner is occupied by the Allenstown Fire Department. (Photograph by Howard T. Moulton; courtesy Brent Michiels.)

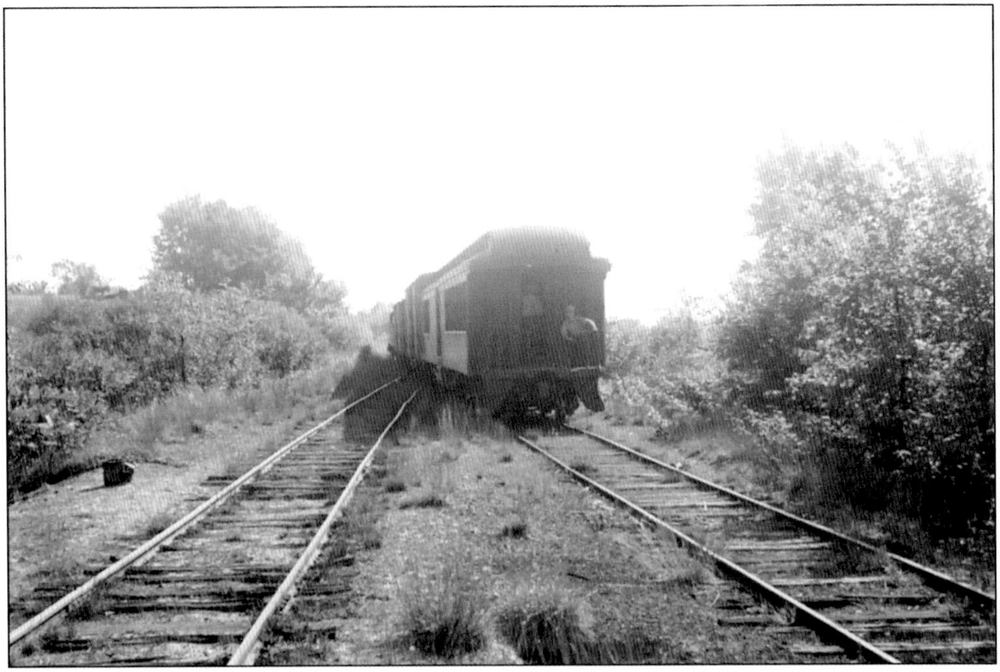

This train is behind farmland on Main Street and heading towards Ferry Street and Suncook depot. The track at right is the old line to Portsmouth that was cut back in 1861. The track at left came from Pittsfield. (Photograph by Howard T. Moulton; courtesy of Brent Michiels.)

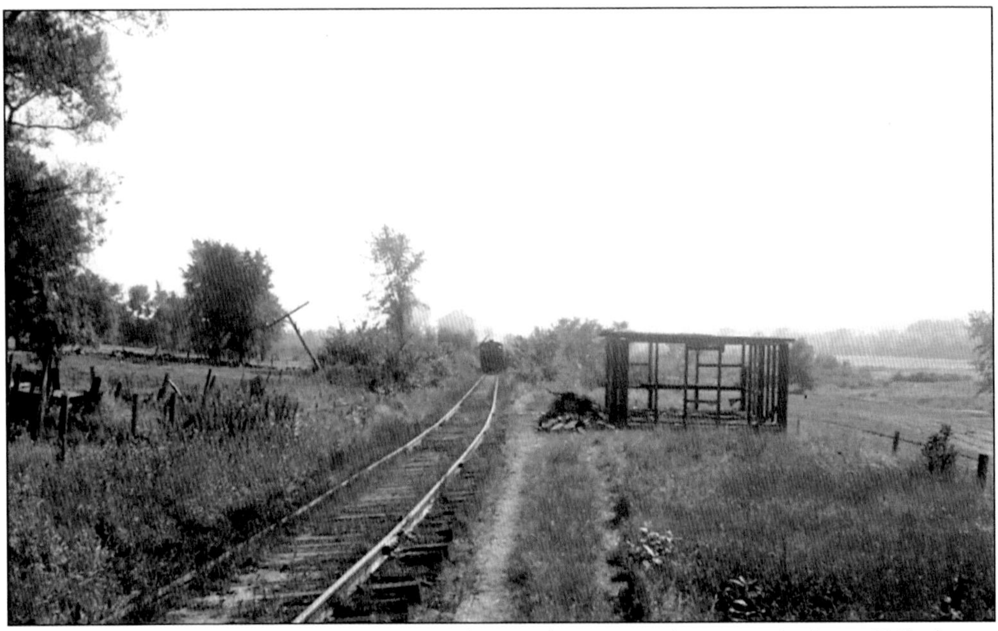

The railroad tracks and water tower near the Hooksett town line were built in 1861 during railroad line relocation through Manchester to Portsmouth. Prior to 1935 this track connected with the mainline railroad in Hooksett village across a series of covered bridges that were destroyed in the 1936 flood. The railroad was cut back in 1945 and Pembroke Water Works supplied water for Suncook Valley No. 1 at the Suncook station. (Courtesy of Brent Michiels.)

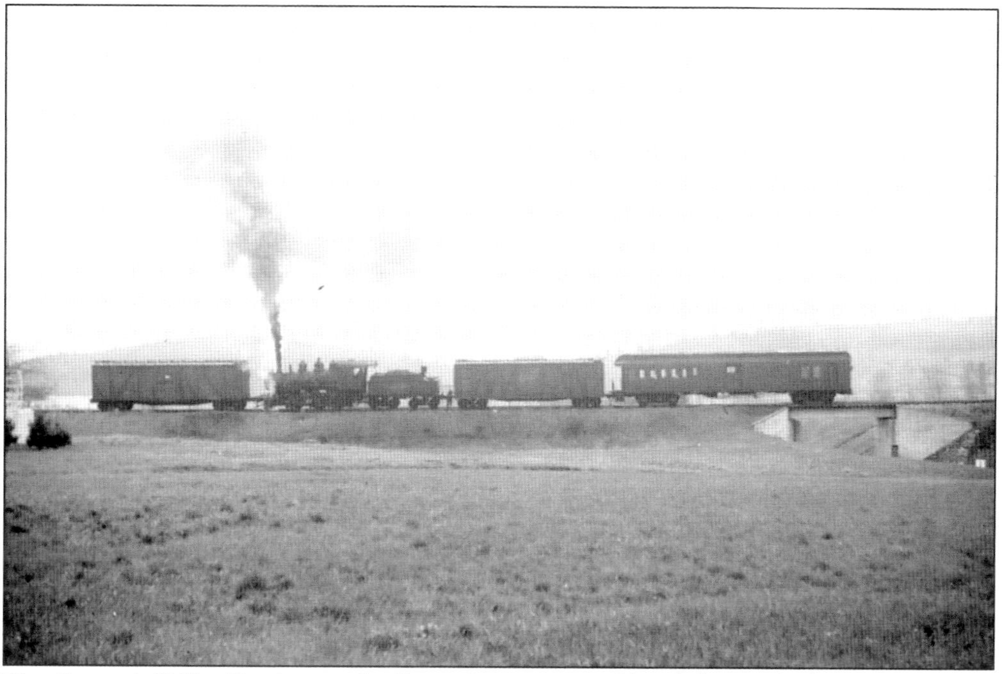

The Suncook Valley No. 1 is on the Route 3 overpass and headed towards the Bailey Lumber Company in 1946. The Route 3 overpass was removed when the intersection of Routes 28 and 3 was reconfigured. (Photograph by Howard T. Moulton; courtesy of Brent Michiels.)

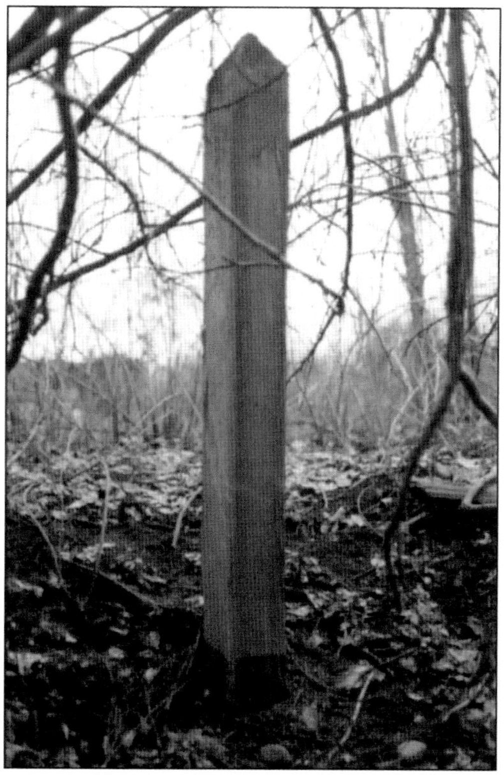

The wooden whistle post at Letendre Avenue is pictured on April 14, 1978. Whistle posts were placed about 200 feet from intersections. The engineer used two long whistles, one short whistle, and one long whistle as a warning at intersections. (Courtesy of Brent Michiels.)

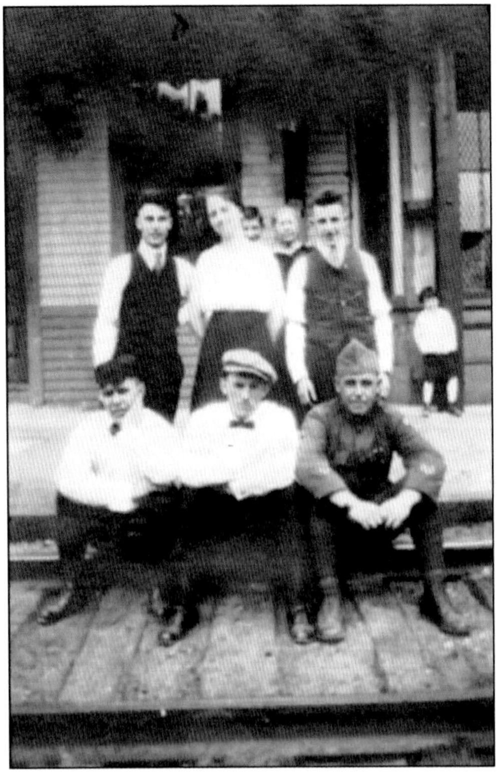

Shown at Suncook station, the Concord and Montreal Railroad connected with Concord, Portsmouth, Manchester, Boston, Maine, Vermont, and Montreal. These passengers were waiting for the train to arrive around World War I. (Courtesy of Roland Martel.)

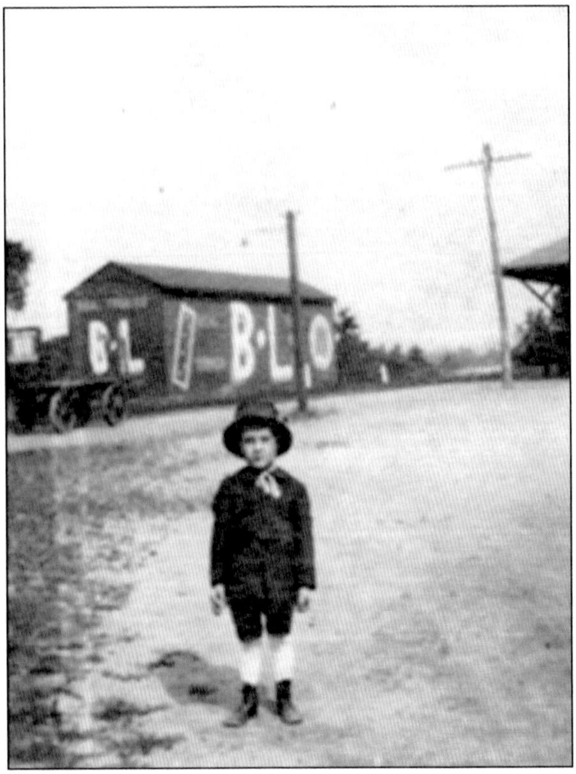

A young child poses for this photograph at the Suncook station around 1912. The Suncook depot is to the far right and directly behind the child is the Frank Blodgett Company coal storage shed. (Courtesy of Roland Martel.)

Four

C. A. BAILEY COMPANY, GRANITE, BRICKS, AND LUMBER

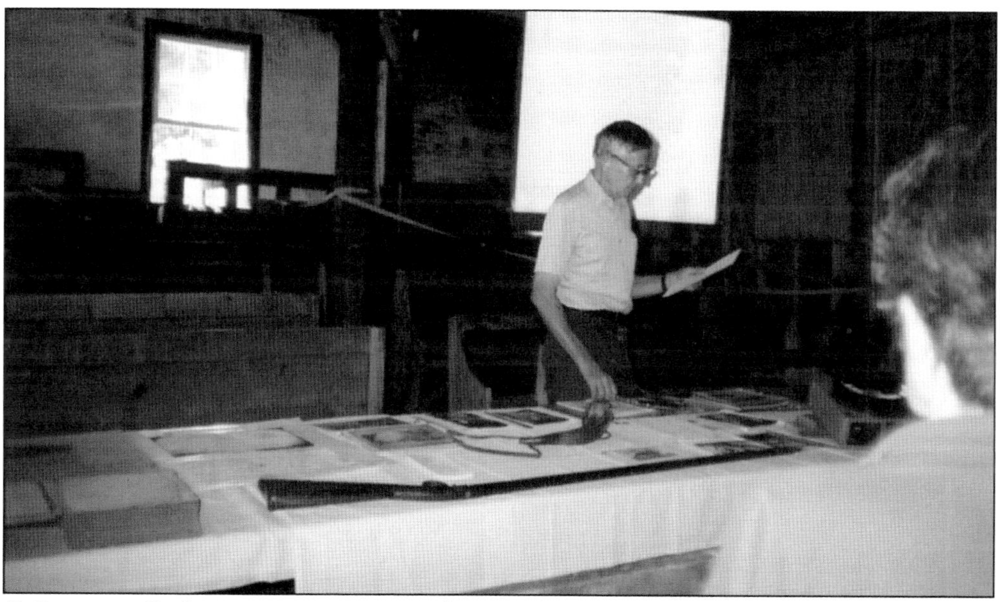

C. Benjamin Bailey gives a presentation about Bailey company history at the Old Allenstown Meeting House in 1994. The artifacts displayed on the table were from his grandfather. Bailey's transcript stated, "Charles A. Bailey bought the quarry in 1878 which included one derrick with blocks, guys, and ropes. He built his own railroad to make the shipping by rail connection with the Suncook Valley Railroad." (Author's collection.)

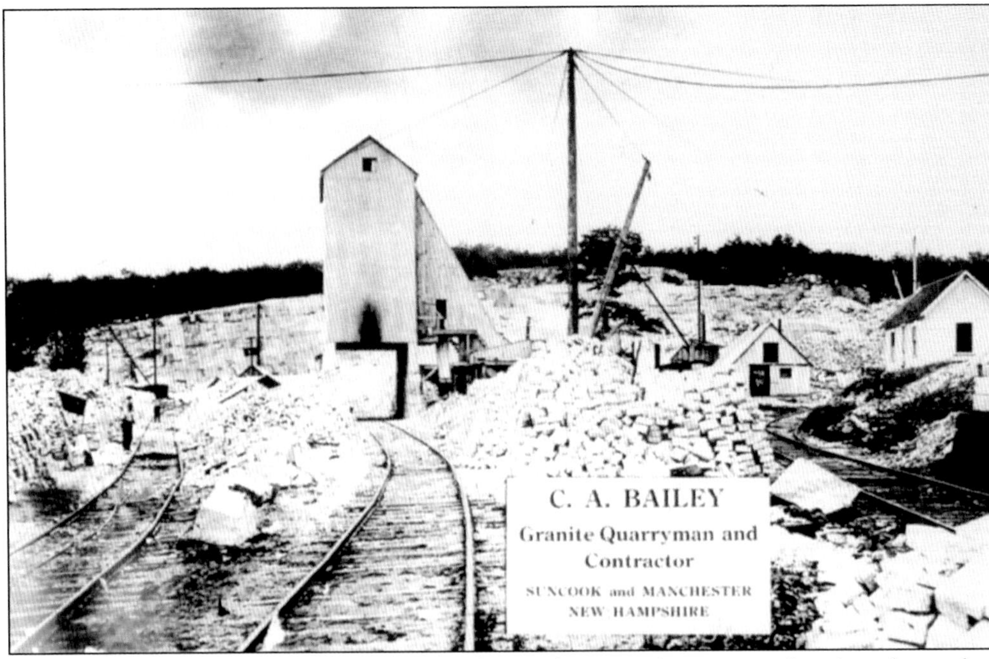

The C. A. Bailey Granite Quarry stone crusher is shown with private railroad tracks used to transport stone to the finishing shed or to the Suncook Valley Railroad interchange in Allenstown where it would be transported by other trains. The quarry was located at the intersection of Granite Street and River Road. (Author's collection.)

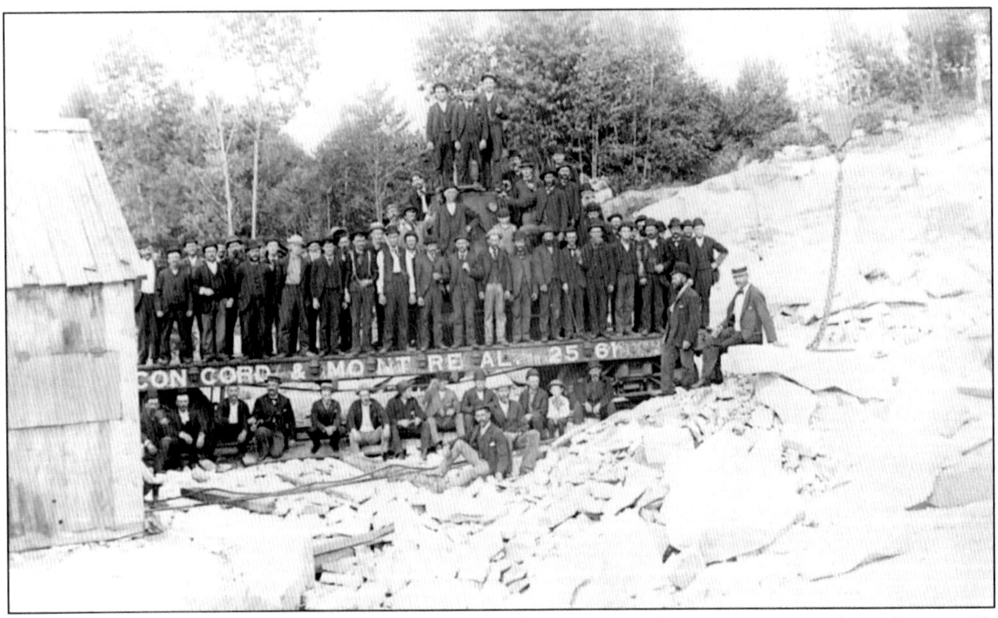

The railroad line grand opening at the C. A. Bailey Granite Quarry is pictured on August 17, 1891. The new track connected to the Suncook Valley Railroad line. In the photograph, quarry employees are standing on the new railroad line. The celebration featured an employee picnic that began the annual tradition of a company picnic that was held for many years. (Courtesy of Brent Michiels.)

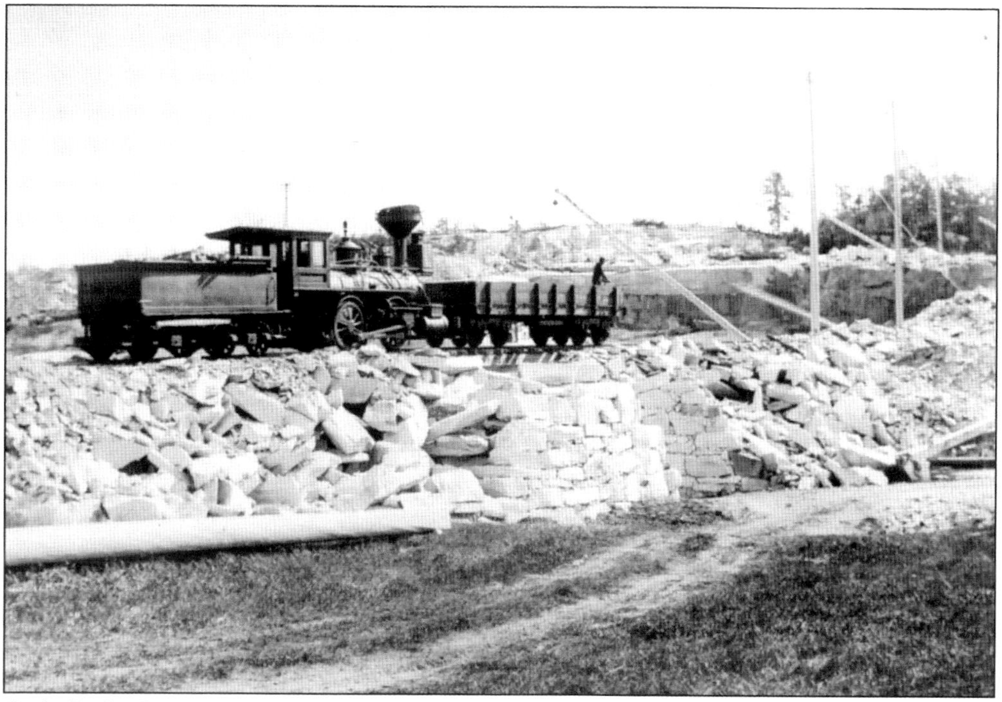

C. A. Bailey Locomotive No. 1 is on the Bailey line tracks around 1900 with a gondola at the quarry next to several derricks and piles of granite paving blocks. It was the first locomotive to join the Bailey line in 1891. (Courtesy of Brent Michiels.)

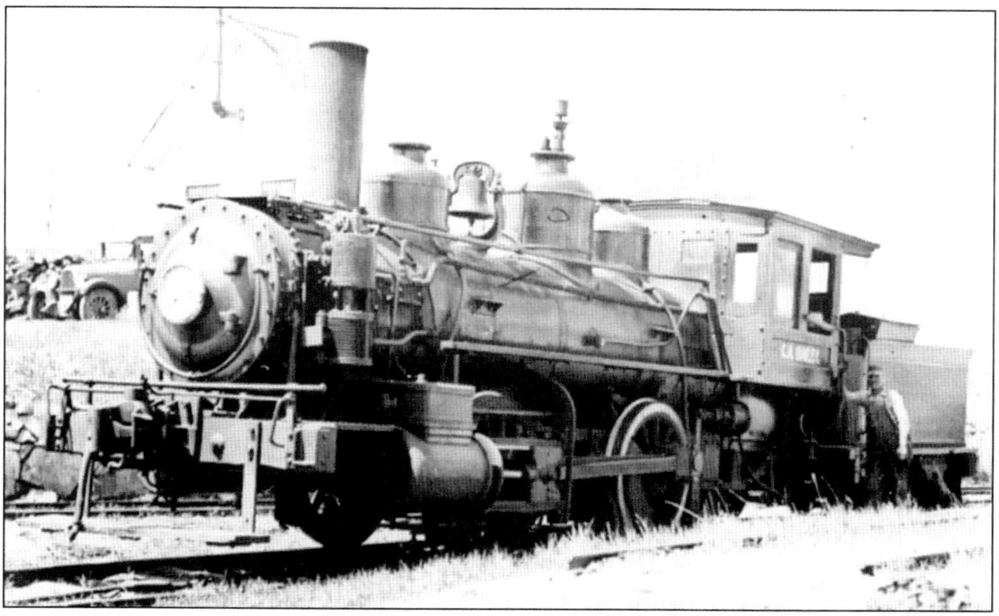

The engineer stands beside C. A. Bailey Locomotive No. 2. (Courtesy of Brent Michiels.)

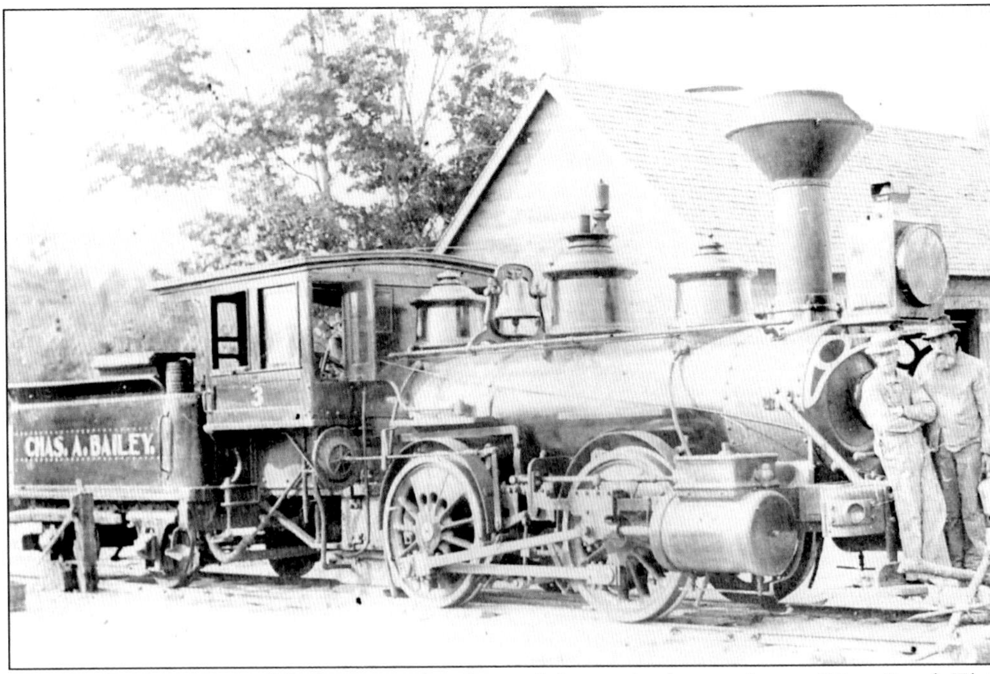

C. A. Bailey Locomotive No. 3 is paused in front of the engine house close to River Road. This engine was probably formerly Boston and Maine No. 15. (Courtesy of Brent Michiels.)

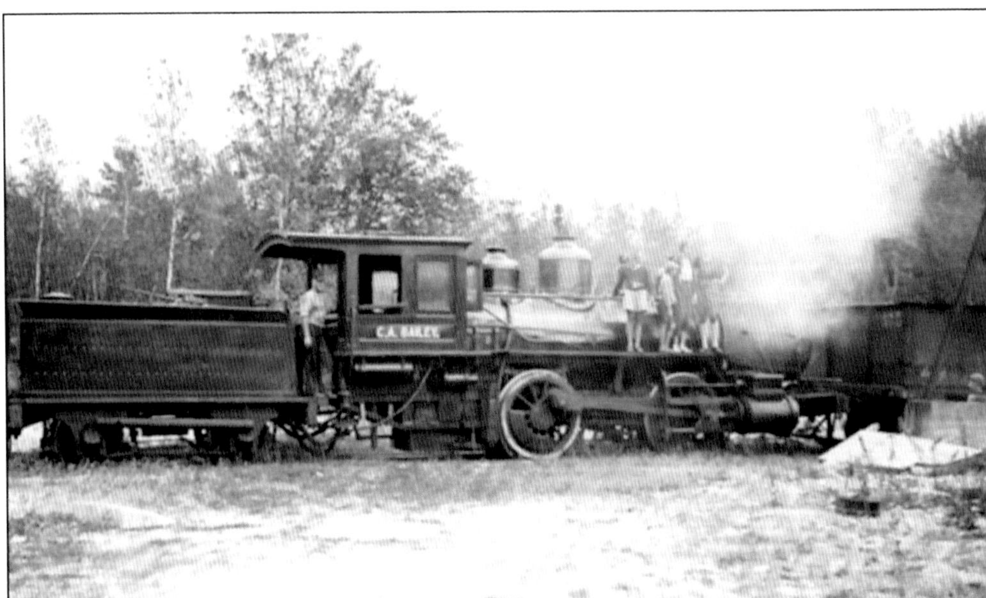

The engineer stands next to locomotive No. 2 with young women and children standing on the locomotive. This photograph was most likely taken at one of the quarry picnics. (Photograph by L. Peter Cornwall; courtesy of Brent Michiels.)

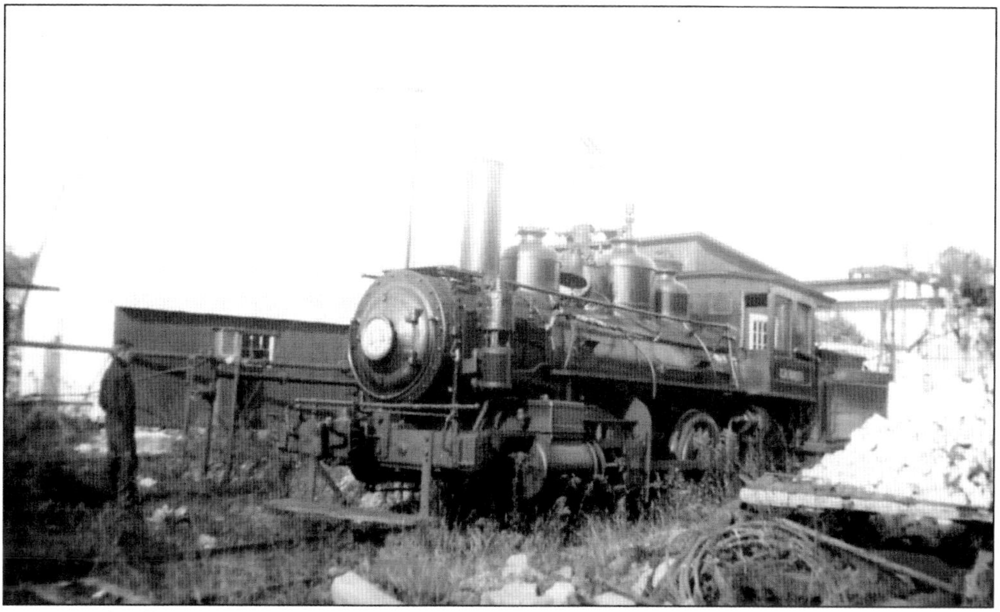

C. A. Bailey locomotive No. 2 is on the tracks in front of the overhead curb crane, loading street curbing for shipment. In 1900 the quarry shipped 2,200 carloads of granite including curbing, paving or cobble stones, building blocks, crushed stone, and rip rap. (Courtesy of Brent Michiels.)

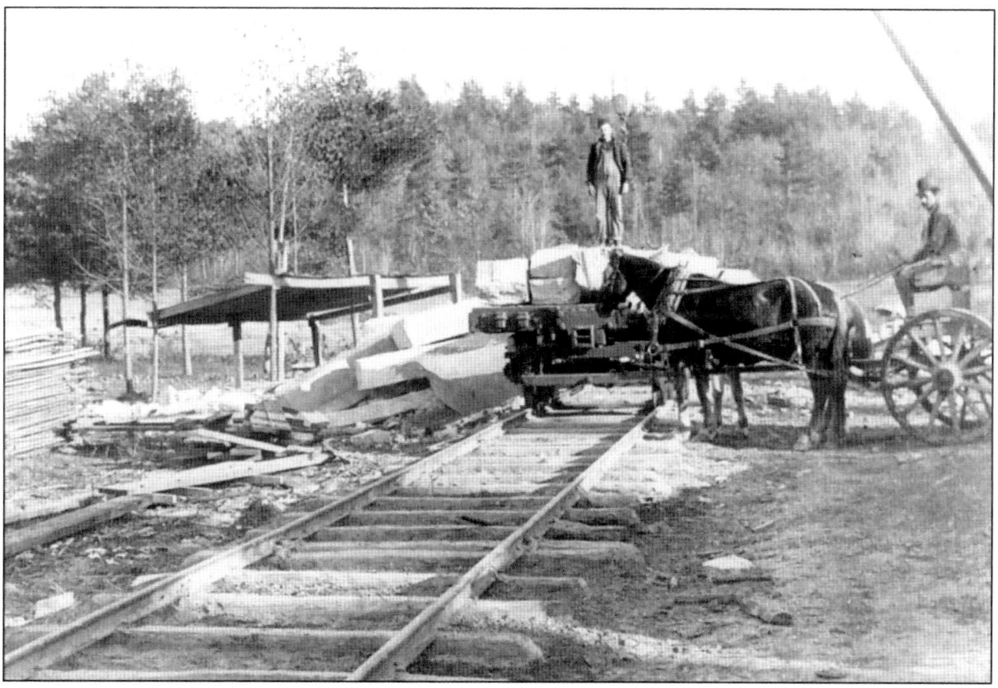

A railroad flatcar and horse and wagon are at the siding close to the stone finishing shed. Stone was transported by railroad directly to the finishing shed or it was left at this siding located northwest of the shed. (Photograph by C. Benjamin Bailey; courtesy of Brent Michiels.)

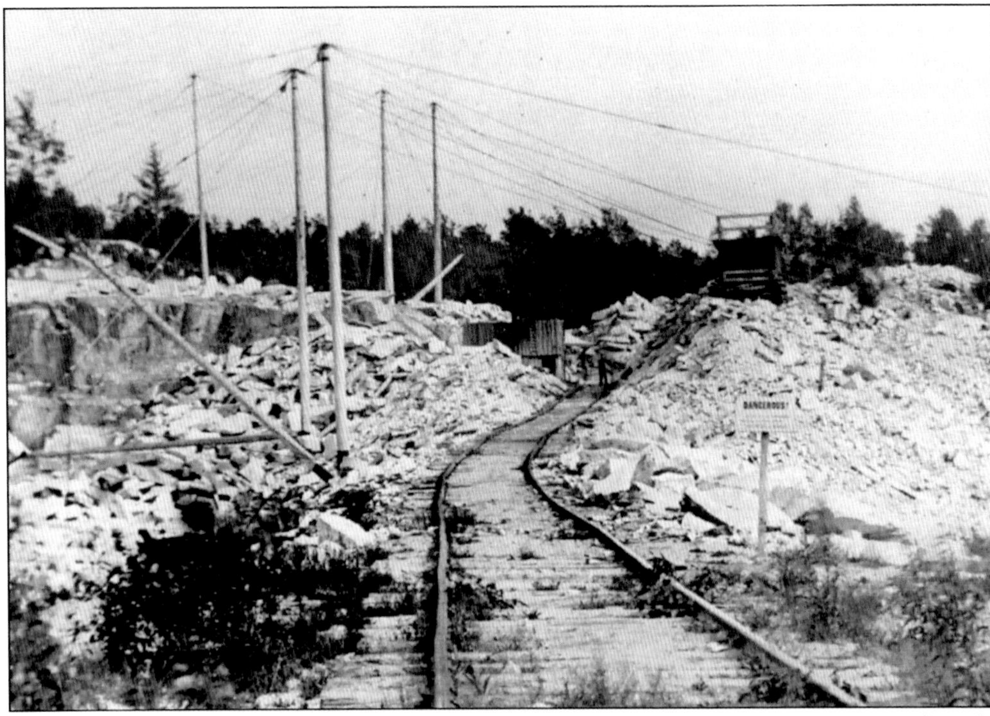

Quarry derricks are positioned close to the Bailey railroad line. There were numerous derricks installed in clusters or rows throughout the granite quarry. (Courtesy of Brent Michiels.)

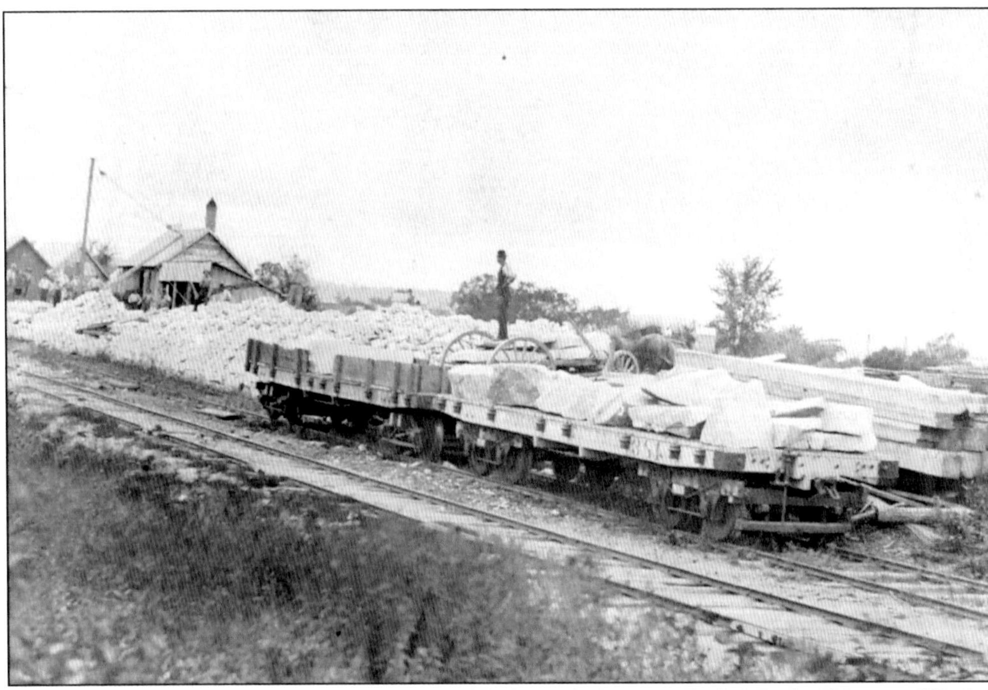

The Bailey cars are loaded with granite. The blacksmith shop on the left had a "Granite Works" sign on the roof of the building. (Courtesy of Brent Michiels.)

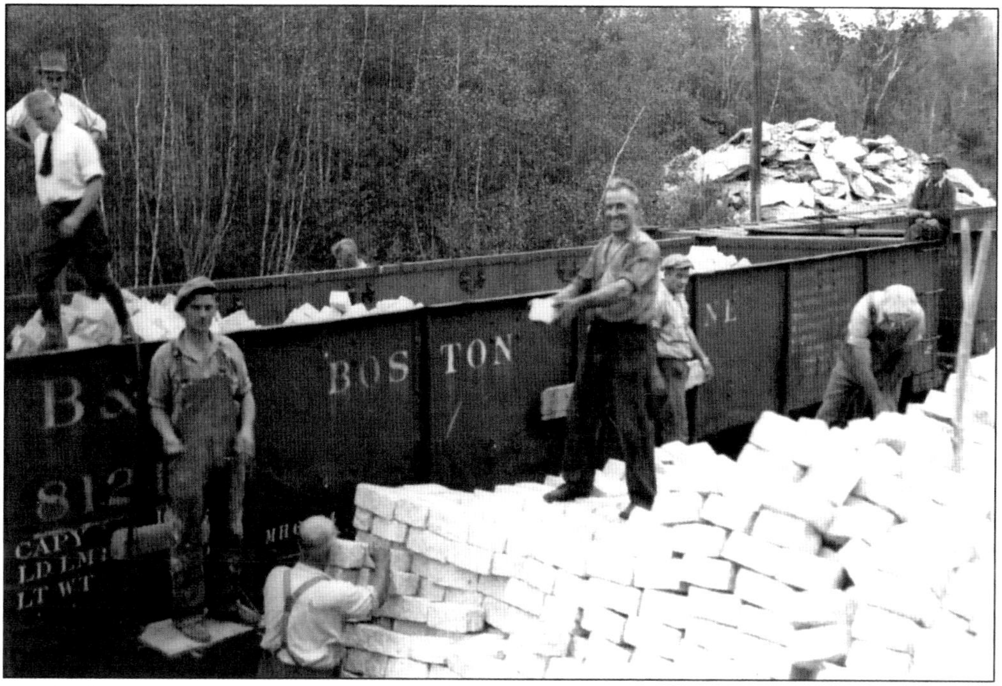

The Bailey quarry crew loads granite cobblestones into an open railroad car. (Photograph by Peter Cornwall; courtesy of Brent Michiels.)

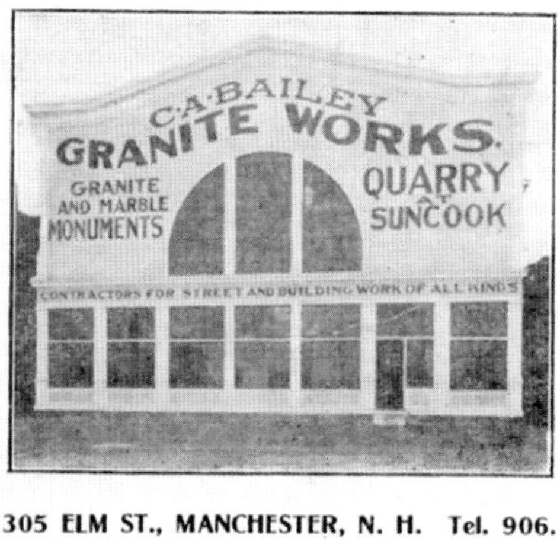

The C. A. Bailey Granite Works storefront was located on South Elm Street in Manchester. The sign states, "Contractors For Street And Building Work Of All Kinds." The Amoskeag Mills and the China Mill are living monuments of Bailey Granite. (Courtesy of Brent Michiels.)

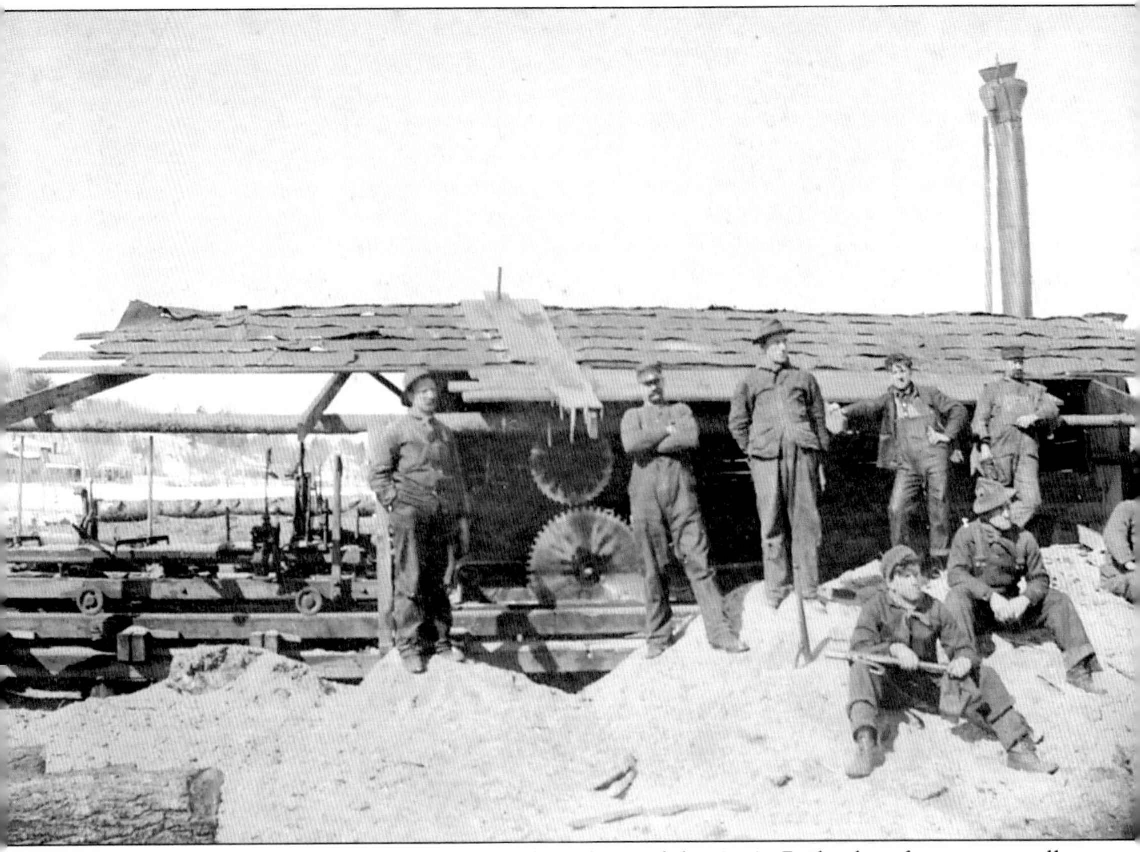

John Murby, with his arms crossed, stands in front of the C. A. Bailey box factory sawmill on Turnpike Street. The C. A. Bailey Lumber and Box Company was established in 1901. The first mill was situated about 100 feet east of the Turnpike Street bridge on Glass Street. It was purchased from Addison Osgood by Charles A. Bailey and Hall E. Bailey. This mill had the capabilities of finishing 50- to 60-foot timbers. The spire for St. Jean the Baptist church came from the first mill. In 1903, a fire destroyed the original mill; the Baileys built another on the same site. In July 1934, the Bailey lumber steam boiler exploded, shaking the countryside and hurling the Erie boiler 500 hundred feet. Herman Lauzier, age 31; Armand Amyot, age 32; and B. L. Randall, age 60, lost their lives. Those injured were Oliver Lavertue, age 19; Rudolfe Lefevre, age 19; Alcide Boisvert, age 5; and company president Hall Bailey, age 50, were seriously injured. The cause of the accident was never determined. (Courtesy of Allenstown, New Hampshire, Historical Society.)

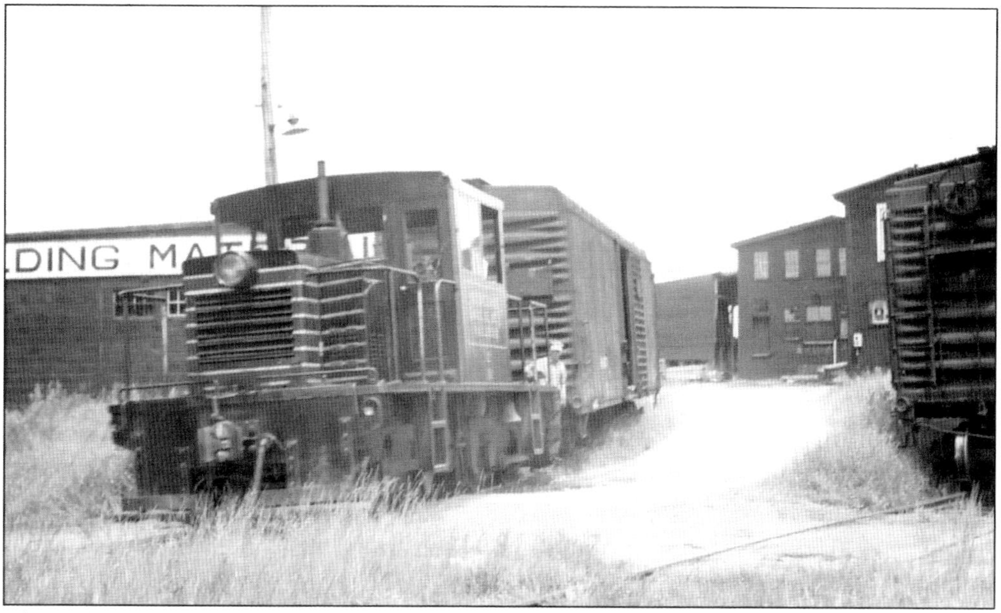

The Bailey Lumber and Box Company was located on Turnpike Street in Allenstown. In this photograph, the Suncook Valley Railroad diesel No. 2 was leaving the lumber company after delivering bags of cement. (Photograph by Norton D. Clark; courtesy of Brent Michiels.)

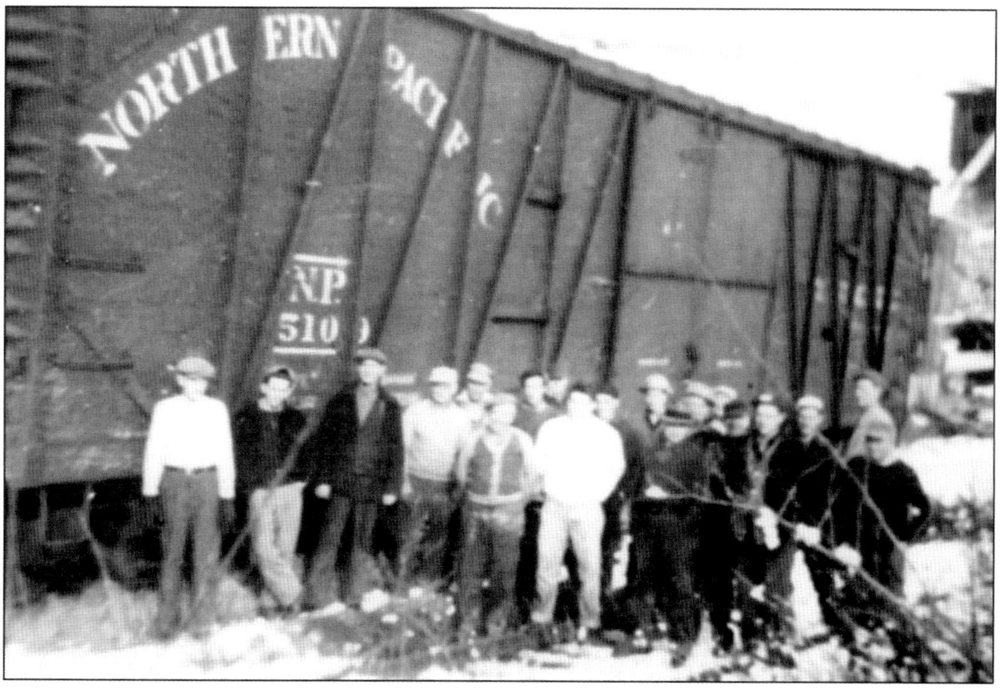

One of the C. A. Bailey crews is pictured after loading the Northern Pacific Railroad boxcar on December 15, 1952. This was the last loaded boxcar to leave C. A. Bailey Lumber and Box Company. (Photograph by C. Benjamin Bailey; courtesy of Brent Michiels.)

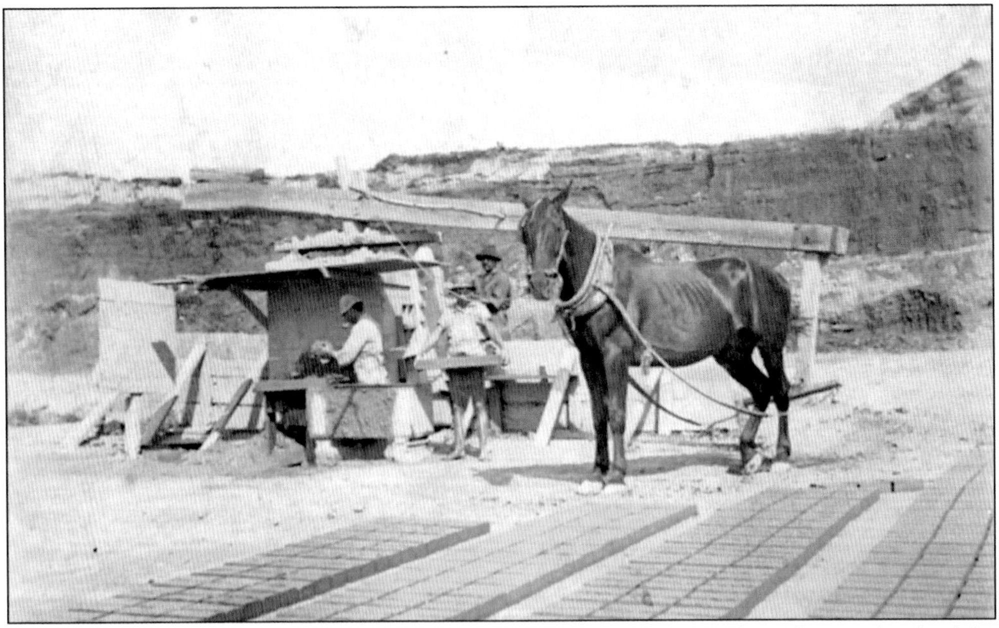

The C. A. Bailey, Warren Sargent, Head, and Gault brickyards were along the east bank of the Merrimack River. The Sargent and Head brickyards covered the Bailey Farm area. Charles A. Bailey owned the operation in partnership with Sargent and Gault. Most of the Amoskeag Mills were built from these bricks and the granite sills and foundations came from the Bailey Quarry. (Courtesy of Arlene and Victor Fleury.)

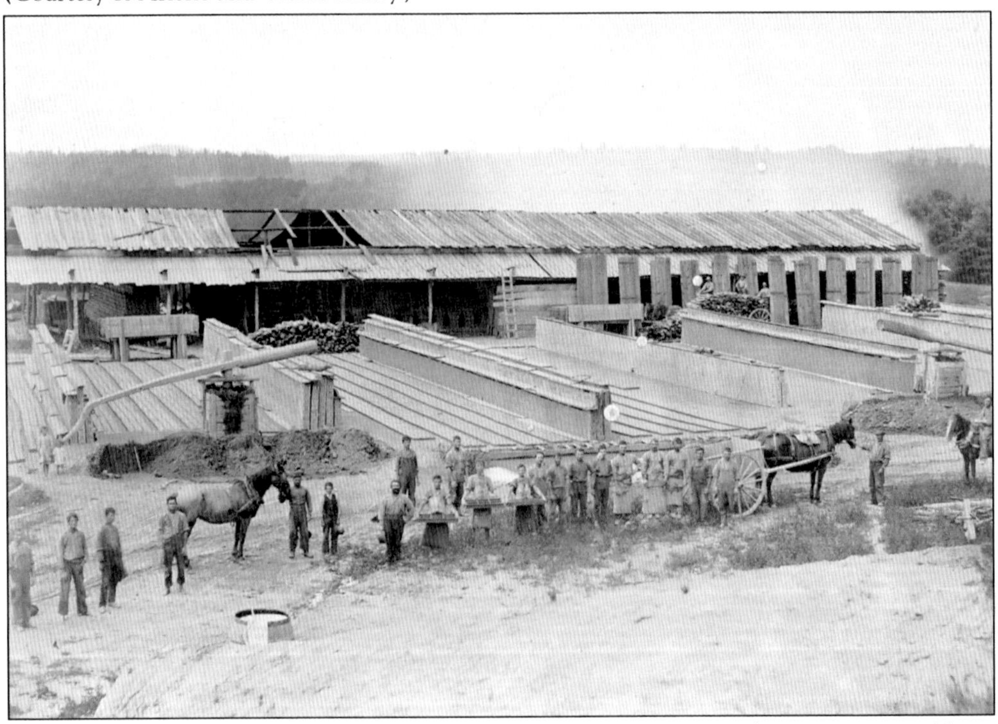

One of Suncook's many brickyards along the clay banks of the Merrimack River is pictured here. (Courtesy of Pembroke Historical Society.)

Five

NEIGHBORHOODS, THE CAST SYSTEM

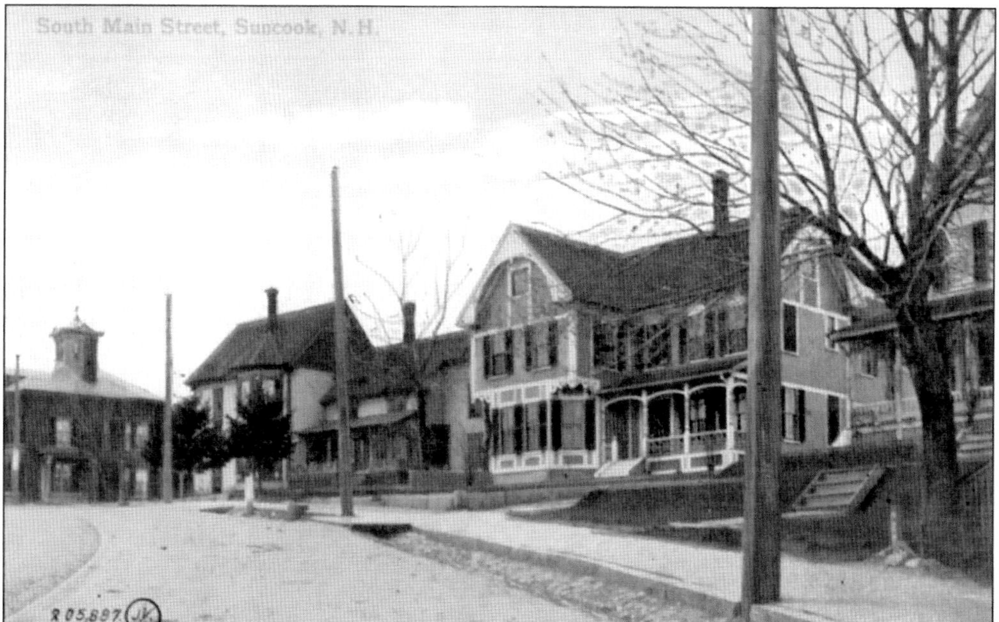

Many prominent business owners and bosses lived in elaborate homes along Main Street. Often referred to as "the street of the bosses," this area was one of several distinct neighborhoods, mostly owned by the Suncook Mills. Webster and Whitten Streets were known as "the street of the supervisors." Between Church and Main Streets were "the corporations," and on Glass Street "the company houses." Adjacent to the China Mill on Canal Street was "China Village" and the neighborhood near the Catholic parish was called "Le Petit Canada." Later, Le Petit Canada was used to reference the heart of Suncook Village. (Courtesy of Connie French.)

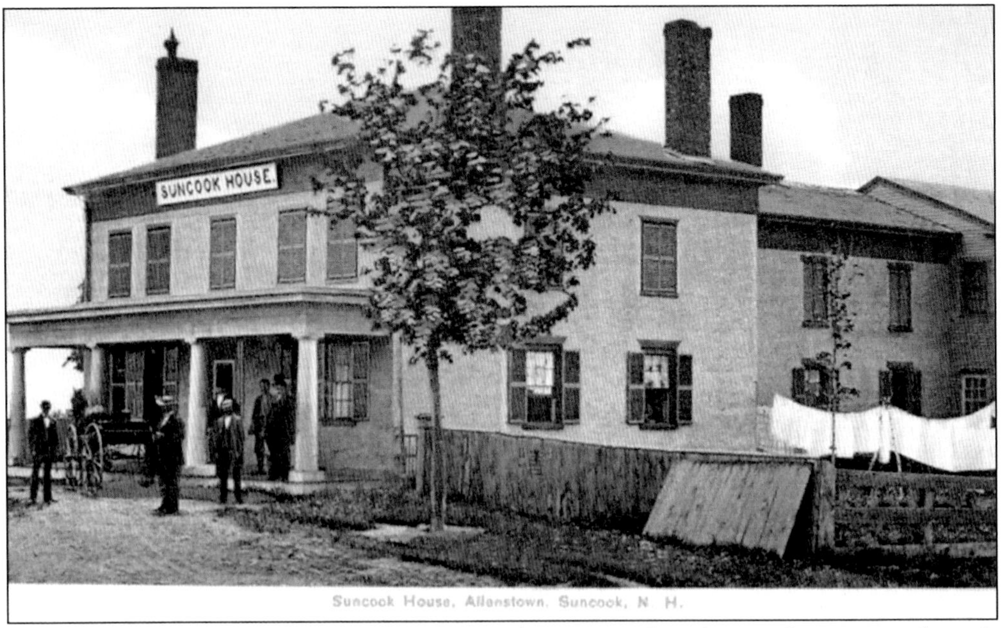

The Suncook House on Main Street was a popular resting place for travelers passing through Suncook Village. Oral tradition claims the Suncook House underwent significant architectural changes in the mid-1800s when it became the Suncook Mills agent's residence. (Courtesy of Connie French.)

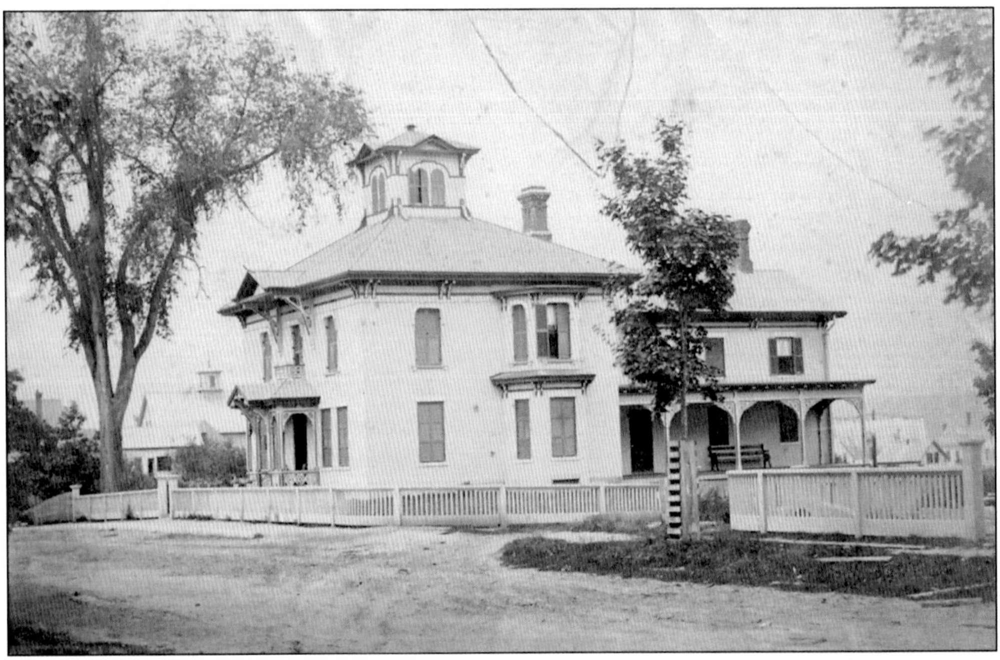

Pictured here is Suncook Mills agent David Lymen Jewell's residence on Main Street. In this image, dating from the late 1800s, the building had a stucco exterior. According to Mary Sargent Head, her father, Maj. Sterling Sargent built the house and sold it to the Suncook Mills in 1842. The building was destroyed by fire on July 18, 2001. (Courtesy of Allenstown, Old Allenstown Meeting House Collection.)

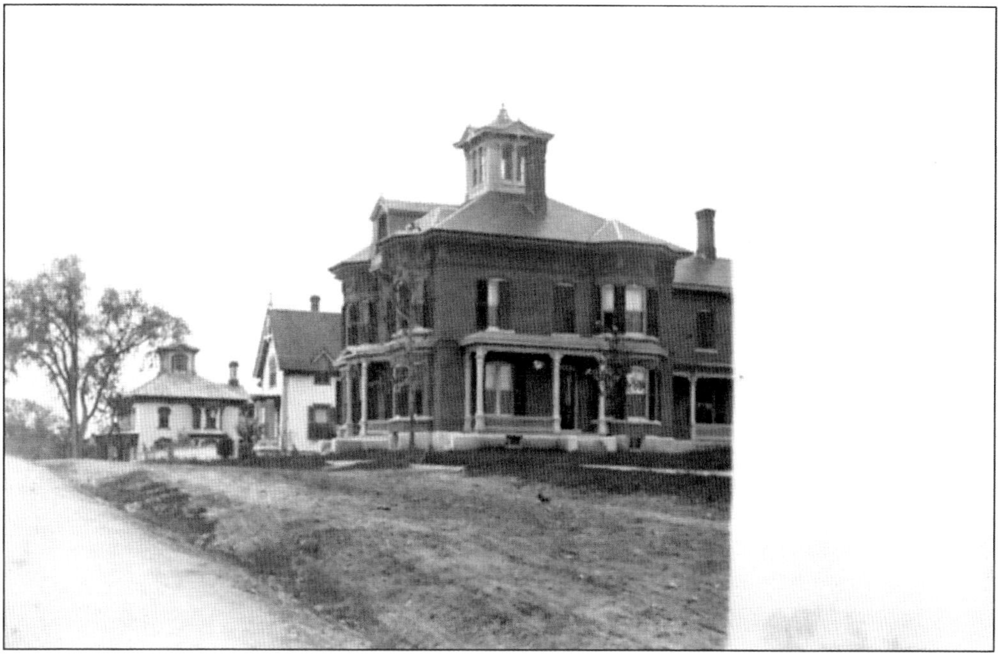

The Phillip Sargent residence on Main Street was built around 1880. He was in the brick-making business. The bricks for his home came from his own yards. In the background is the Suncook Mills agent's home. (Courtesy of Pembroke Historical Society.)

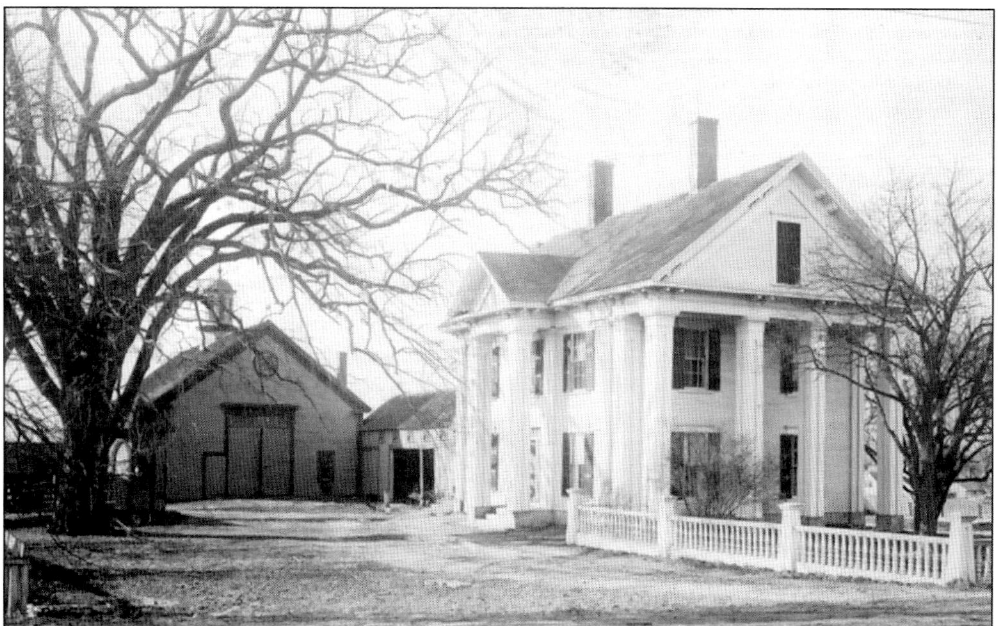

The residence of Philip Fowler and Lizzie Francis Johnson Fowler at 36 Main Street is seen above. Lizzie was a descendent of Nathaniel Baker, who served in the American Revolution. (Courtesy of Allenstown, New Hampshire, Historical Society.)

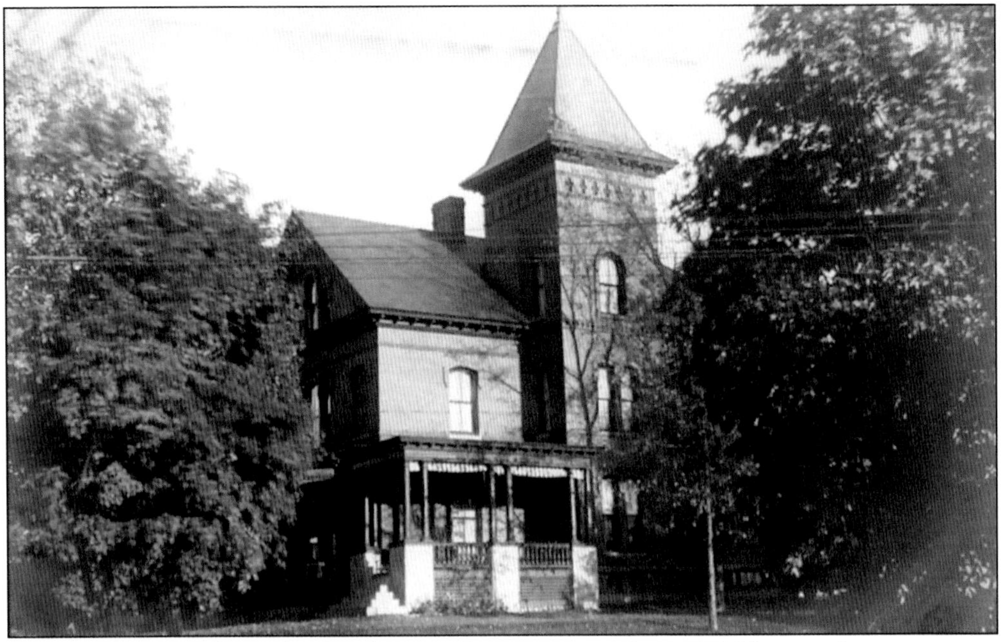

The Head estate is located in Hooksett at the gateway to Suncook Village at the intersection of Main and Merrimack Streets just before the Allenstown and Hooksett line. (Courtesy of Pembroke Historical Society.)

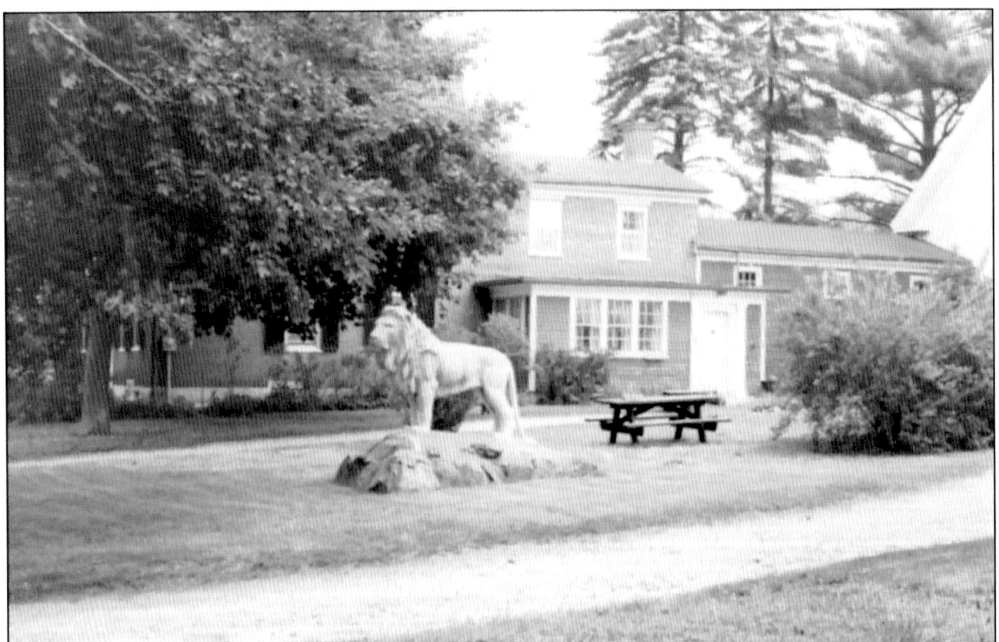

Warren Sargent's residence at 1 Main Street was on the Allenstown and Hooksett line. He owned a brickyard along the banks of the Merrimack River across from his home. In later years, the house was owned by Judge George Cofran. The lion was placed there by an antique dealer who owned the property prior to the Cofran purchase. (Courtesy of Roland Martel.)

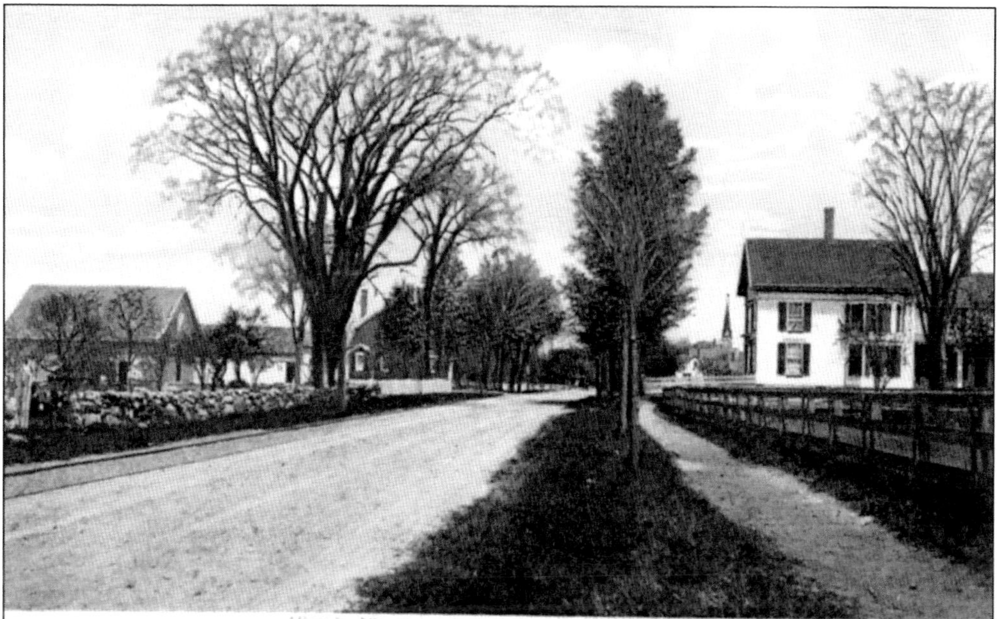

This is a view of the Dycas farm on the left side of Main Street, looking north. The Dycas barn was destroyed by fire in the mid-1950s. (Courtesy Connie French.)

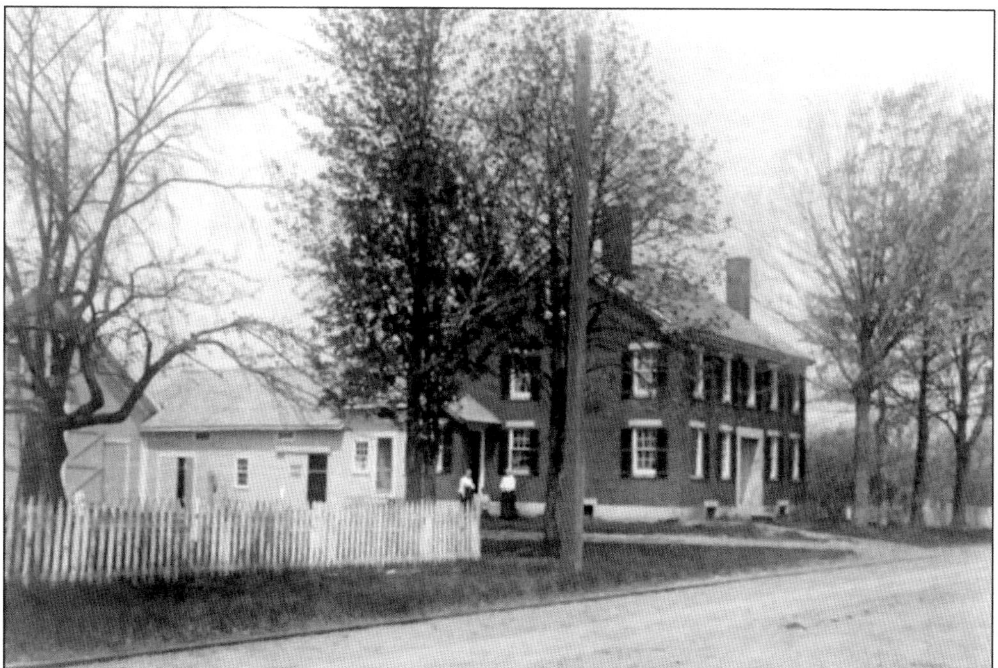

The Dycas farm, residence, and barn on Main Street are pictured here. The Dycas hayfields were located along Main Street and behind the farm. (Courtesy of Pembroke Historical Society.)

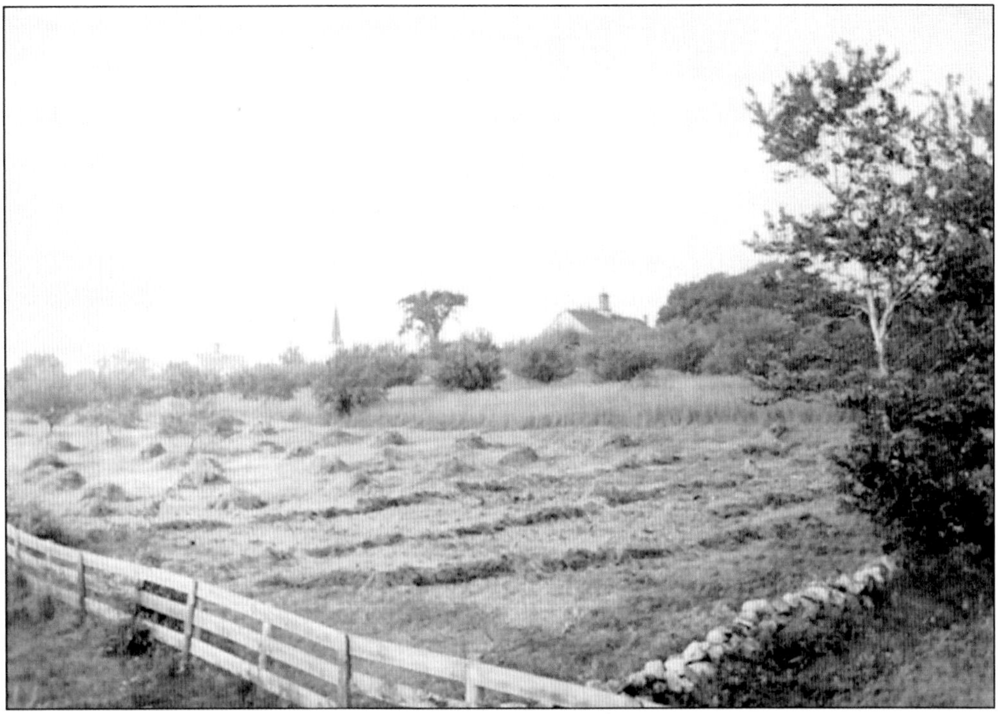

Dycas farm fields are seen here during the haying season. The steeple from the St. Jean the Baptist Church is visible in the distance. (Courtesy of Allenstown, New Hampshire, Historical Society.)

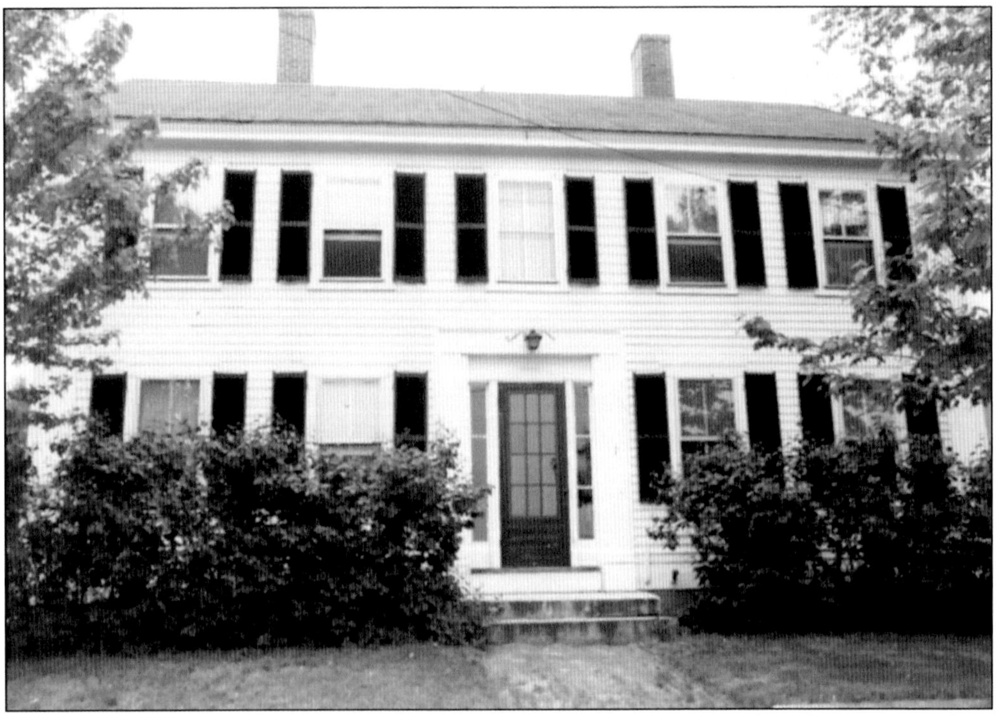

The McNamara dairy farm and residence on Main Street had pastureland on the opposite side of the road along the Merrimack River. (Photograph by Dan Chase; courtesy of Roland Martel.)

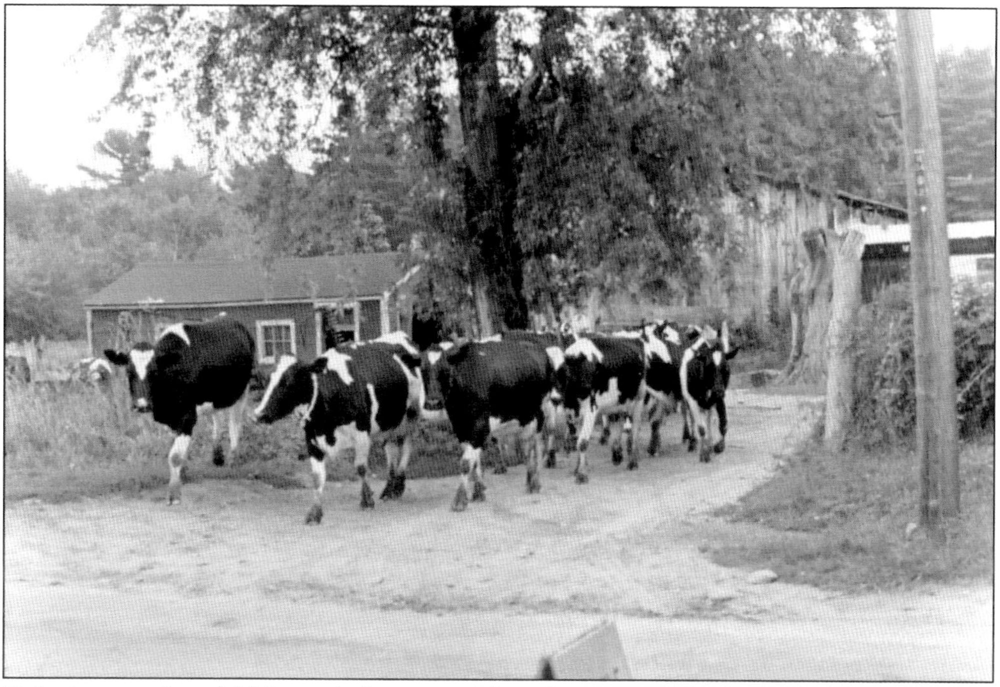

Holstein cows from McNamara's farm cross Main Street in 1975. This was a familiar site for many years. (Photograph by Brent Michiels.)

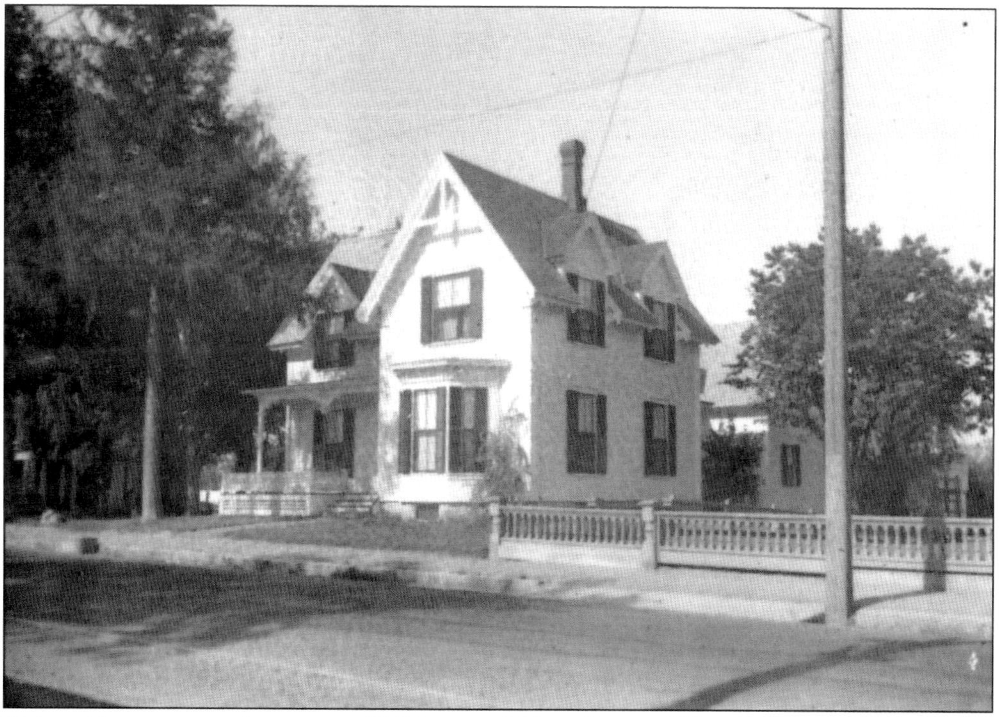

This residence was at the corner of Whitten and Main Streets. Whitten Street was one of "the streets of the supervisors." In 1937, the Suncook Mills auctioned off 14 dwellings on Whitten Street. (Courtesy of Brent Michiels.)

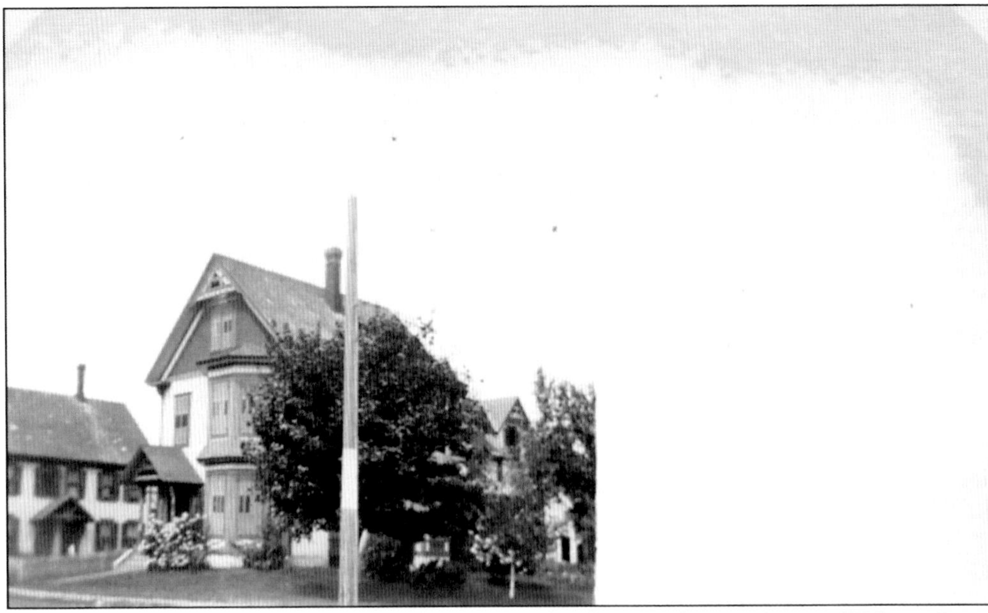

The Bergevin residence was located at the corner of Webster and Main Streets. Webster Street was also known as "the street of the supervisors." The Suncook Mills sold 12 dwellings on Webster Street at the 1937 auction. (Courtesy of Pembroke Historical Society.)

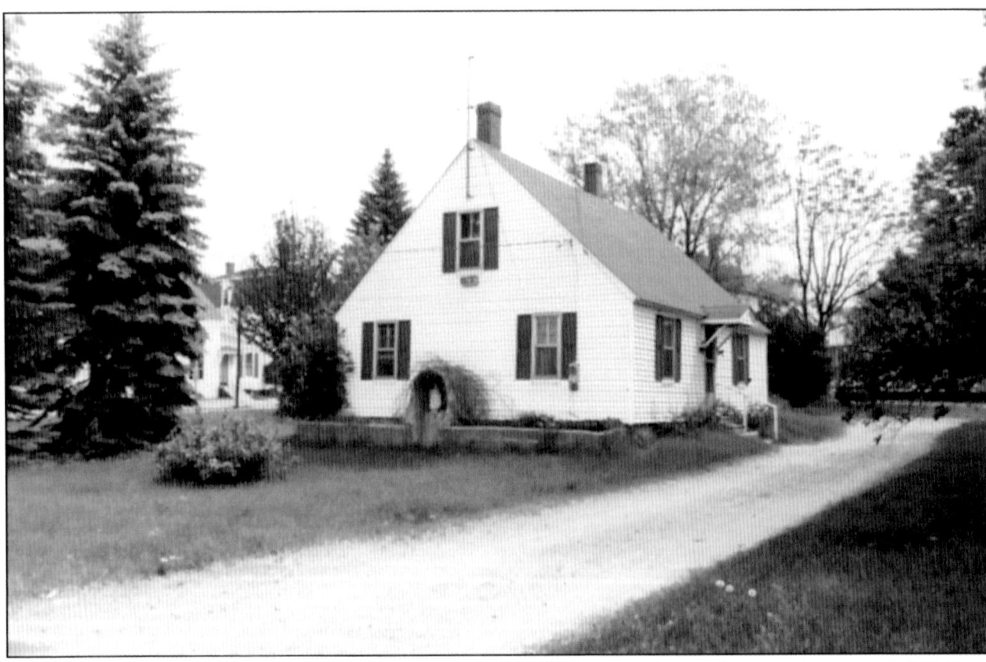

This home at the corner of Main and School Streets was the residence of William Haseltine Jr. This residence is believed to be the oldest house in the village; the structure displayed a sign dated 1723 for many years. In 1858, Haseltine also owned the land on the opposite side of Main Street. School Street was considered part of the neighborhood known as Le Petit Canada. (Photograph by Dan Chase; courtesy of Roland Martel.)

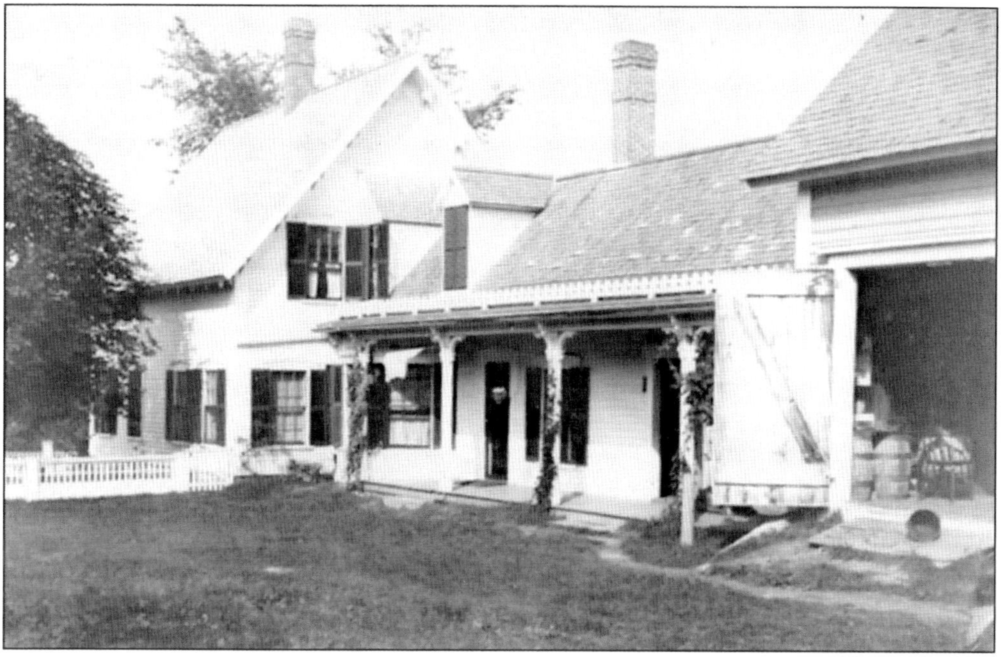

The old home of King Darius Stewart was located at the corner of Main and Cross Streets. King Darius was the son of William and Ann (Sargent) Stewart. The home was built by King Darius, where he lived until he died on January 13, 1882. The house was later owned by Joseph Lamiette. The photograph was taken by George W. Stewart on October 1, 1898. (Courtesy of Richard and Carol Merrill.)

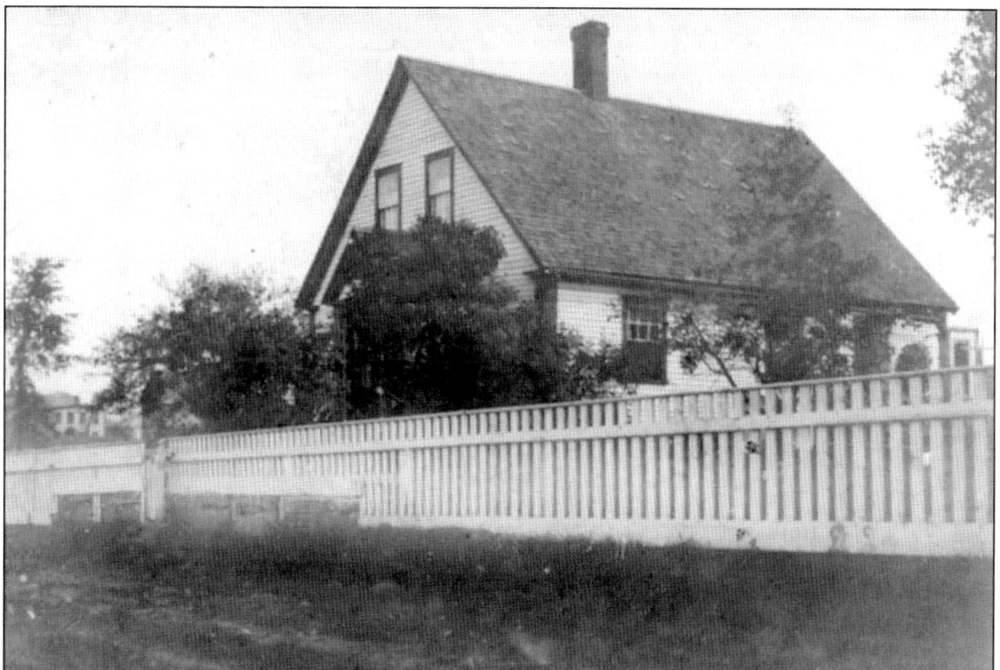

This photograph of Alanson Stewart's home on Main Street was taken by his son George W. on October 1, 1898. (Courtesy of Richard and Carol Merrill.)

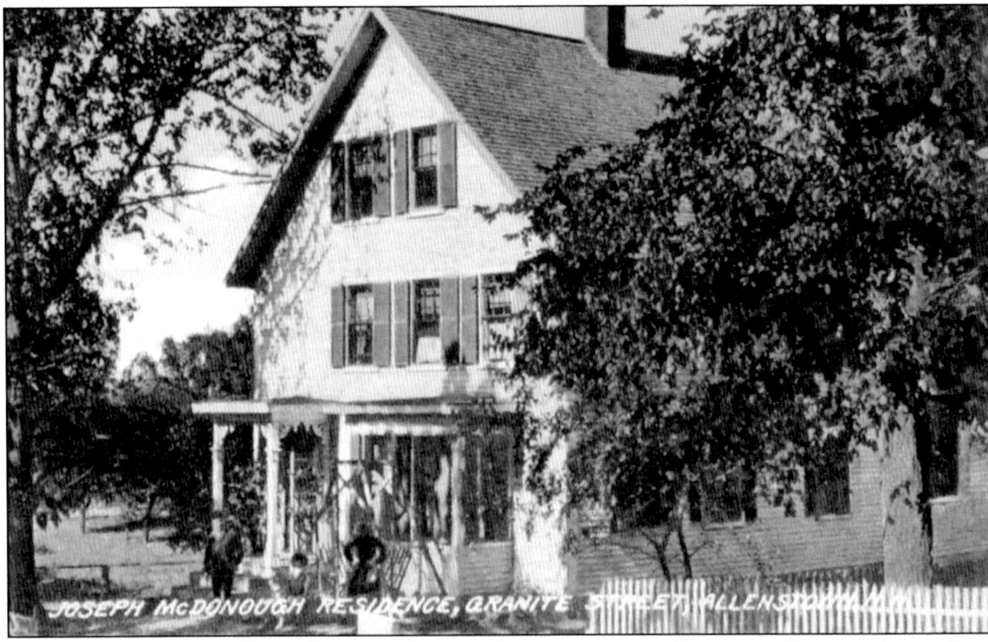

The Joseph McDonough residence on Granite Street is seen in this postcard image dating from the early 1900s. Granite Street led to the Bailey Quarry. (Courtesy of George Rainville.)

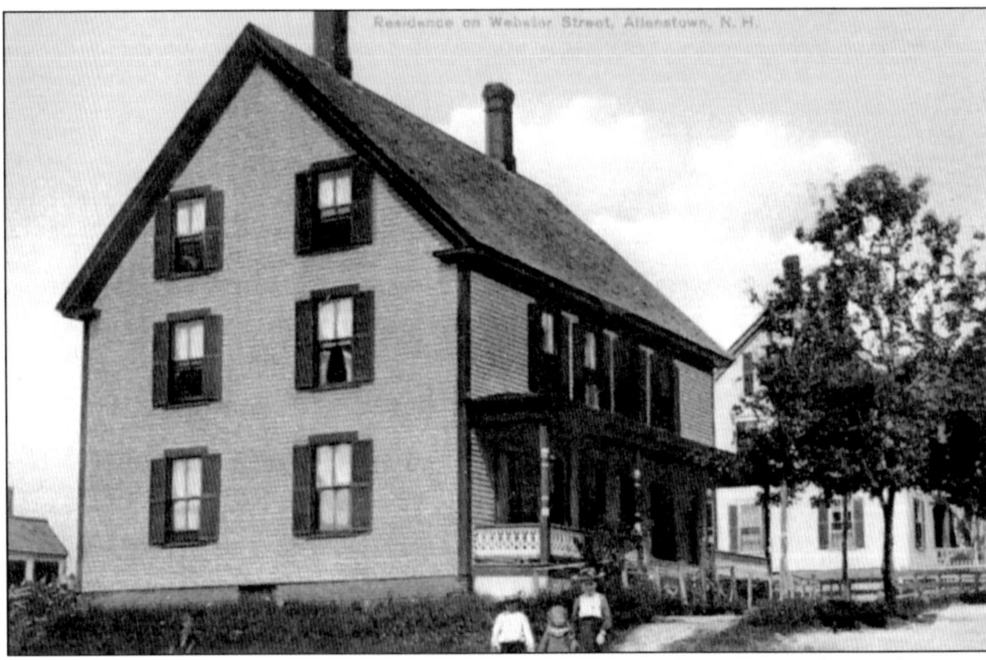

This photograph, taken in the early 1900s, is of a residence on Webster Street. This residence was most likely one of the many dwellings sold by the Suncook Mills at the 1937 auction. (Courtesy of George Rainville.)

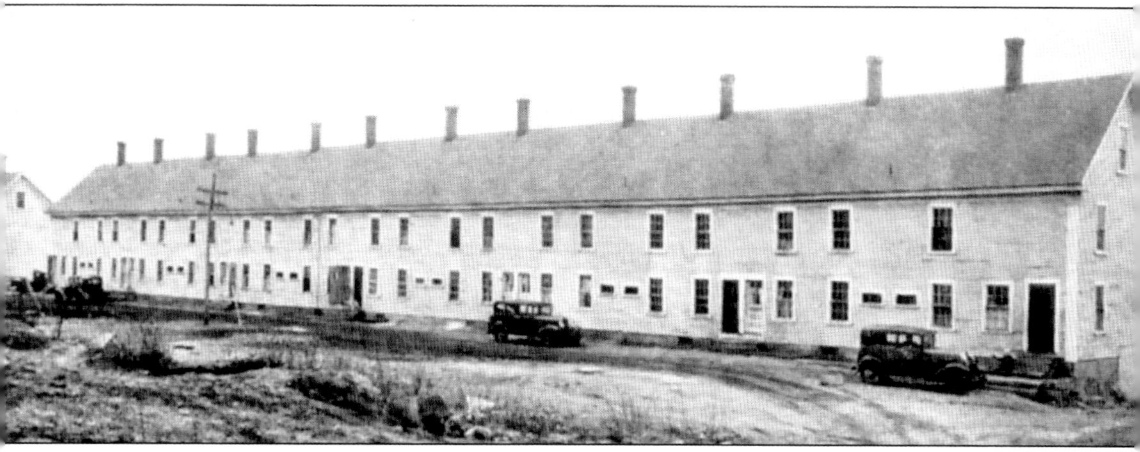

Shown in this photograph are two of the nine China Mill tenement buildings known as China Village, that were located between the China Mill and Canal and Ferry Streets. Each building contained six, five-room apartments. Many employees, mostly workers that had recently immigrated to Suncook, were housed in these tenements. An early school was set up in one of the buildings. On March 31, 1894, a giant conflagration destroyed five of the China Mill tenements, including a boardinghouse. The *Lowell Dailey Sun* reported on April 2, 1894, that the fire displaced 38 families and left 400 people homeless and without all their belongings. The mill and three warehouses narrowly escaped destruction. The blaze occurred during the night but, miraculously, everyone escaped, including many small children. Only a few minor burns were reported. The newspaper also added it would take the town of Suncook years to recover from the blow. In later days, the remaining tenements were destroyed by fires and floods. (Courtesy of Allenstown, New Hampshire, Historical Society.)

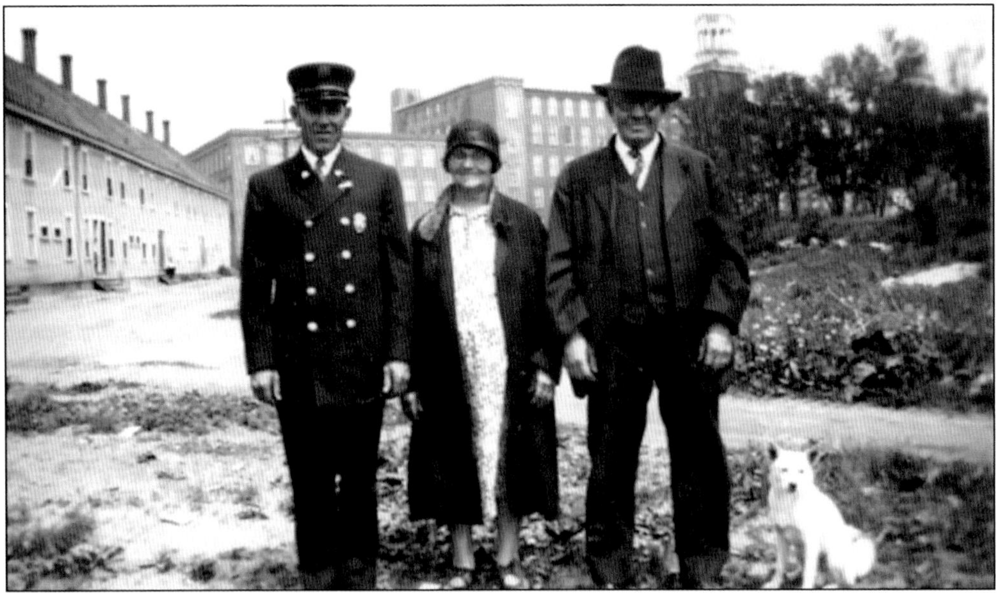

From left to right, George Verville, Marie (Joyal) Verville, George H. Verville, and an unidentified friend pose next to one of the China Mill tenements. Each tenement had a small woodshed and a garden plot behind the building. (Courtesy of Armand and Claudette Verville.)

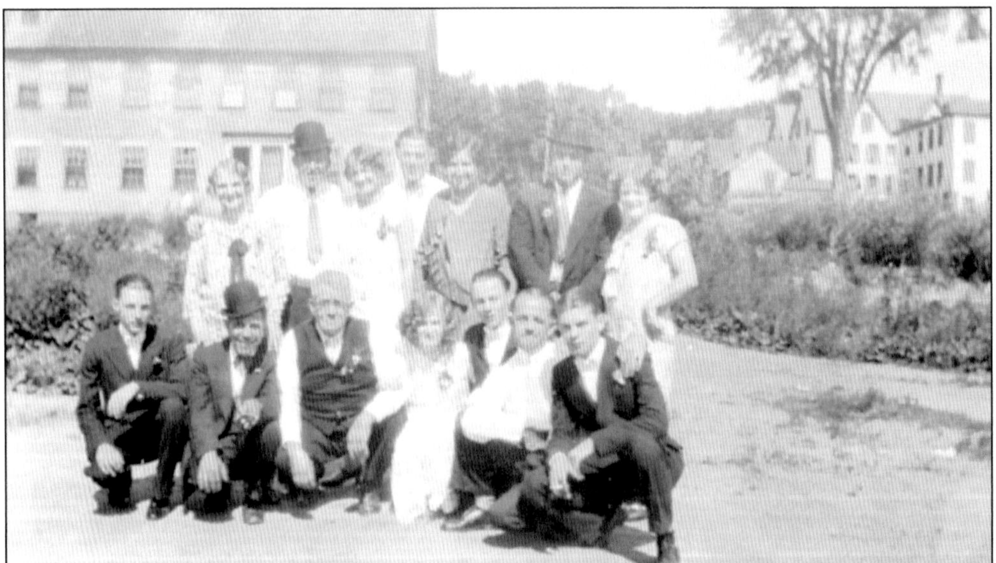

This is the Canal and Ferry Streets tenement block. The Verville family posed for this photograph in front of their residence, one of the last remaining tenements in China Village. (Courtesy of Armand and Claudette Verville.)

Norman "Jazzy" Connor and his sister Arlene Connor Cassidy were on one of their first sledding expeditions. Many years later Jazzy became a long-standing police chief in Allenstown. (Courtesy of Armand and Claudette Verville.)

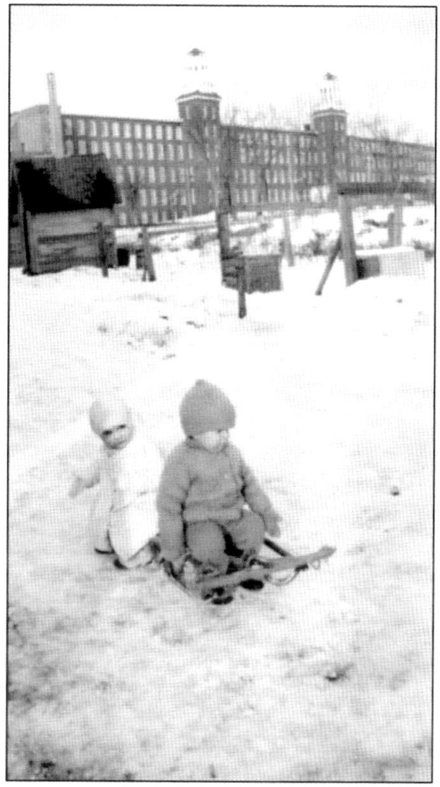

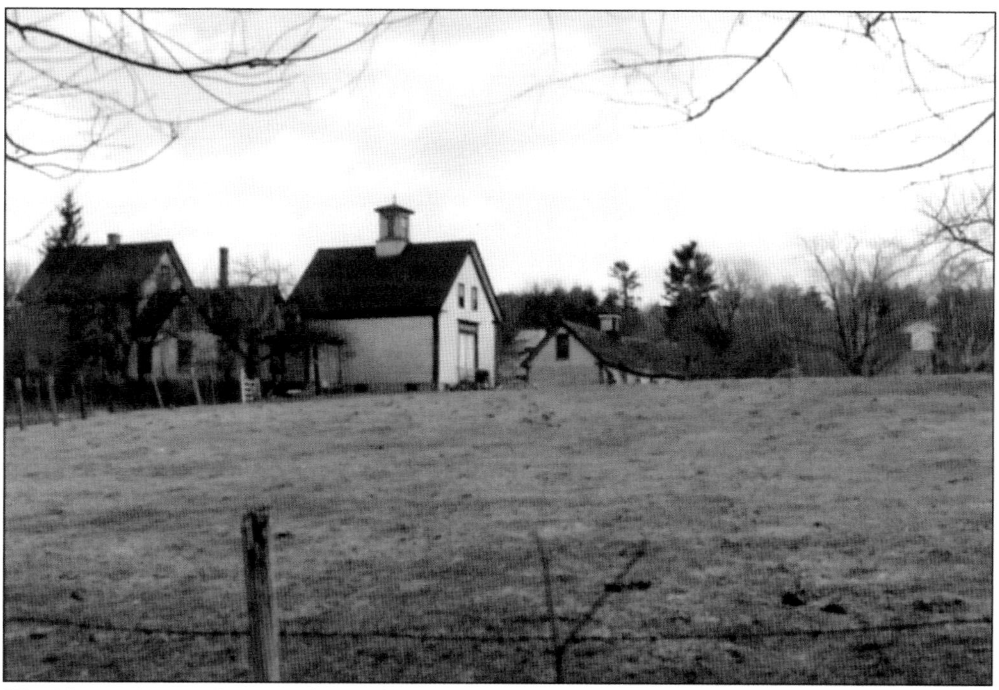

The Harriet Young farm was located between School Street and Granite Street. The farm was destroyed by fire on June 13, 1985. (Photograph by Brent Michiels.)

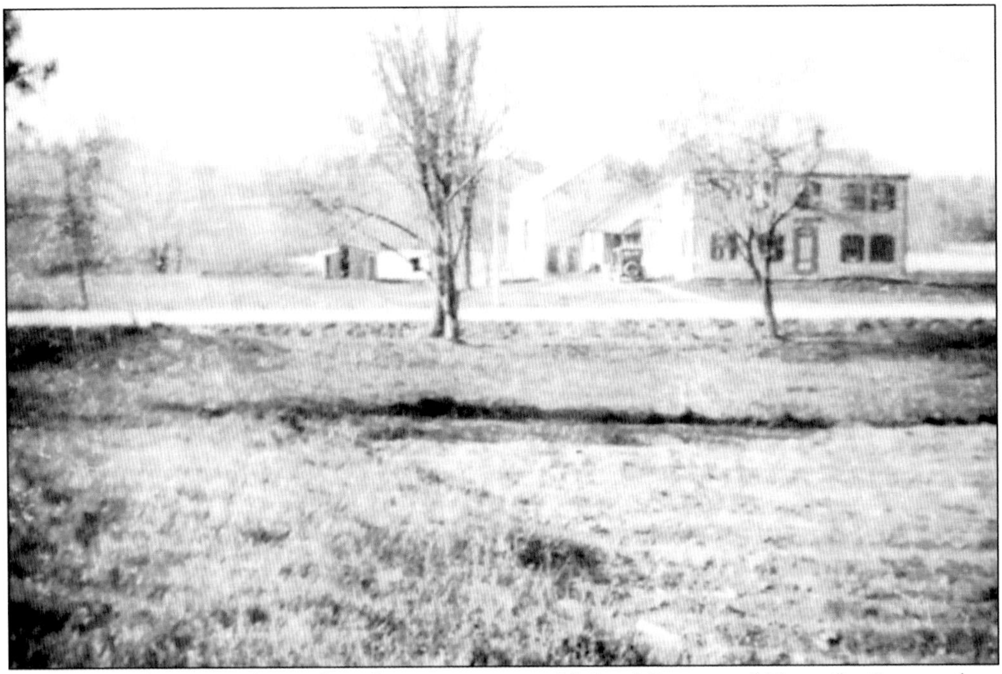

The Harvey home was located at the intersection of School Street and Turnpike Street, close to Iris Pond. The house was removed when Route 3 was constructed in 1931. (Courtesy of Brent Michiels.)

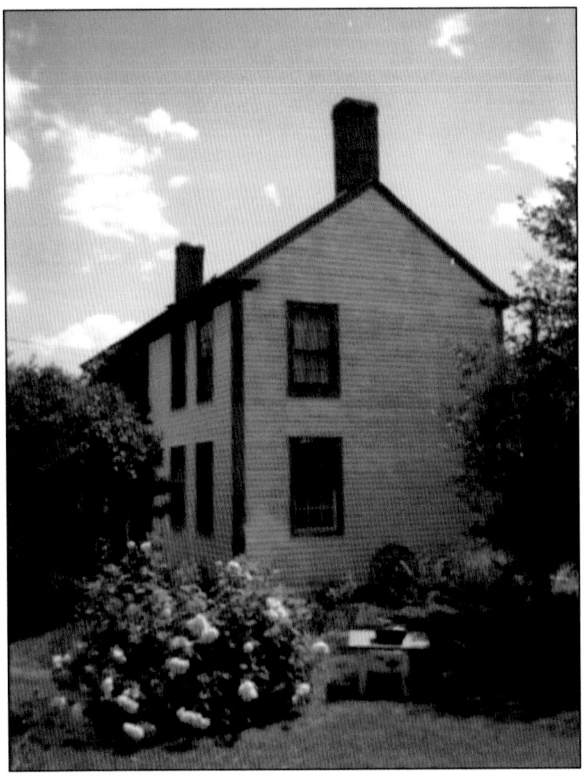

The Charles and Owen Osgood residence was located at 51 Turnpike Street on Osgood's Island. Prior to the flooding of Iris Pond for the Webster Dam impoundment, a large field was located behind this house. After the flooding, the house was on an islandlike peninsula, which became known as Osgood's Island. This home was destroyed by fire on August 25, 1989. (Courtesy of Brent Michiels.)

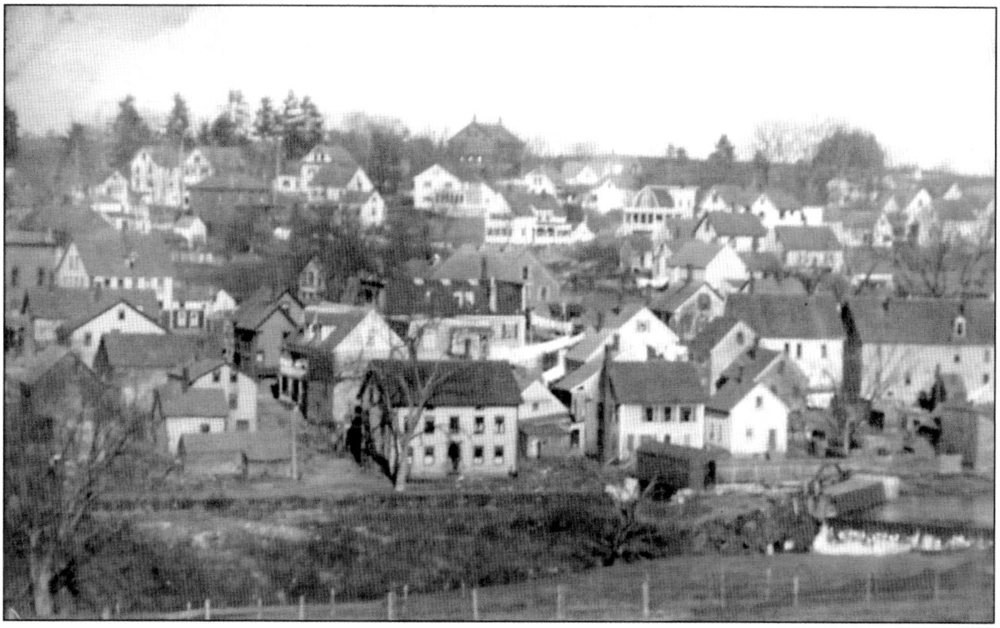

The "company houses" on Front and Glass Streets varied in size and design. (Courtesy of Pembroke Historical Society.)

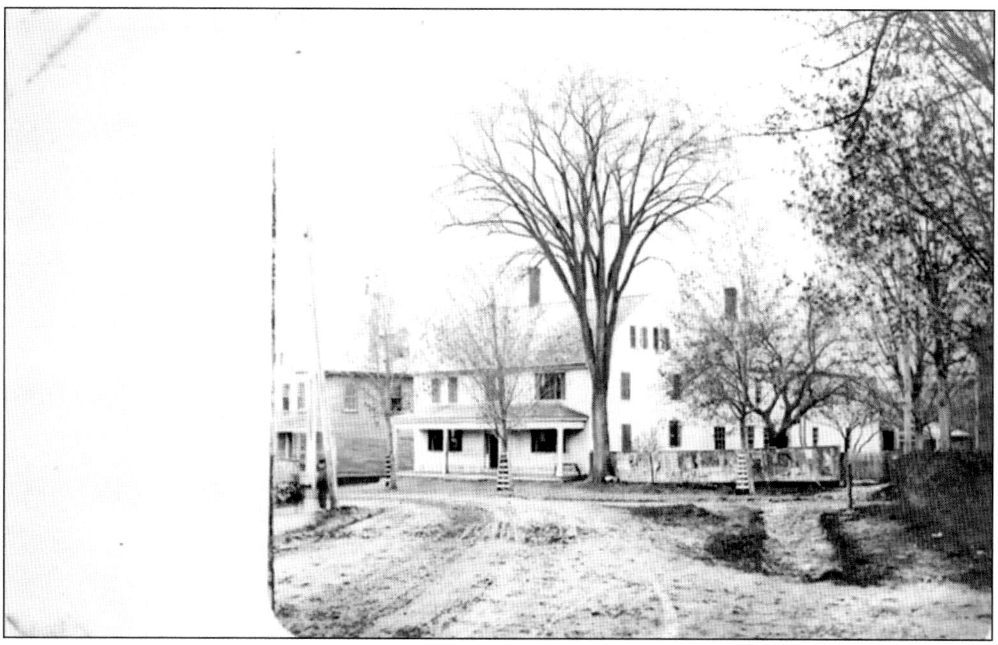

Osgood's Inn was located on Main Street at the site of the present Methodist church. (Courtesy of Pembroke Historical Society.)

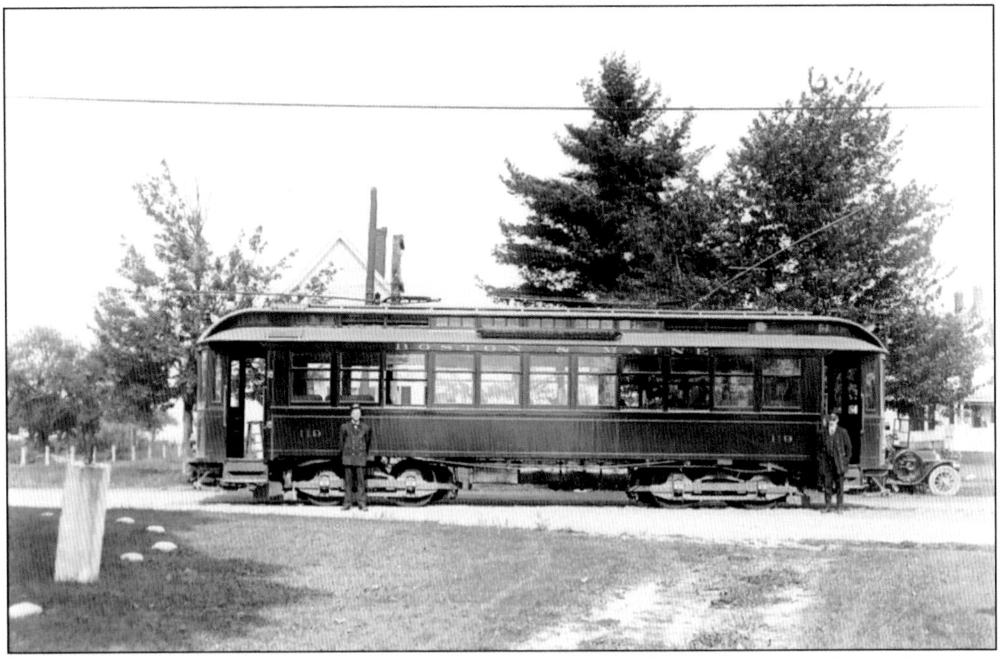

Boston and Maine Railroad trolley No. 119 is seen here at the intersection of Broadway and Pembroke Street. Suncook's trolley system traveled Main and Pembroke Streets, connecting with other lines in Concord and Hooksett. Electric cars operated in the village from 1903 until 1933, being replaced by buses. The bus run was dropped in 1975 by Concord Trailways and today operates between Concord and Boston via Interstate 93. (Courtesy of Brent Michiels.)

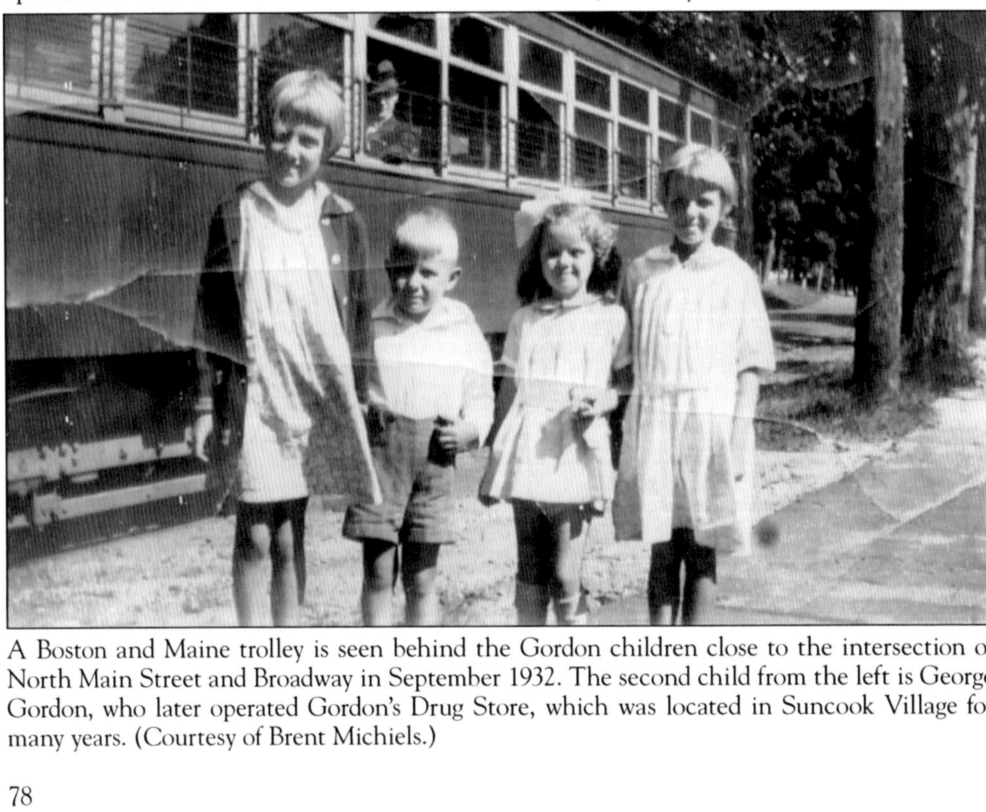

A Boston and Maine trolley is seen behind the Gordon children close to the intersection of North Main Street and Broadway in September 1932. The second child from the left is George Gordon, who later operated Gordon's Drug Store, which was located in Suncook Village for many years. (Courtesy of Brent Michiels.)

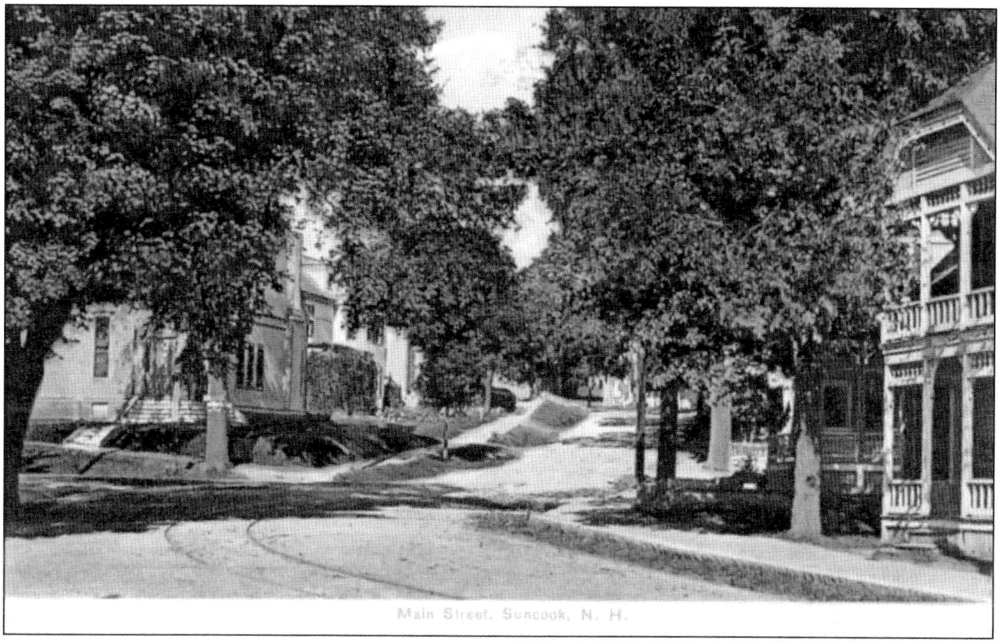

This is a view of the North Main Street intersection looking east with the Baptist church on the left and the Petit and Martel residences on the right. This was the location of the trolley in the previous photograph. (Courtesy of Connie French.)

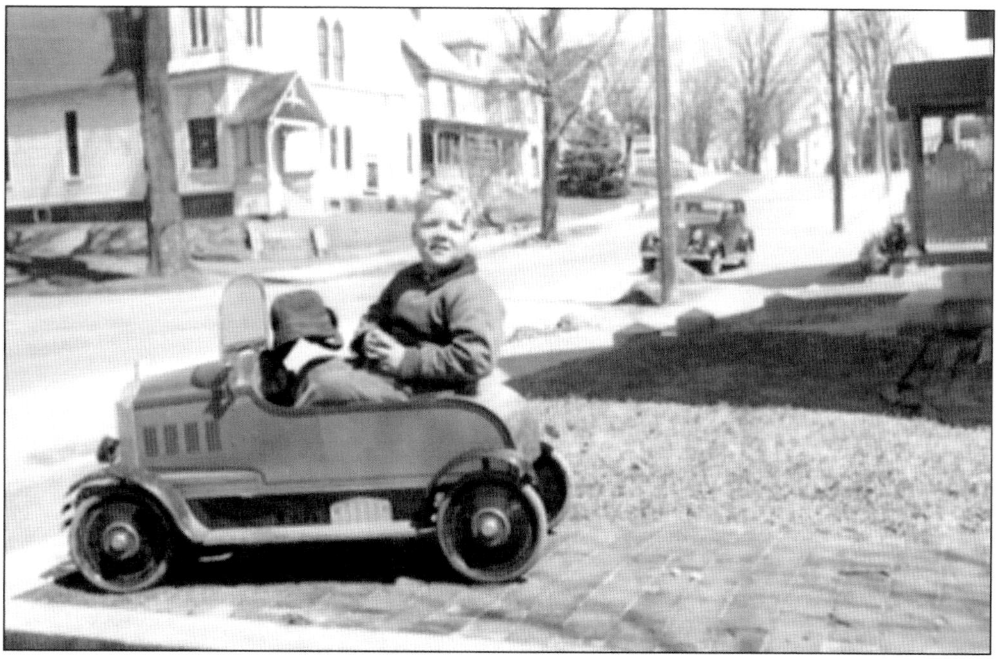

Geddy Petit rides his car in front of his family home on North Main Street in 1943 or 1944. Petit was probably headed to Martel's Garage for service. The Baptist church and North Main Street was in the background and Martel's Garage was around the corner. (Courtesy of Roland Martel.)

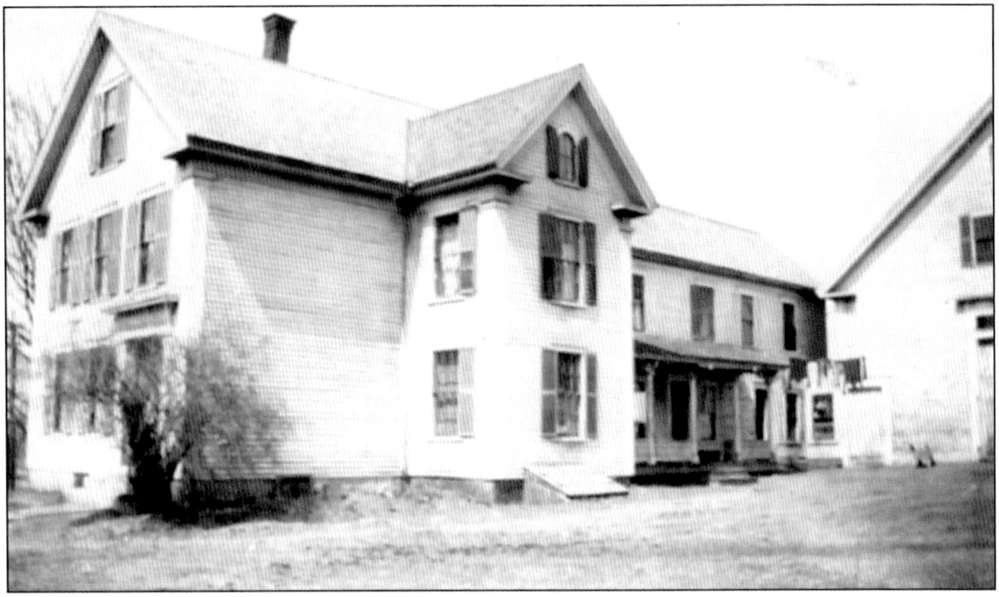

The Gustave and Roseanna Roy residence, pictured here around 1900, was located on Exchange Street across from the Suncook Railroad station and depot. (Courtesy of Roland Martel.)

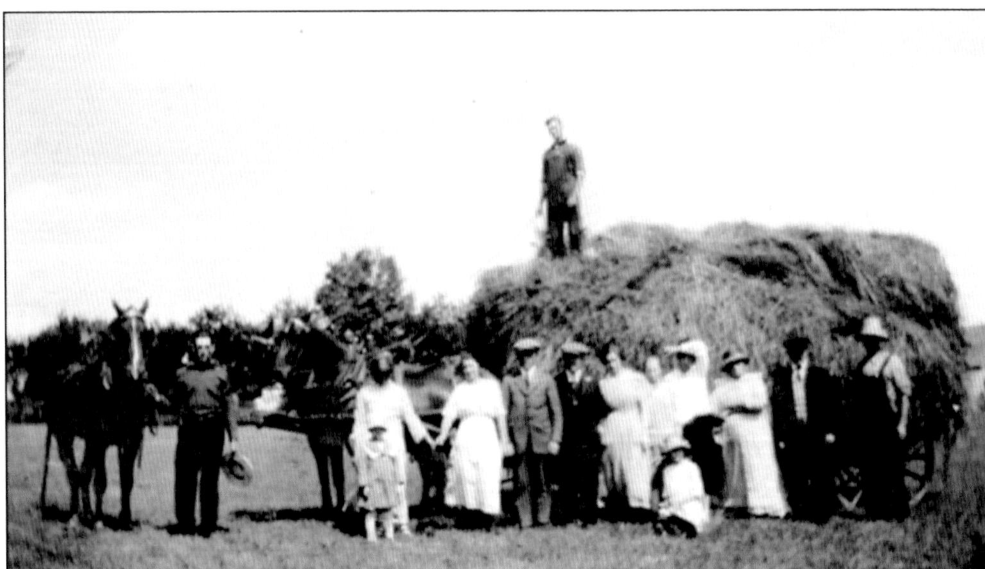

This Roy family photograph was taken in the vicinity of Exchange Street and Memorial Field during the haying season around 1910. The visitors had just arrived most likely by train. (Courtesy of Roland Martel.)

Six

SUNCOOK VILLAGE COMMERCE

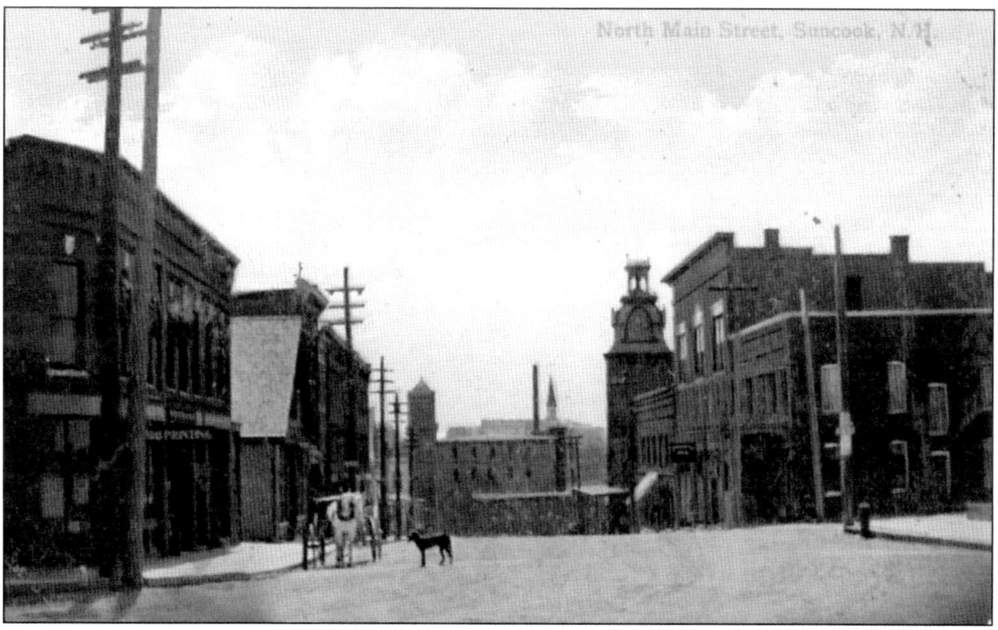

Suncook Village's business district was the center of commercial and social activity for surrounding communities. Village stores sold jewelry, groceries, hardware, toys, candy, dry goods, baked goods, shoes, clothing, and home furnishings. Other businesses included a bank, opera houses, halls, restaurants, hotels, ice cream parlors, saloons, bowling allies, a Chinese laundry, a movie theater, and a drug store. The horse and wagon seen here belonged to the American Express Company. (Courtesy of Connie French.)

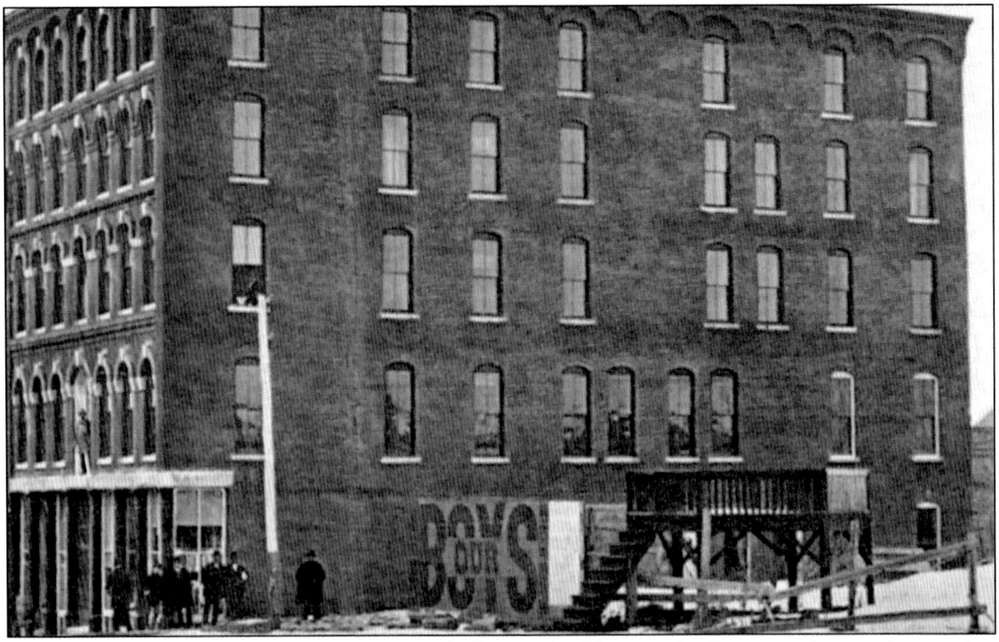

The Bartlett Hotel and Opera House was the largest building in the business district. Located at the southwest corner of Union and Main Streets, the building stood five stories tall. The Boston Philharmonic Club performed for the grand opening of the opera house on December 4, 1877. The hotel contained a restaurant in addition to the opera house. It was destroyed by fire on December 11, 1886. (Courtesy of Connie French.)

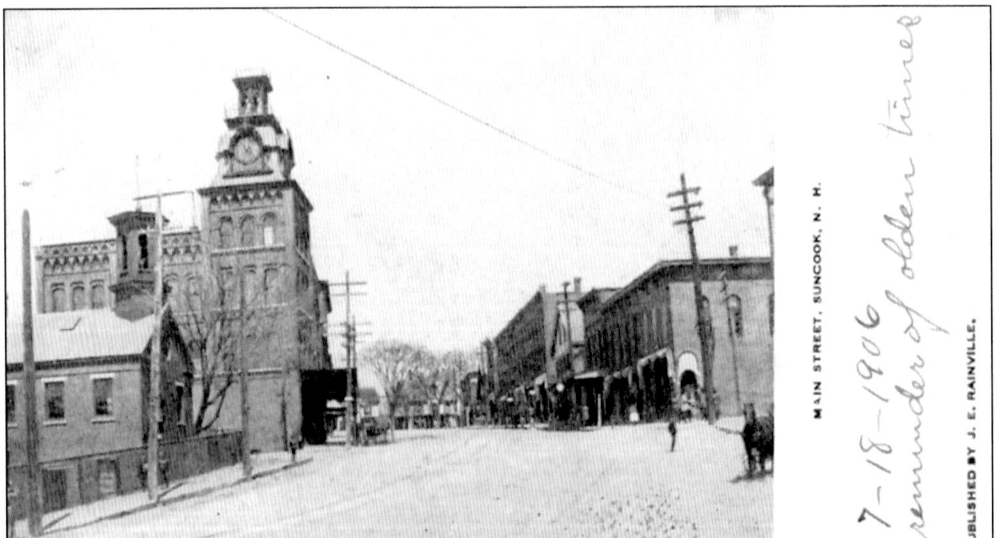

Charles Williams's and J. L. Hosmer's Clock Tower building on Main and Front Streets was built in 1879. Local merchants Charles Williams and J. L. Hosmer commissioned architect and builder Samuel Ordway to design and build the privately-owned Clock Tower building. The town of Pembroke raised money to purchase the clock and has since owned it. The timepiece was made by E. Howard Clock Company of Boston in 1879. (Courtesy of Connie French.)

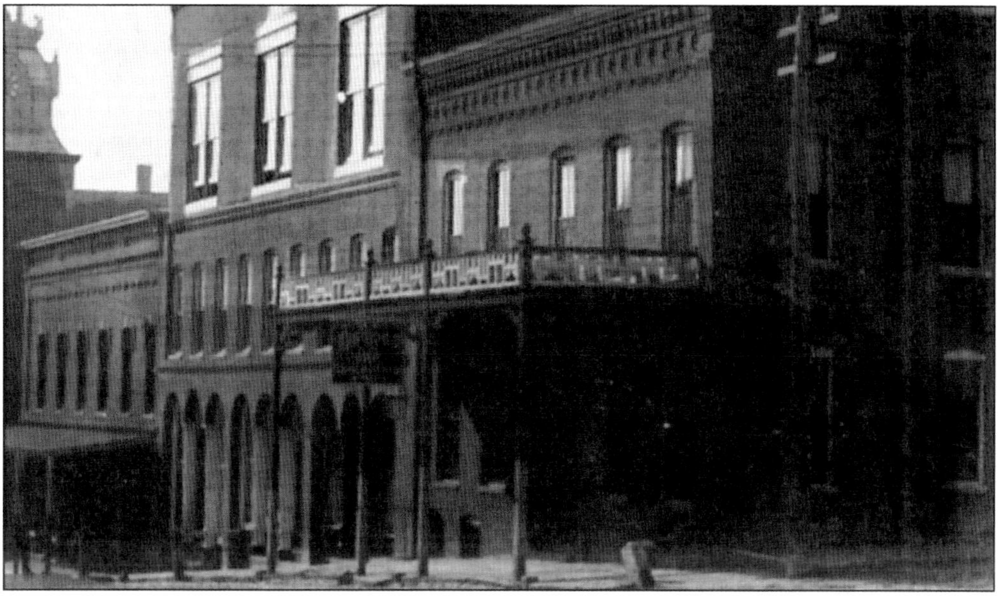

The west side of Main Street was built in 1886. The original building owners and businesses, from left to right, are the T. J. Otterson block, which included a bakery, a tobacco shop, and Suncook Hall; the Addison N. Osgood block, which housed Simpson Miller and Company groceries and millinery, and the International Order of Odd Fellows on the third floor (lost in a 1914 fire); and Osgood's Inn (owned by Addison Osgood), which included a laundry, bowling alley, and pool room. (Courtesy of Connie French.)

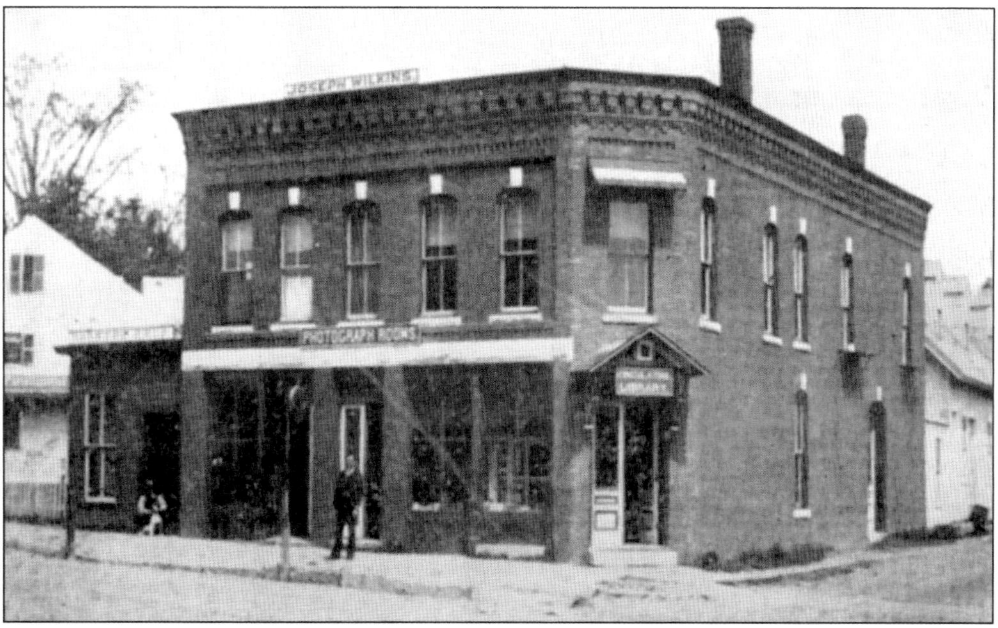

The Joseph Wilkins block is seen here on the southeast corner of Main and Central Streets. Joseph Wilkins's photography studio was on the second floor. The post office for Allenstown and Pembroke was located in the corner office until a new post office was built in 1963. The American Express Company was above the post office. The building also housed a dry goods store and a circulating library. (Courtesy of Connie French.)

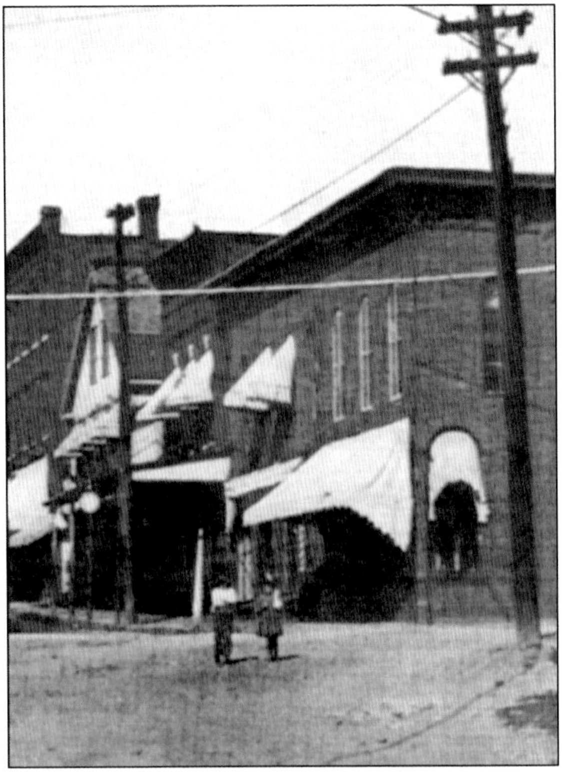

This photograph shows the blocks on the lower east side of Main Street. From left to right the commercial wooden structure built in 1884 is next to a smaller structure, both buildings replaced the historic Gen. Caleb Stark house built in 1812; next is the Jacob E. Chickering block built in 1868, occupied by a jewelry store; and on the corner of Main and Glass Streets is the Natt B. and J. Morrill Emery block built in 1869 that housed a grocery store and post office. This was known as Emery Corner. (Courtesy of Connie French.)

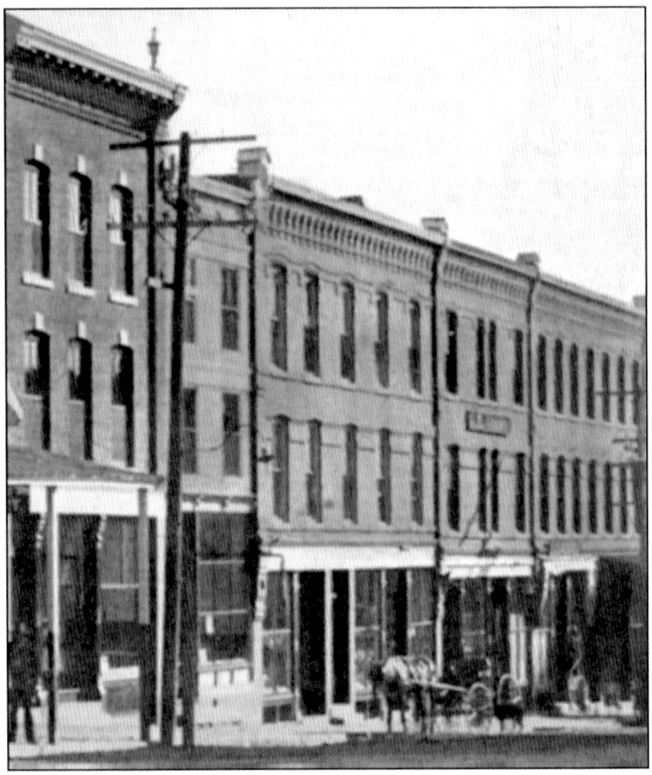

Pictured here are the five blocks on the upper east side of Main Street. From left to right the Thomas Green block built in 1895, housed a saloon; the John Bartlett block built between 1892 and 1893, was utilized as a barbershop and insurance office; the Osgood Block built in 1879, Addison Osgood owner operated a dining room; the Gordon-Piper block was built in 1879, owned by William H. Piper and occupied by G. E. Gordon Company; and the Tennant block built in 1879, was owned by John Tennant and occupied by a laundry and a fancy grocery store. (Courtesy of Allenstown, New Hampshire, Historical Society.)

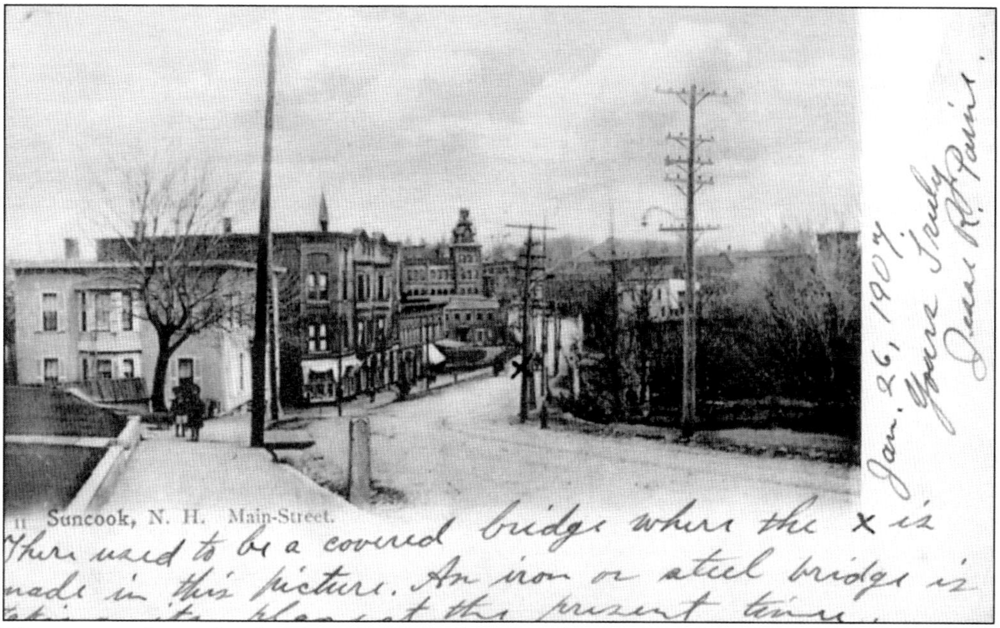

This image shows South Main Street looking north. Hayes Hall and Opera House is the second building on the left. The C. P. Morse Company is located in the two-story adjoining structure. Trolley tracks are visible in the street. The steep grade and curve in the road caused many accidents on this section of Main Street. Later a sign with skull and crossbones warned pedestrians and drivers to exercise caution. (Courtesy of Connie French.)

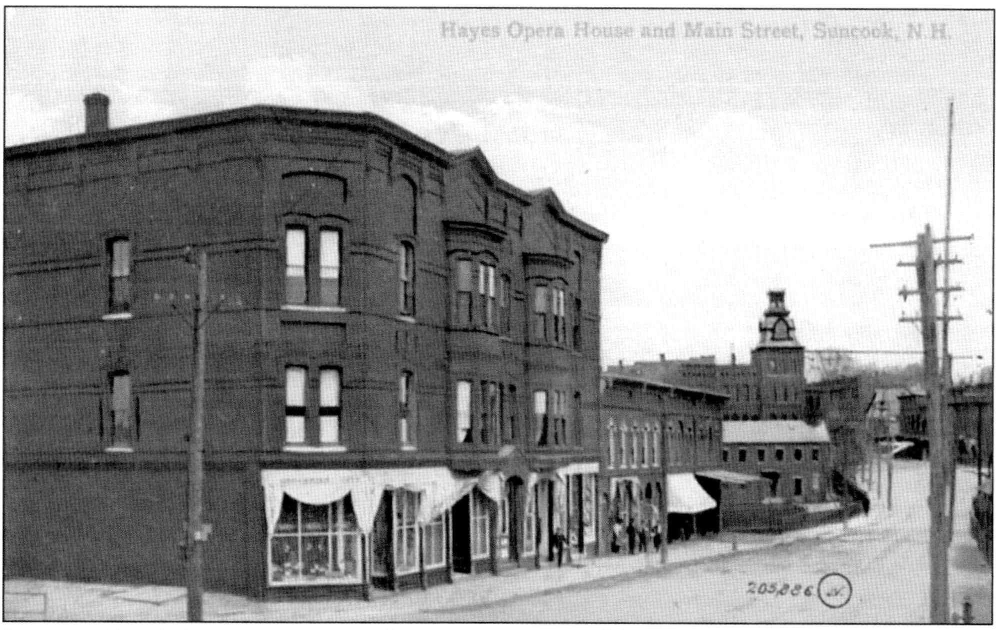

Hayes Hall and Opera House was adjacent to the C. P. Morse building on Main Street. The Hayes Opera House offered dramatic presentations, traveling troops, concerts, and teas. On July 28, 1877, the Jubilee Singers, one of the many entertainments, were advertised as "a genuine slave band emancipated by Abraham Lincoln's proclamation." From 1876 on, the hall was also used for Allenstown's public meetings and voting. (Courtesy of Connie French.)

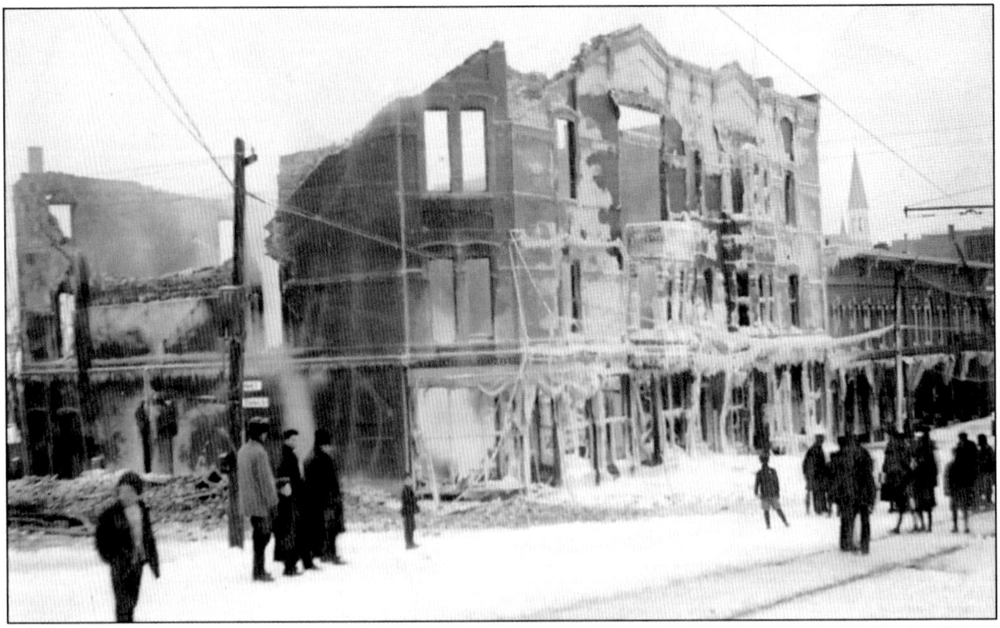

Hayes Hall and Opera House was destroyed by fire on February 8, 1910. By 1915, the building was replaced by the Sansterre Block. (Courtesy of Brent Michiels.)

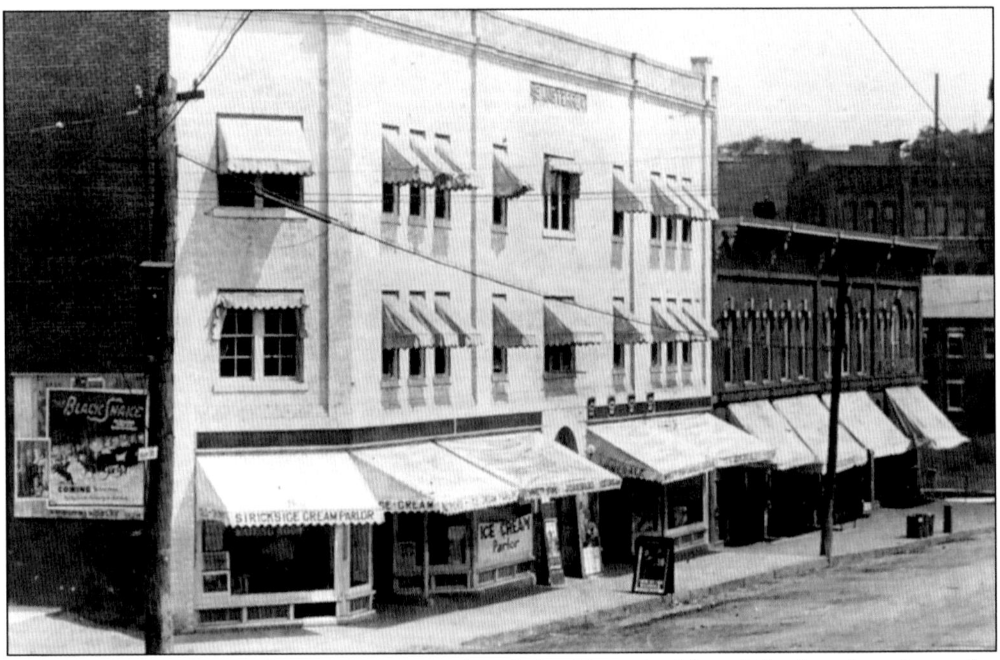

The Sansterre Block and Opera House replaced the Hayes building. The first floor housed a movie theater and ice cream parlor. In 1928, the movie theater advertised a holiday attraction for Wednesday, May 30, called *Sailors Wives*, with Loyd Hughs and Mary Astor. In later days, the building became the Knights of Columbus hall. The Sansterre Block was destroyed by fire in the early 1970s. (Author's collection.)

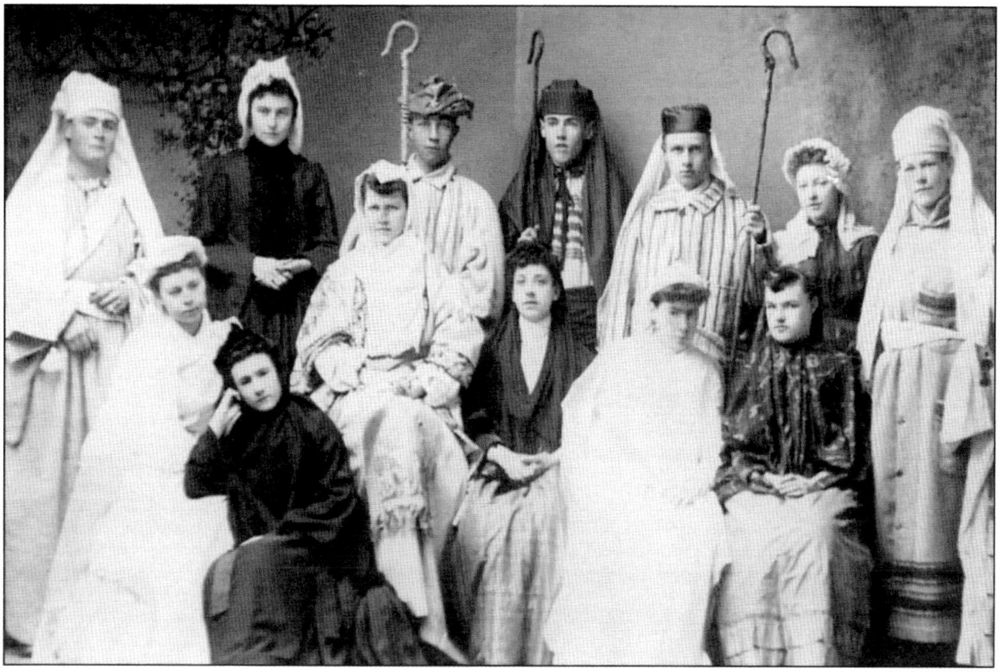

This photograph was taken at Joseph Wilkin's studio on February 20, 1890. This performance was one of many operas, concerts, and plays in Suncook Village. The Christmas presentation was most likely held at the Methodist church or Hayes Opera House. (Courtesy of Brent Michiels.)

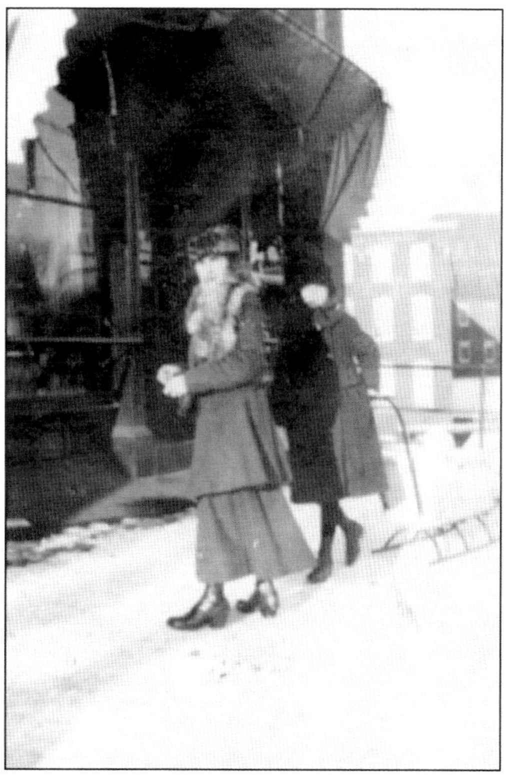

This photograph of the river side of the C. P. Morse Furniture building, built in 1878 on Main Street, shows the storefront prior to renovations around 1900. The child is pulling a sled to carry packages home. In the early 1920s, Victor Leblanc purchased F. W. Morse Furniture, formerly C. P. Morse Furniture. (Courtesy of Roland Martel.)

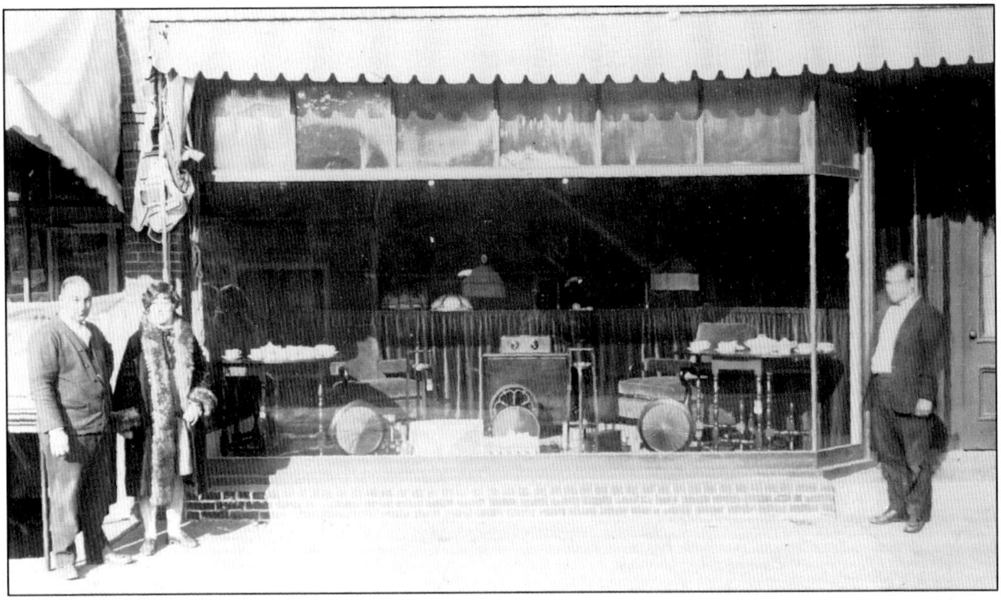

Pictured here from left to right in front of Morse Furniture on Main Street is Victor E Leblanc, Eva Leblanc, and at far right, her husband, Paul Leblanc (Victor's brother). In the early 1920s, Victor purchased F. W. Morse Furniture. The building housed three family-owned businesses, including Morse Furniture on the Main Street level, Leblanc Funeral Home on the second floor, and Leblanc Plumbing in the basement. (Photograph by Lester Leblanc; courtesy of Gloria Reeves.)

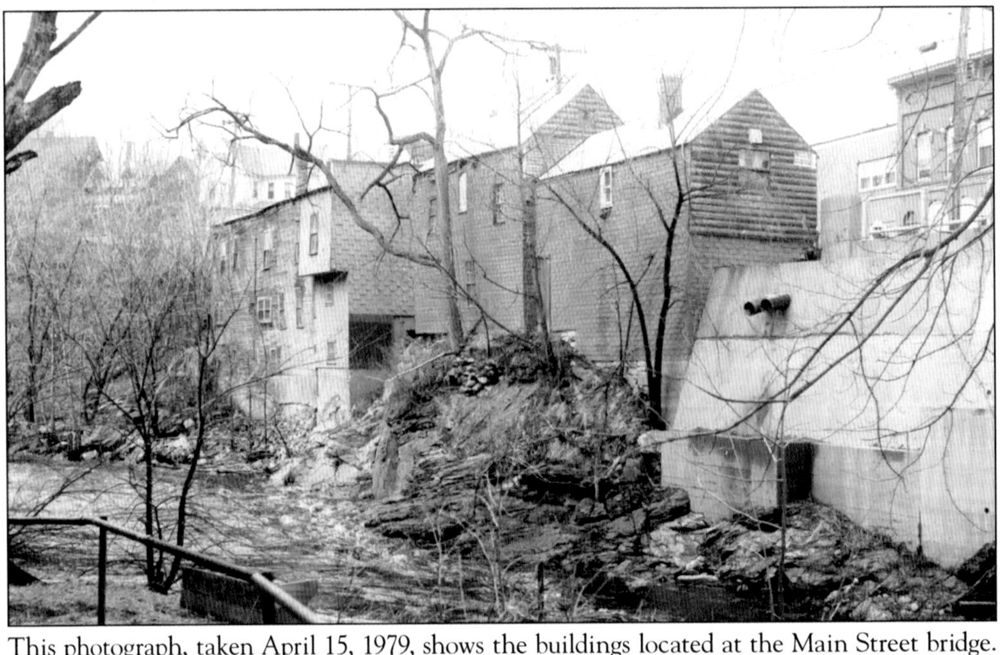

This photograph, taken April 15, 1979, shows the buildings located at the Main Street bridge. There are indications that the Webster Mill may have owned these buildings. In the 1950s, a bakery, a barbershop, a television repair shop, and the Suncook Rod and Gun Club occupied the structures. The buildings were removed when the new Main Street bridge was constructed in 2004. (Photograph by Brent Michiels.)

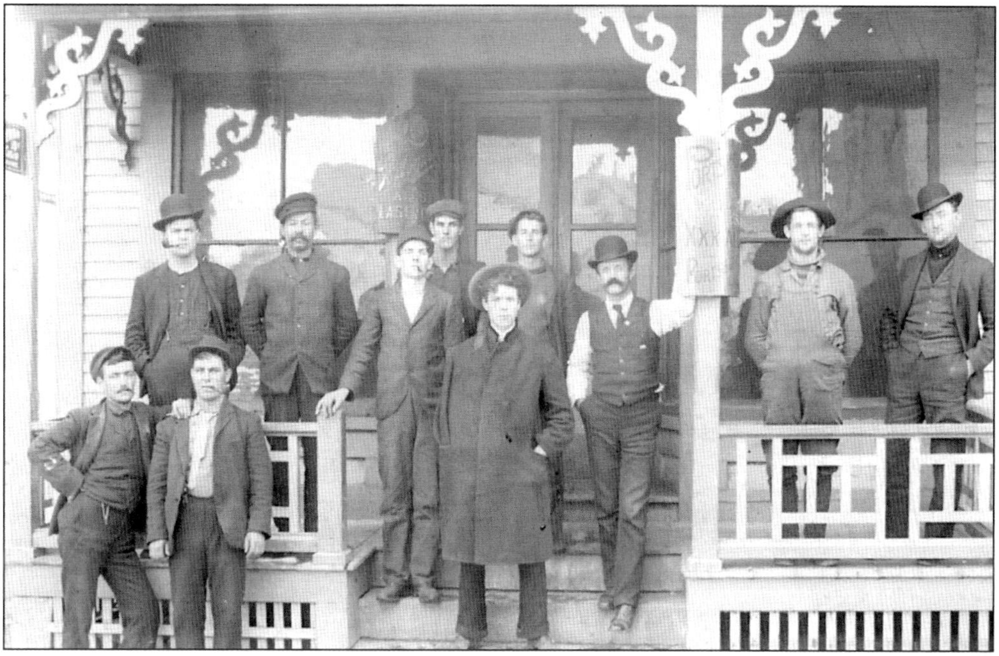

This is Lavallee's Saloon in Suncook. Standing from left to right are (first row) Peter Mahair and Joe Lefebvre; (second row) unidentified, Thomas Brasley, and George Labelle; (third row) Paul Harnois, Farmer Duclos, Joseph Cantara, unidentified, Crème Duclos, and Felix Connor Jr. (Courtesy of Pembroke Historical Society.)

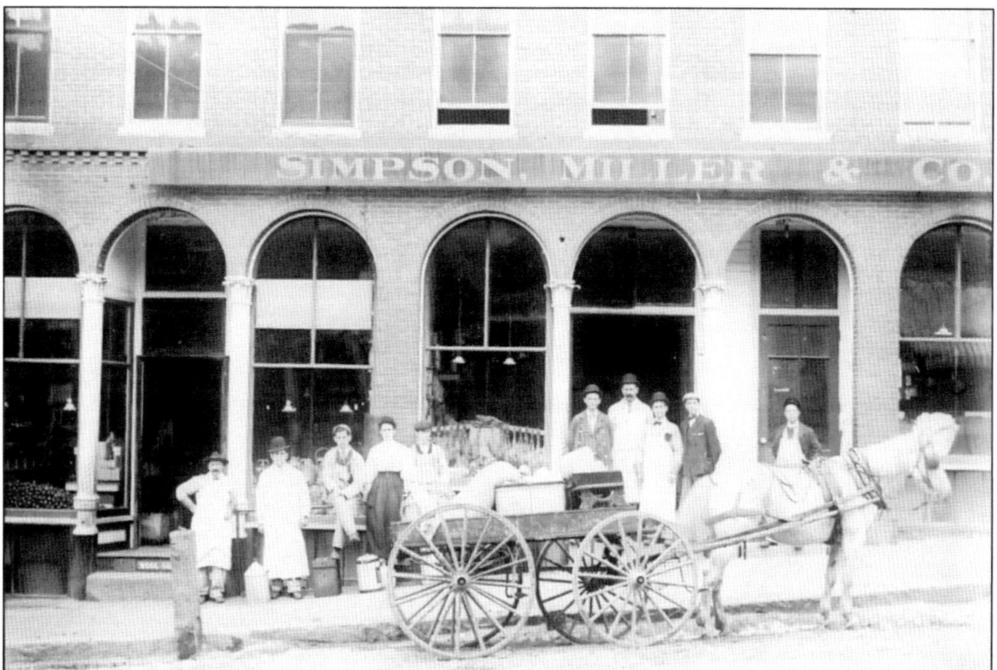

Simpson, Miller and Company was located on the west side of Main Street. The company spanned three storefronts. The American Express Company horse and wagon is picking up or delivering. (Courtesy of Pembroke Historical Society.)

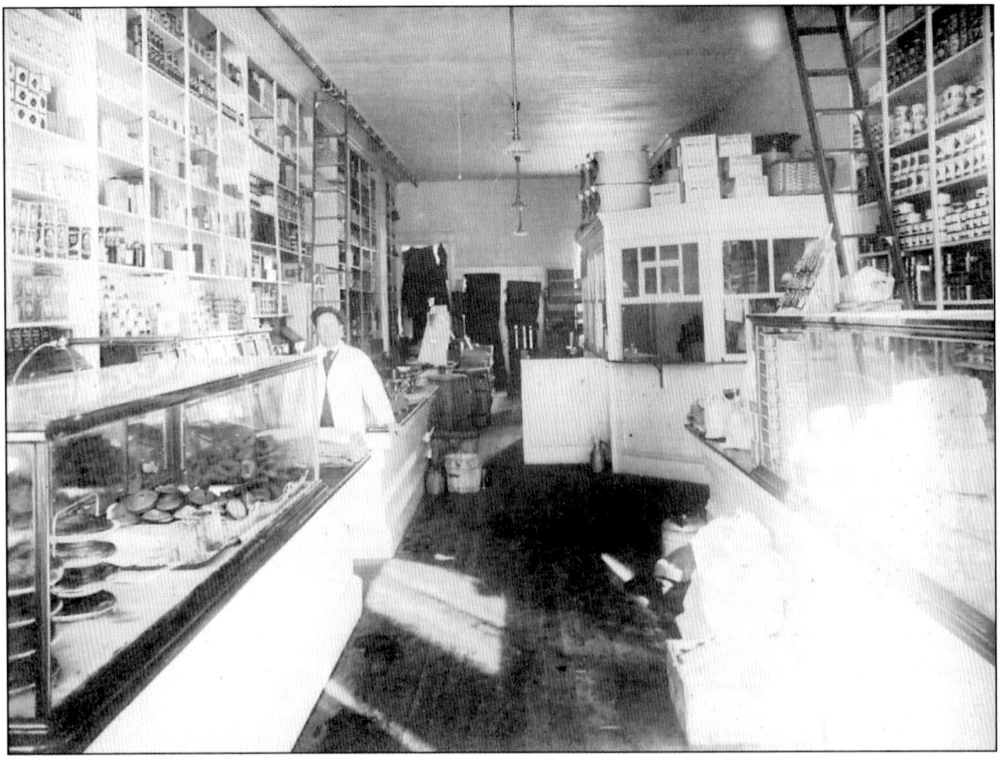

Simpson, Miller and Company carried baked goods, groceries, meats, dry goods, furniture, hardware, and millinery. (Courtesy of Pembroke Historical Society.)

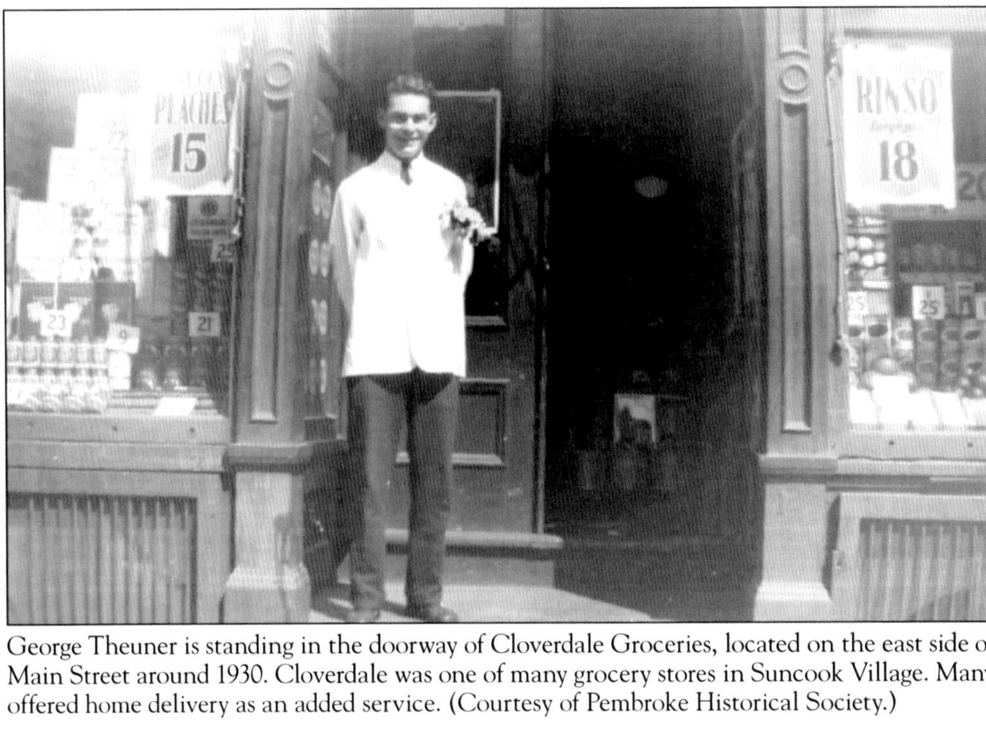

George Theuner is standing in the doorway of Cloverdale Groceries, located on the east side of Main Street around 1930. Cloverdale was one of many grocery stores in Suncook Village. Many offered home delivery as an added service. (Courtesy of Pembroke Historical Society.)

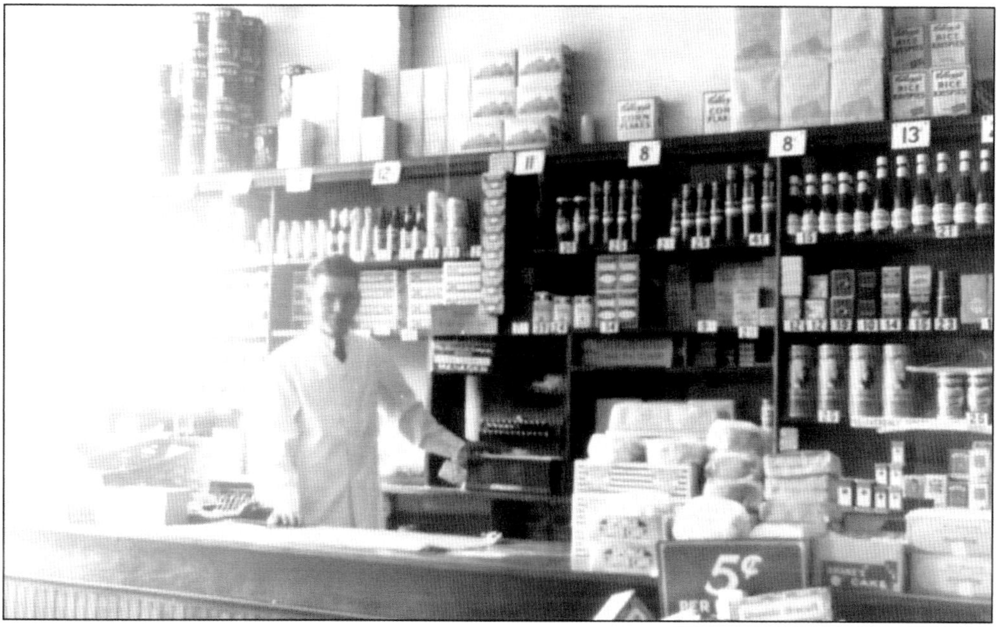

George Theuner is minding the store behind the counter at Cloverdale Groceries around 1930. (Courtesy of Pembroke Historical Society.)

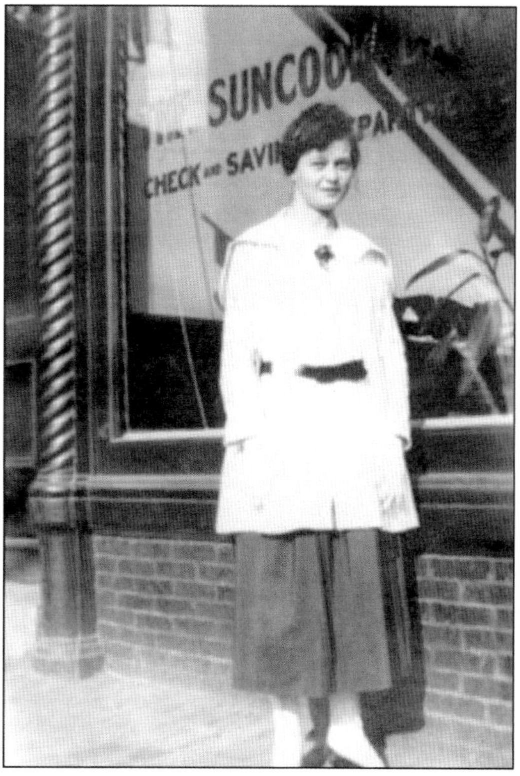

The Suncook Bank was located on the corner of Main and Glass Streets. The bank opened for business in September 1916. Later the bank moved to the corner of Glass and Church Streets in 1955. The Hoosett branch opened in 1972 and the Epsom branch opened in 1975. When this photograph was taken the bank offered four percent interest on savings accounts. Prior to the opening of the Suncook Bank, the Suncook Mills established the China Savings Bank. (Courtesy of Roland Martel.)

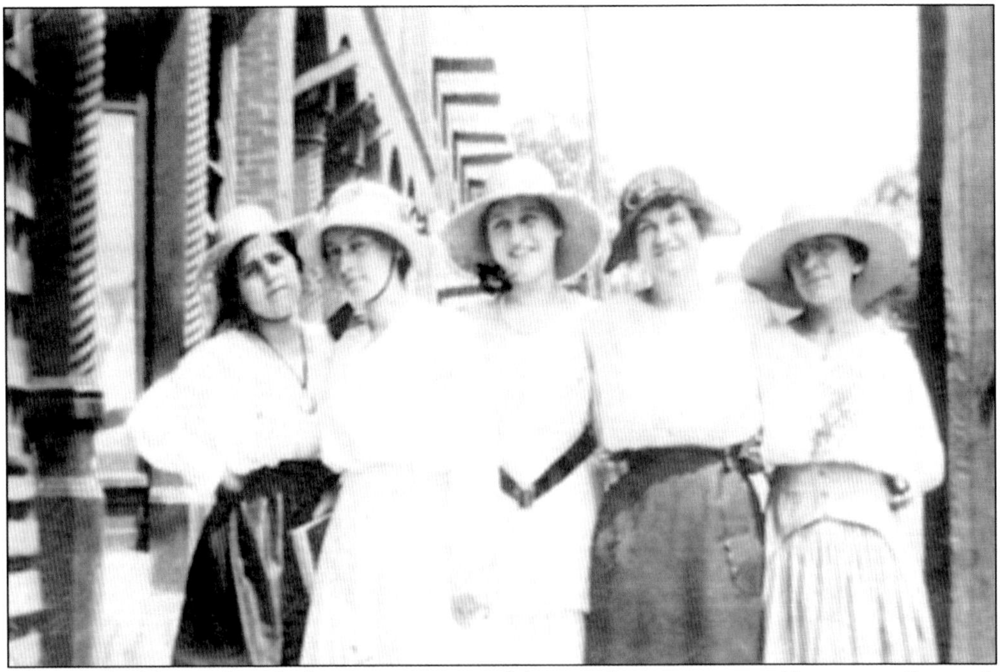

At the end of the workweek, shopping was part of the social entertainment. Downtown Suncook offered everything needed plus an opportunity to interact with friends and neighbors. Many shoppers came from surrounding communities, particularly towns connected by the railroad. While women shopped, men discussed the news of the day in local businesses or saloons. (Courtesy Roland Martel.)

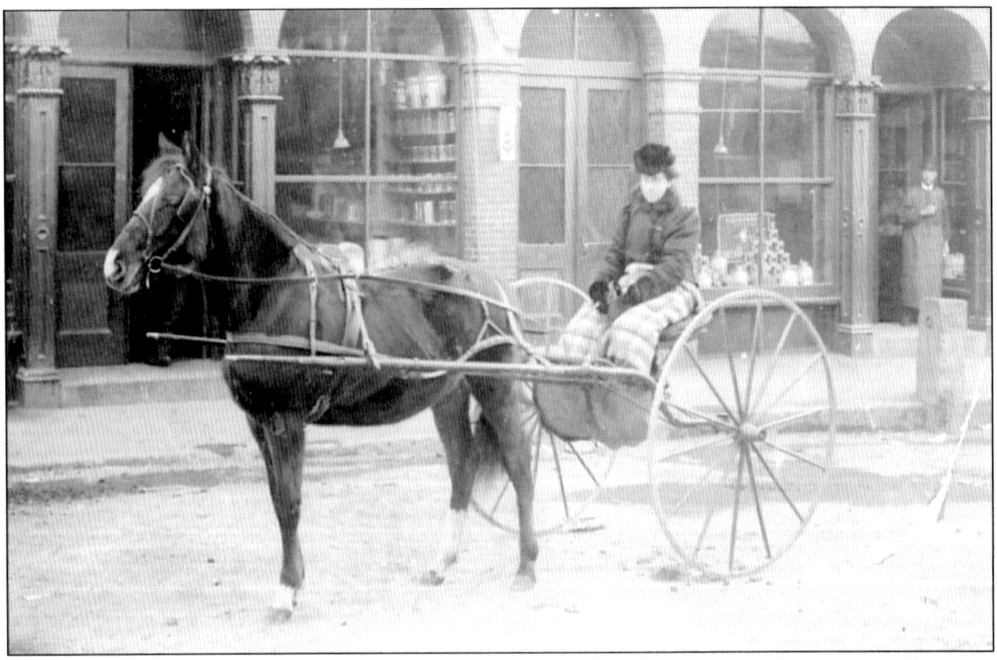

Mrs. Wilkes is driving the horse and cart around 1911 in the Glass Street or Main Street business district. (Courtesy of Armand and Claudette Verville.)

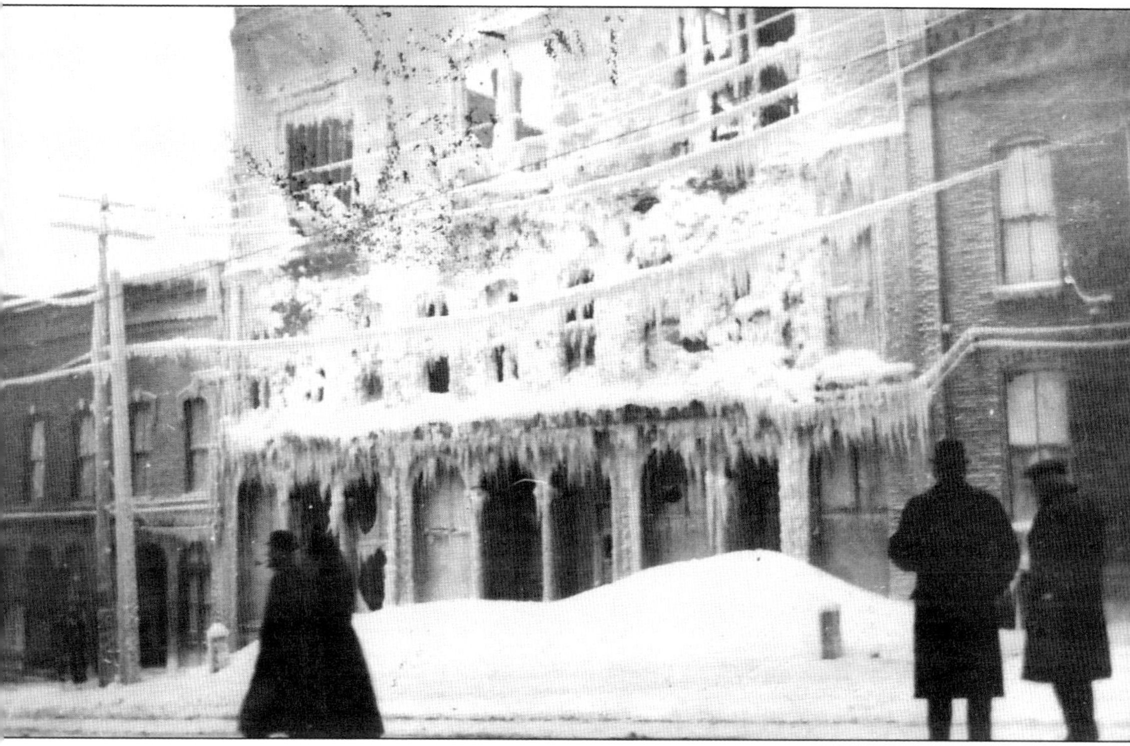

Seen here is the fire aftermath of Addison Osgood's block during the winter of 1914. The third floor of this building housed the International Order of Odd Fellows, Howard Lodge. Between 1873 and 1886, three major conflagrations devastated the business district. The first, January 25, 1876, destroyed wooden buildings on the west side of the street. Afterward three brick buildings were built, including the five story Bartlett Hotel and Opera House. A second fire occurred August 14, 1878, destroying the wooden structures on the east side of the street. Brick buildings were then built alongside the Chickering and Emery blocks. The third conflagration, December 11, 1886, obliterated the 10-year-old Bartlett Hotel and buildings on the west side of the street. The west side was rebuilt and has remained the same except for the third story of the Osgood block. (Courtesy Armand and Claudette Verville.)

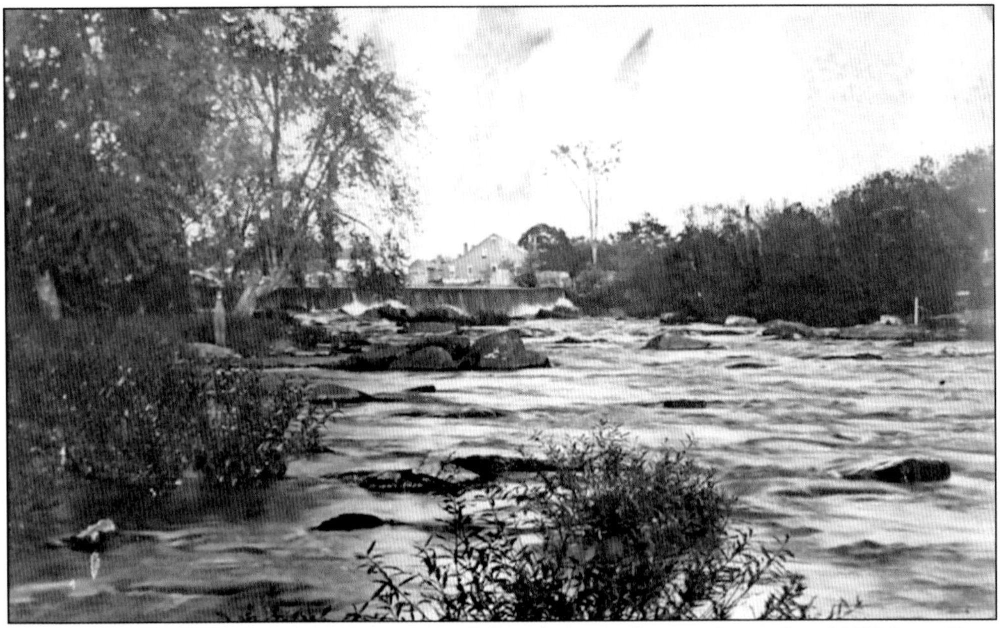

The Suncook Glass Works is at the center of this photograph, just above the old Webster Dam on the Suncook River. (Courtesy of Pembroke Historical Society.)

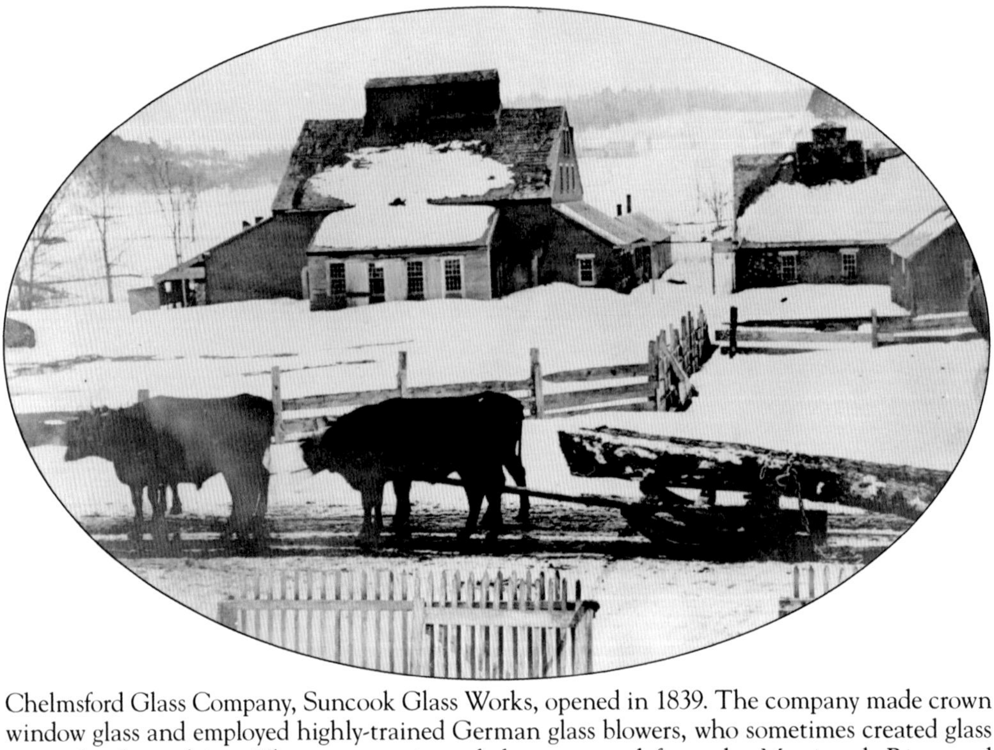

Chelmsford Glass Company, Suncook Glass Works, opened in 1839. The company made crown window glass and employed highly-trained German glass blowers, who sometimes created glass canes, bowls, and jars. The company intended to use sand from the Merrimack River and Massabesic Lake, but the sand proved inferior for the production of glass. Suncook Glass Works closed in 1850. (Courtesy of New Hampshire Historical Society.)

The Fowler Brothers Grain Store was a wholesale and retail business that was behind the Suncook Railroad depot on Exchange Street. The store was owned by George Winthrop Fowler and his brother Edward Fowler. (Courtesy of Pembroke Historical Society.)

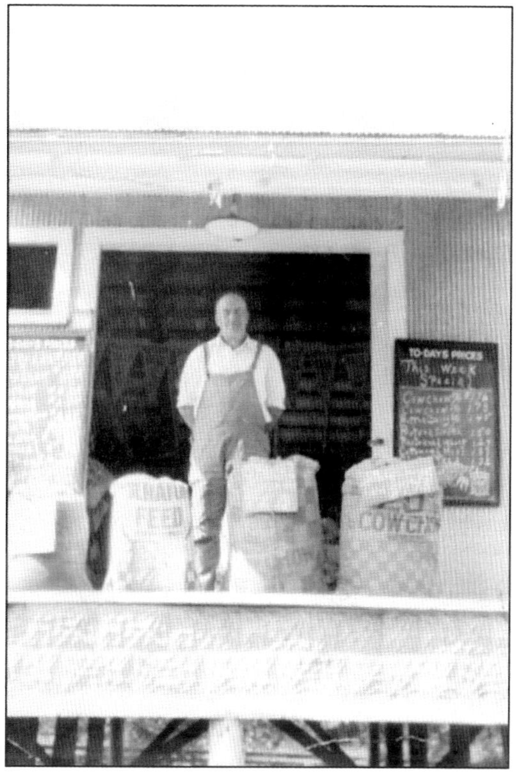

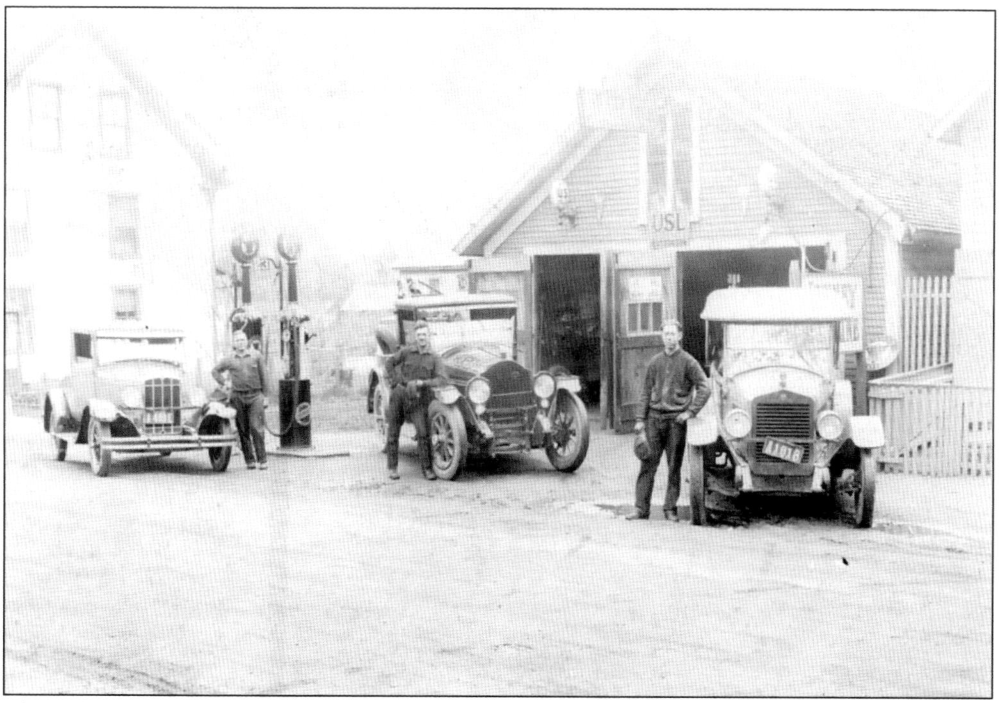

The Glass Street Garage, pictured here, was removed in 1940. (Courtesy of Arlene and Victor Fleury.)

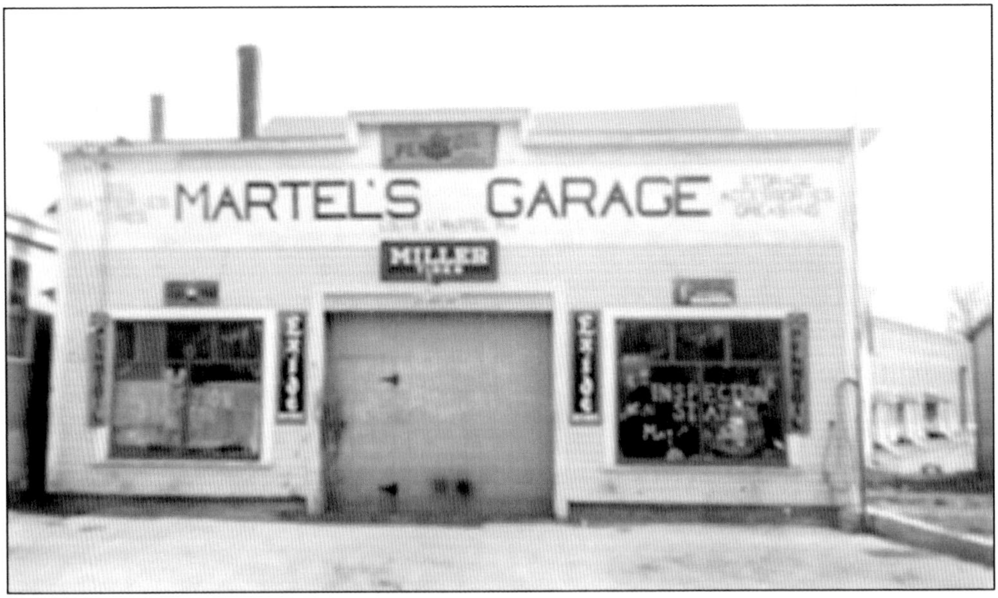

Martel's Garage on North Main Street is seen here around 1940. The garage was owned and operated by Louis Martel. In later days, the building became a laundromat and eventually was torn down. Today a parking lot is where it once stood. (Courtesy of Roland Martel.)

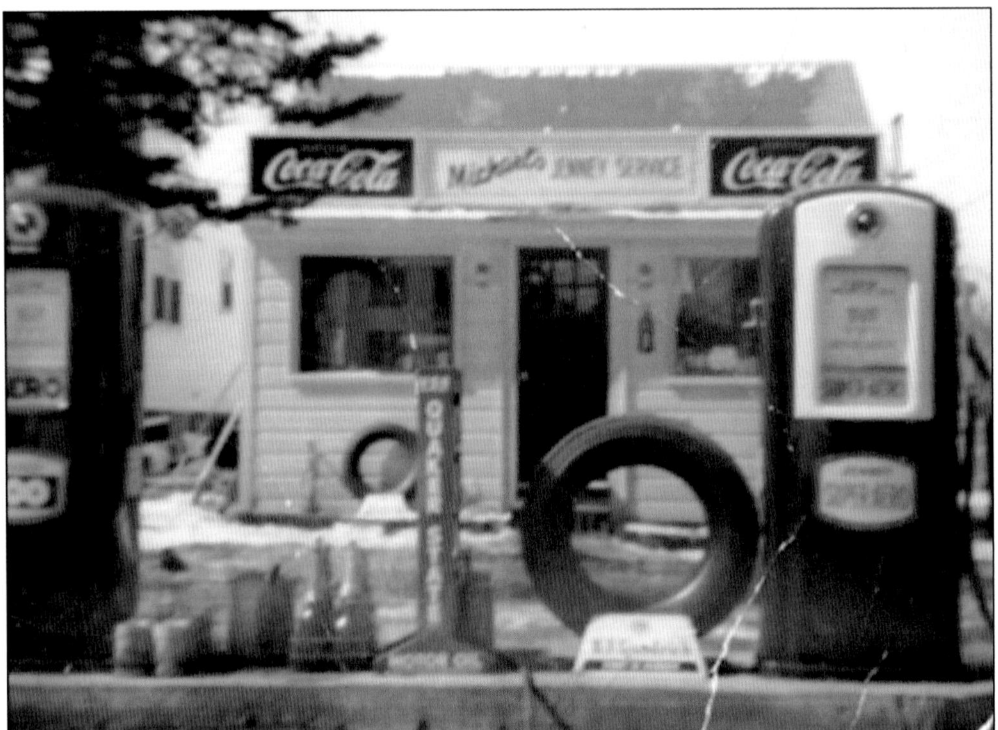

Micheals Jenney Service station, more commonly known as "Mike's," pictured here around 1950, was located at the corner of Ferry and Main Streets. The station was owned and operated by Mike Chroniak. (Courtesy of Bob St. Germain.)

Seven

The Catholic Mission, Churches, and Schools

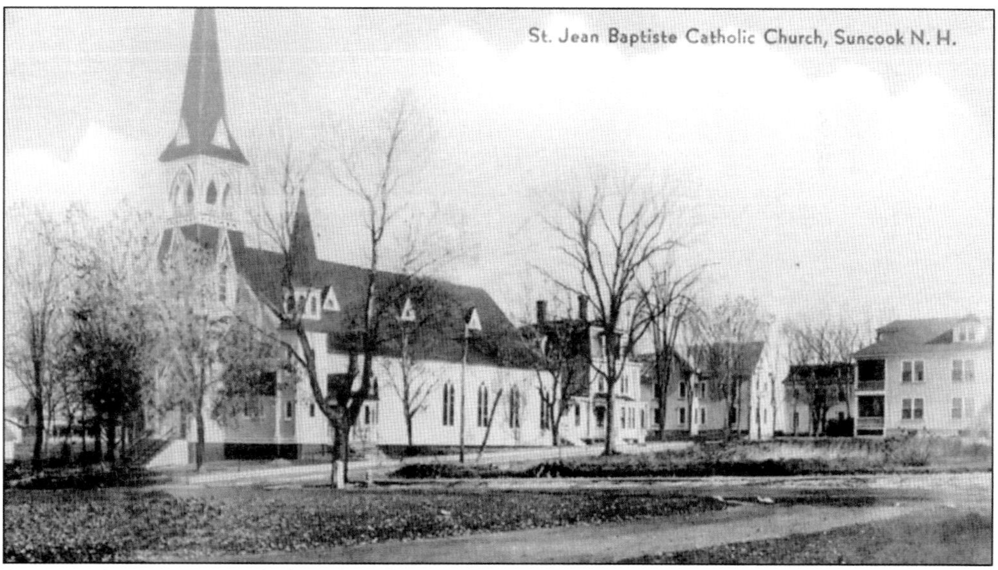

St. Jean the Baptist Catholic Church is seen here in 1923. In 1873, Rev. Jean Baptist Richer acquired land from the China Manufacturing Company and built the church. Stained-glass windows were installed in 1881 and on July 14, 1884, a 1,700-pound bell produced by McShane Foundry of Baltimore, Maryland, was added. The church was renovated in 1923, 1934, 1959, and 1973. The original building still remains within the updated structure. (Courtesy of Connie French.)

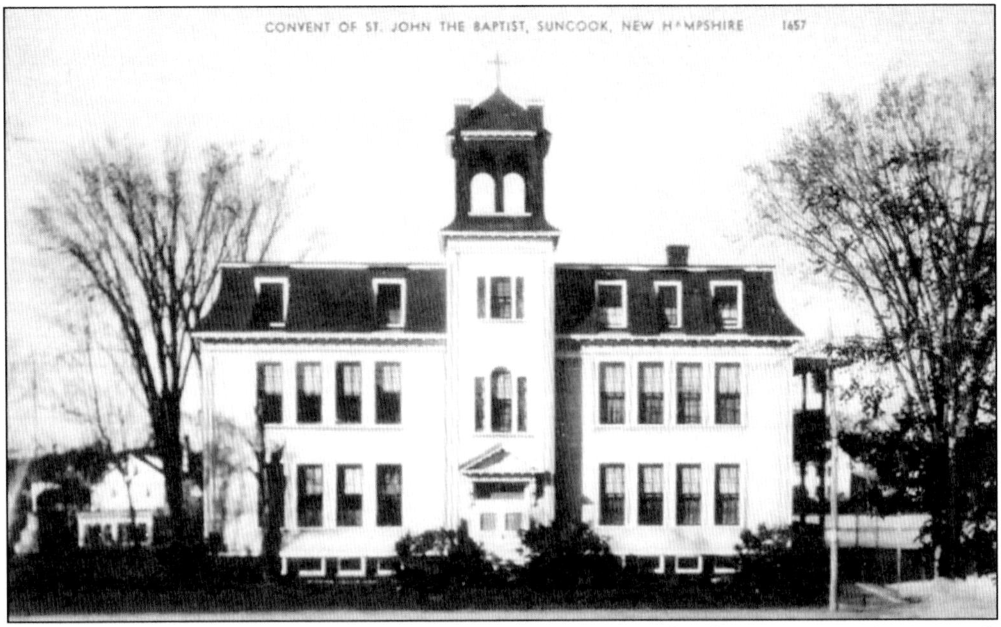

Shown in this picture is St. Jean the Baptist Convent on School Street. In 1861, Suncook became a mission of St. John the Evangelist of Concord. Rev. John E. Barry traveled to Suncook regularly to conduct mass in area homes. Area Catholics made a request to the bishop in 1870 for the establishment of a parish. This request was granted and the first parish building was the church built in 1873. A rectory, convent, and school were built afterward. (Courtesy of Connie French.)

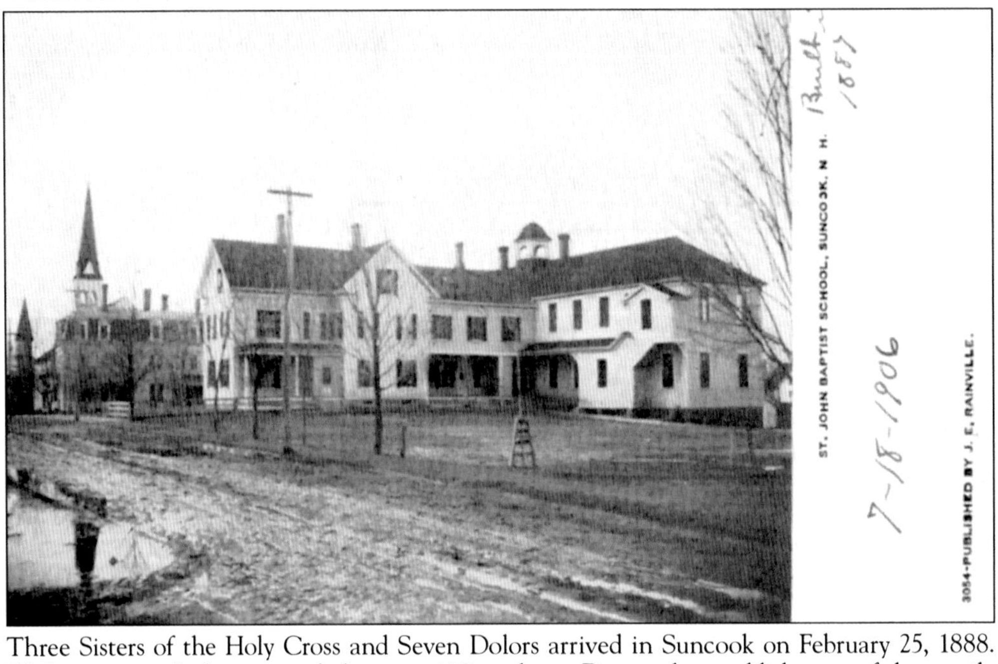

Three Sisters of the Holy Cross and Seven Dolors arrived in Suncook on February 25, 1888. Within one week they opened classes to 192 students. Due to the establishment of the textile mills, population growth increased the need for larger and better schools. Three public and two parochial schools were built to fulfill this need. (Courtesy of Connie French.)

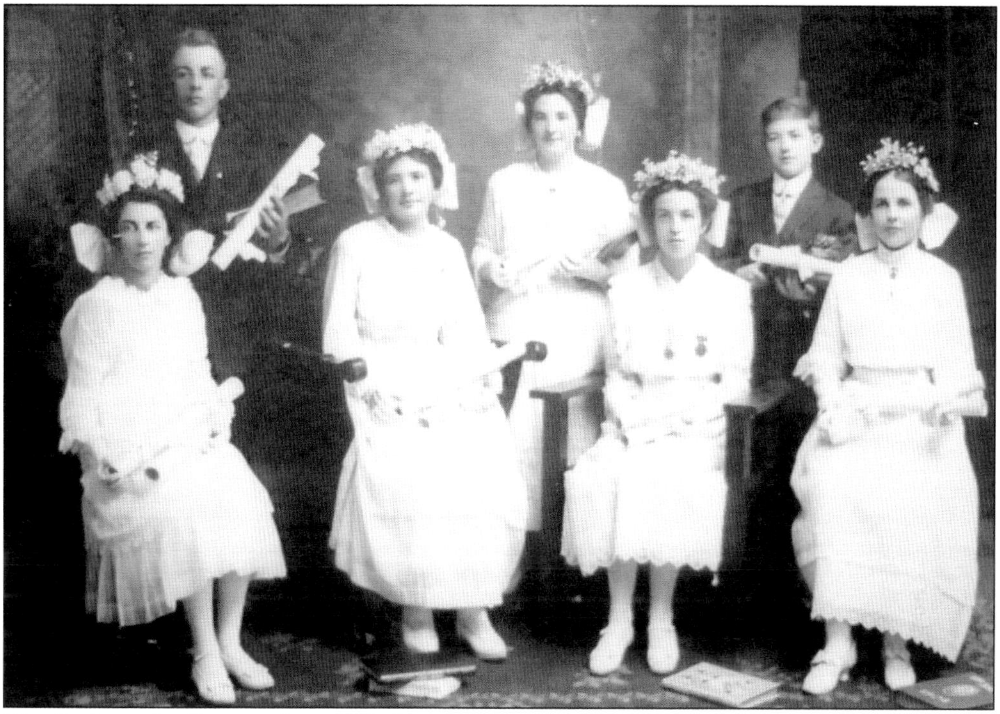

The St. Jean the Baptist class of 1915 is pictured here. From left to right are (first row) Maria Raymond, Anna Letendre, Clothilde Courtemanche, and Maria A. Duval; (second row) M. David Poisson, Juliette Fontaine, and Arthur Trombley. (Courtesy of Larry Perron.)

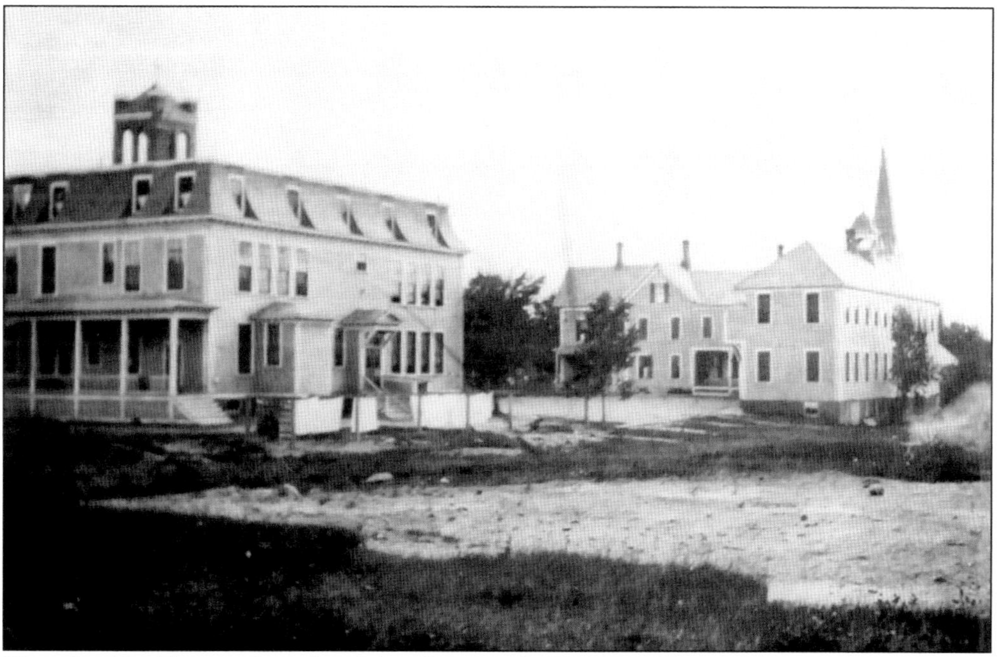

The school building on the right of this photograph was for grades one through six. The convent on the left side of the photograph contained the seventh and eight grade classrooms. (Courtesy of Armand and Claudette Verville.)

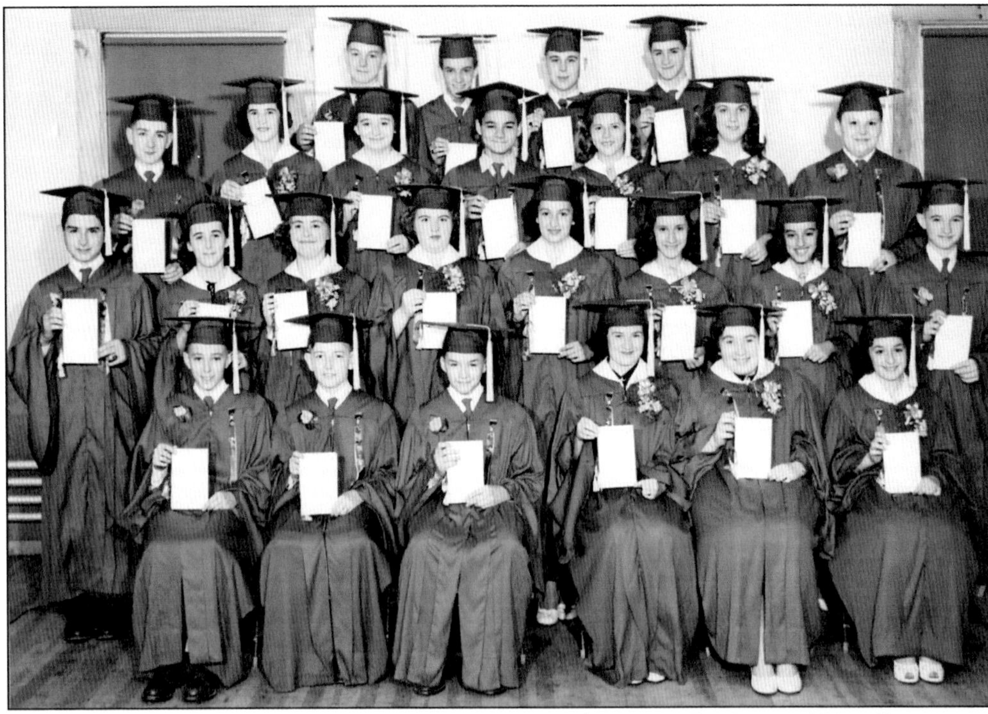

St. Jean the Baptist grammar school graduates are seen here in 1954. Armand Verville is seated second from the left in the first row. (Courtesy of Armand and Claudette Verville.)

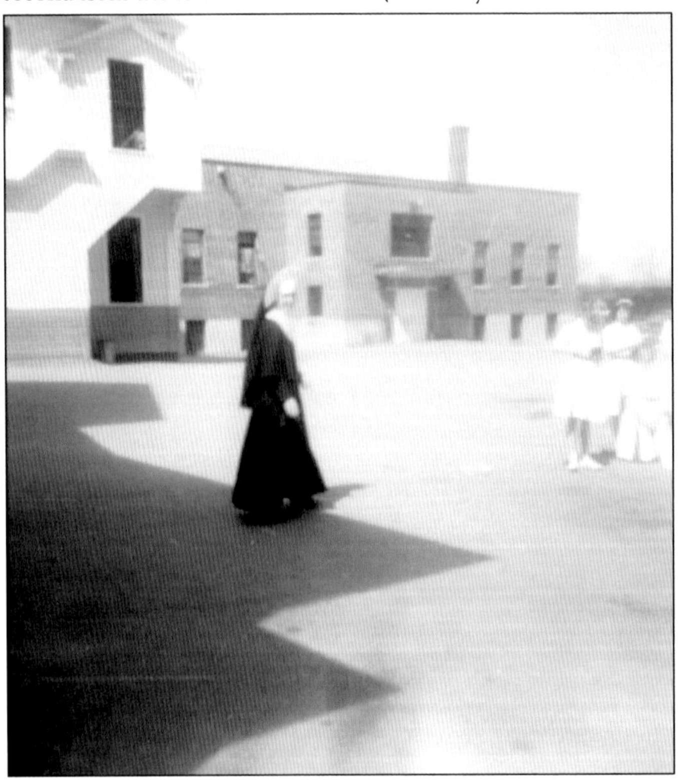

The schoolyard, a sister of the Holy Cross, and students are seen in this May 1960 photograph. In the background is the St. Jean the Baptist gymnasium. Built as a social center for sports and activities, the building housed a bowling alley on the first level and a gymnasium on the second level. A new catholic school was added to the gymnasium in 1973. (Courtesy of Roland Martel.)

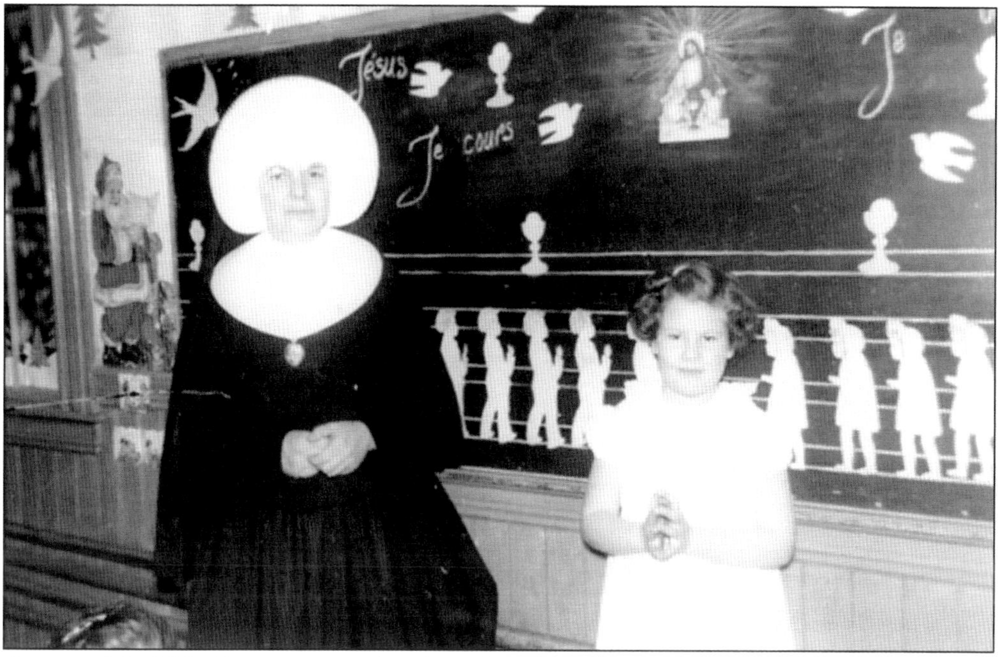

A sister of the Holy Cross is pictured with students in a classroom at St. Jean the Baptist school in this 1950s photograph. The students were taught in French for half the day and in English for half the day. This helped children learn the English language and, at the same time, preserved their French Canadian heritage. (Courtesy of Roland Martel.)

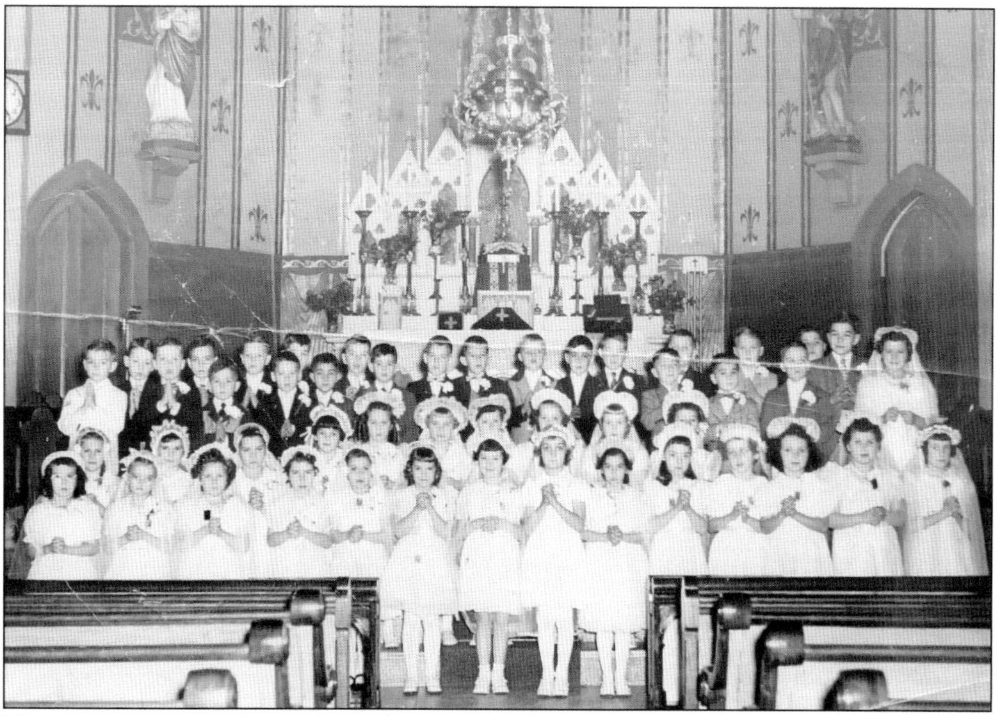

This photograph of the St. Jean the Baptist Church altar during the sacrament of Holy Communion was taken in 1952. (Courtesy of Roland Martel.)

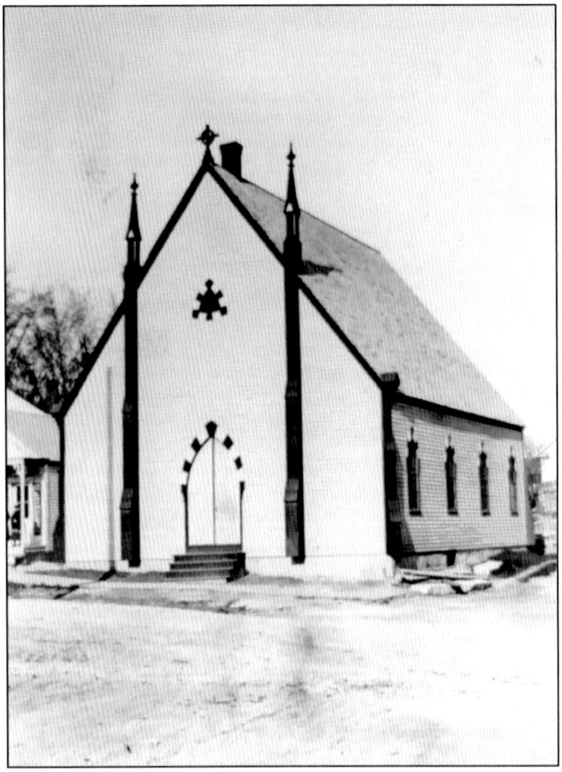

The first Baptist church was built in 1871. The church was located on Main Street in Suncook Village across from the present-day Methodist church. It was destroyed by fire in 1878. The second Baptist Church was built in 1879 at the corner of Broadway and Main Street. (Courtesy of Larry Perron.)

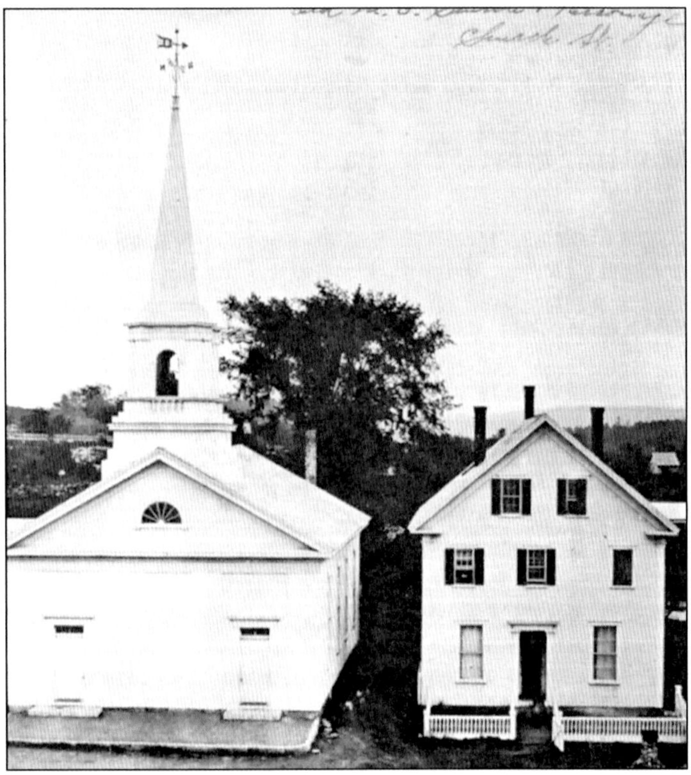

The Methodist church, built in 1849, and the parsonage were located on Church Street. Both buildings were lost by fire October 10, 1882. The second church and parsonage was relocated at the corner of Union and Main Streets in 1884 and again destroyed by a fire on February 15, 1911. The third and present-day Methodist church was dedicated July 27, 1912. (Courtesy of Brent Michiels.)

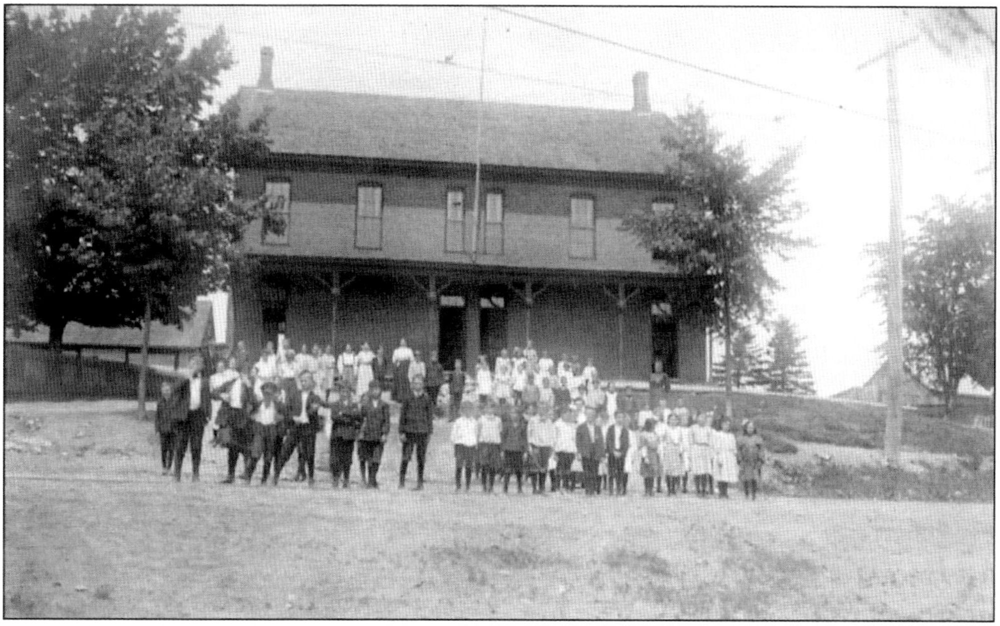

The Village School, built in 1872, was the first graded school in Suncook Village. The school was located at the corner of Turnpike and Main Streets on the Pembroke side of the village. After the new Village School opened in 1907, this structure was remodeled as a gymnasium for community usage. In 1951, Pembroke Water Works converted the space for offices, a garage, and storage. (Courtesy of Pembroke Historical Society.)

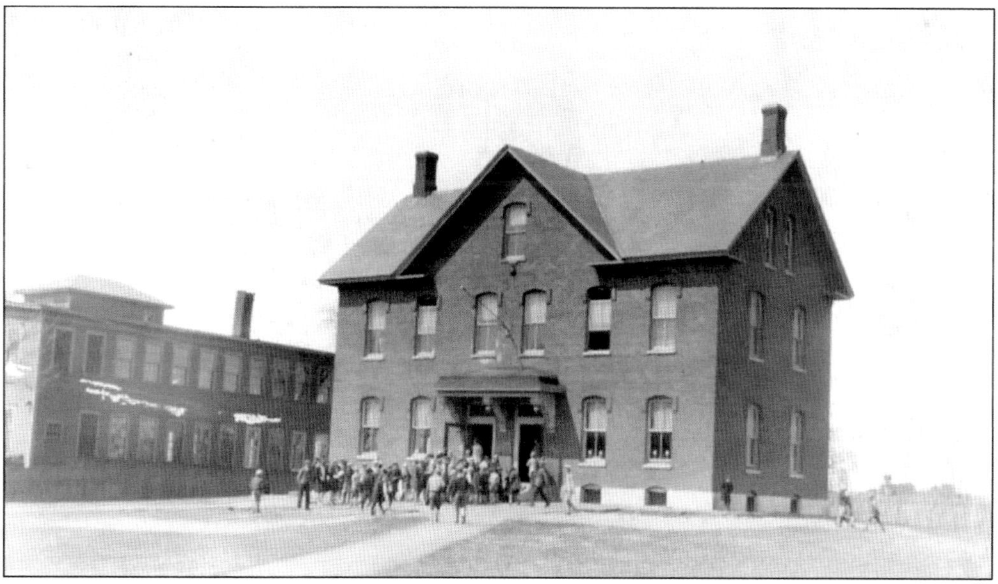

Allenstown Grammar School was built between 1877 and 1878 and dedicated on December 8, 1878. The building had a balconied second floor with classrooms on each side. It was the second school built in the village containing graded classrooms. The brick building next to the school was originally owned by China Manufacturing Company and later became Allenstown Shoe Manufacturing Company. (Courtesy of Allenstown, New Hampshire, Historical Society.)

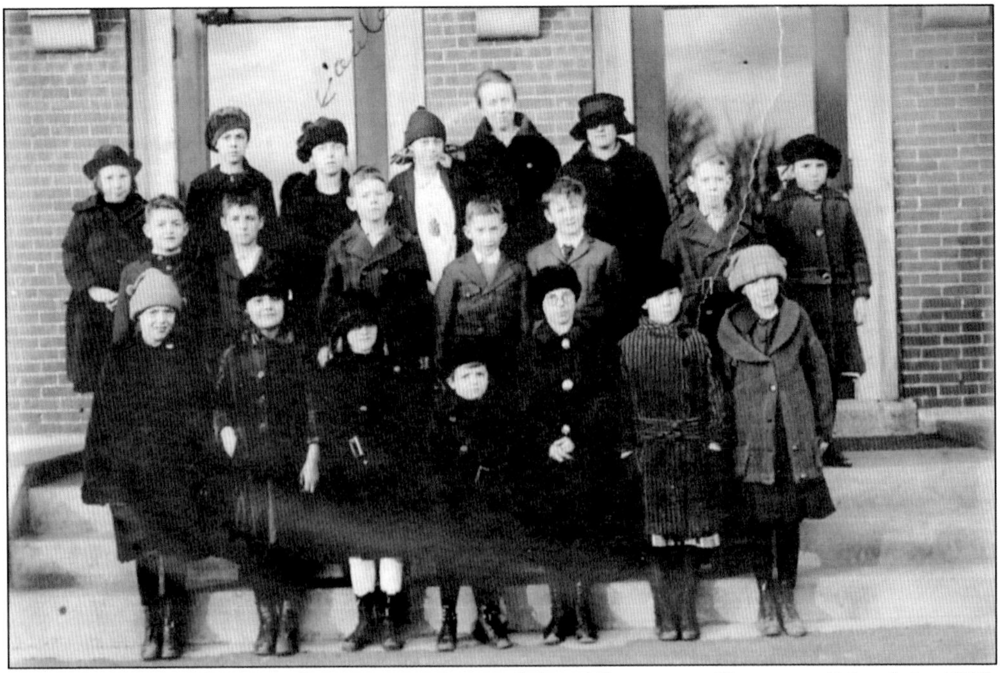

Students are standing on the stairs in front of the Allenstown Grammar School in 1912. Cecile (Lefevre) Verville is under the arrow. (Courtesy of Armand and Claudette Verville.)

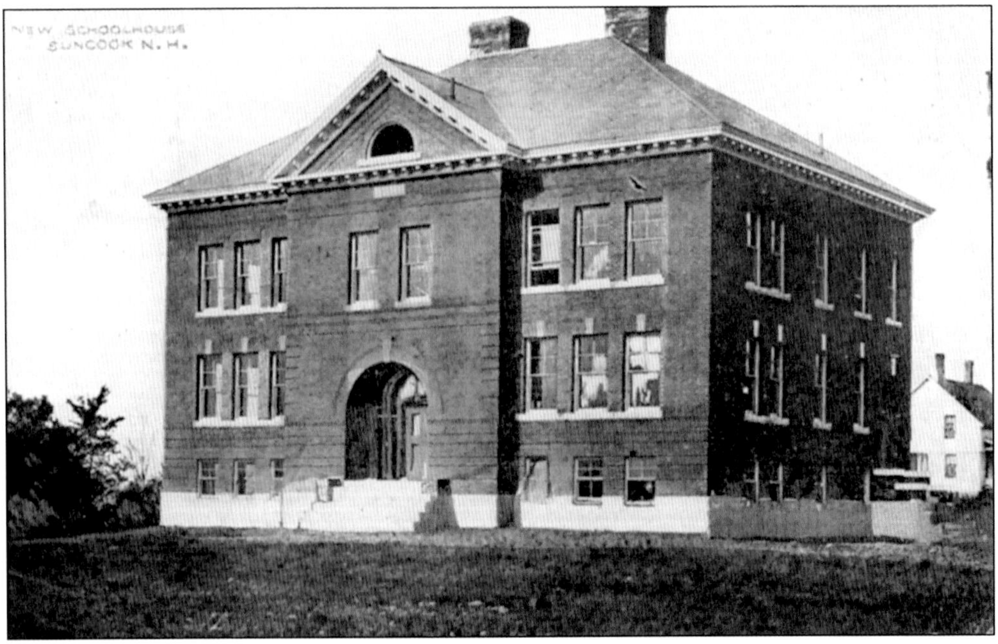

By the early 20th century, the Village School was overcrowded and a larger school was needed. Institutional architect Charles R. Whitcher (1876–1940) was hired to design the building. The new Village School was built in 1907 on a four-acre lot located at the west end of High Street. (Courtesy of Allenstown, New Hampshire, Historical Society.)

Eight

Disasters and Municipal Services

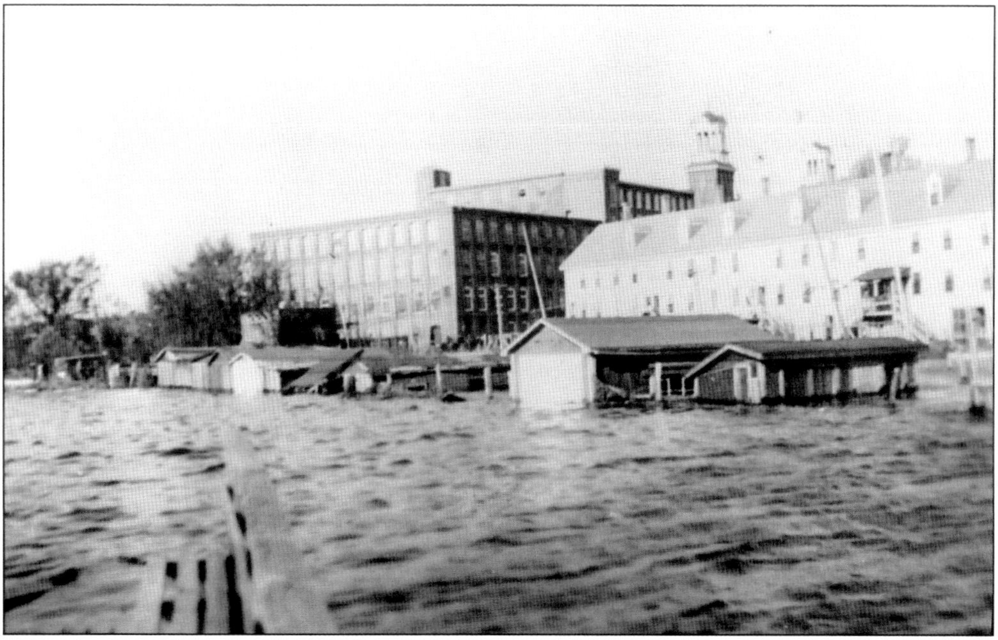

The China Mill and China Village tenements are underwater during the March 19, 1936, flood. The Civilian Conservation Corps, Juniors Company 1123, from the Bear Brook Reservation-Camp responded to the flood emergency, assisting with sandbags, diversion tactics, and clean up. The flood devastated the village and other communities throughout New Hampshire. In Suncook, it was one of the two largest disasters during the 20th century. (Courtesy of Brent Michiels and Albert Mondoux.)

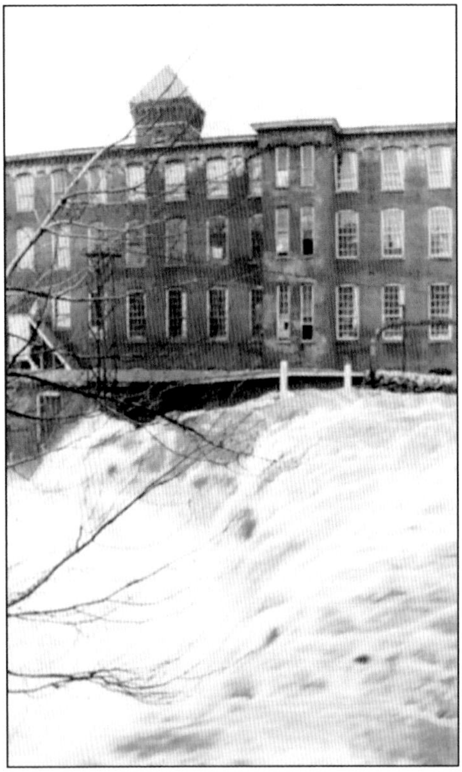

The Pembroke Mill Dam is seen here on March 19, 1936. The right-hand wall was protected by sandbags. (Courtesy of Pembroke Historical Society.)

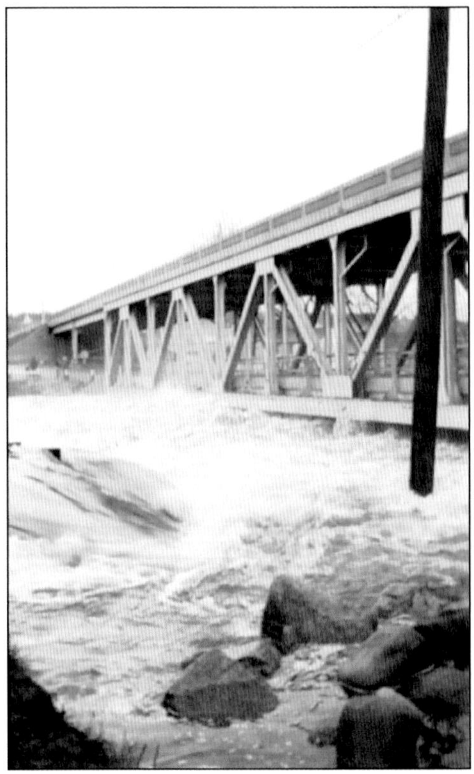

This photograph shows the double-decker bridge on Route 3 and Turnpike Street, looking southwest during the March 1936 flood. The flood destroyed many bridges in the area, but this bridge survived it. A new bridge replaced the old one in 2007. (Courtesy of Pembroke Historical Society.)

The Webster Mill is seen here on August 2, 1982, in the fire aftermath. The closely-developed business district narrowly escaped this quick-moving and enormous mill fire. In earlier days the mill served as an attractive gateway to the Suncook Mills. Later furniture maker Emerson Manufacturing Company occupied the building. After Emerson closed, the Webster Mill sat idle and in disrepair. When approaching the Main Street Bridge, the mill that once seemed welcoming appeared ominous and imposing. (Courtesy of Brent Michiels.)

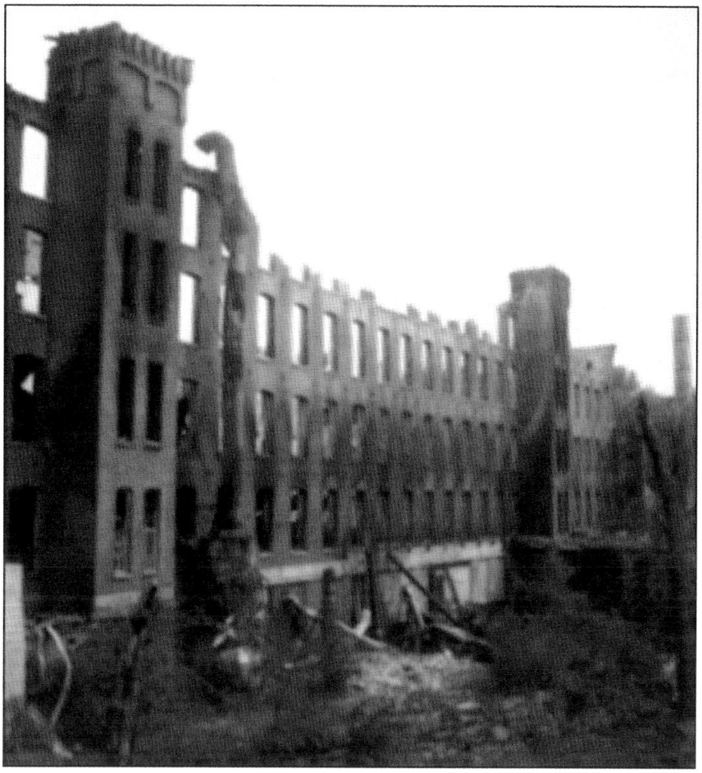

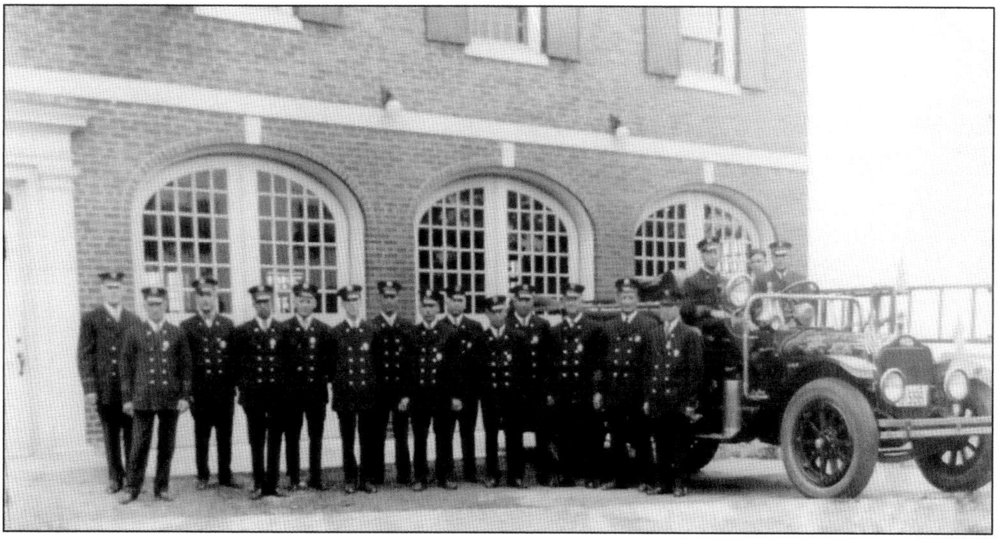

This photograph is of the Pembroke Fire Department in 1931. From left to right are A. Levesque, T. Welch, O. Turgeon, N. Thibeault, A. Ricard, A. Richard, P. Dube, L. Hamel, F. Bouchard, D. Plourde, D. Laberge, A. Tetrault, G. Petit Sr., J. Chase, Chief Walter Edmonds, Rudolph Sansterre, and Asst. Chief W. Smith. (Photograph by Pembroke Fire Department; courtesy of Larry Perron.)

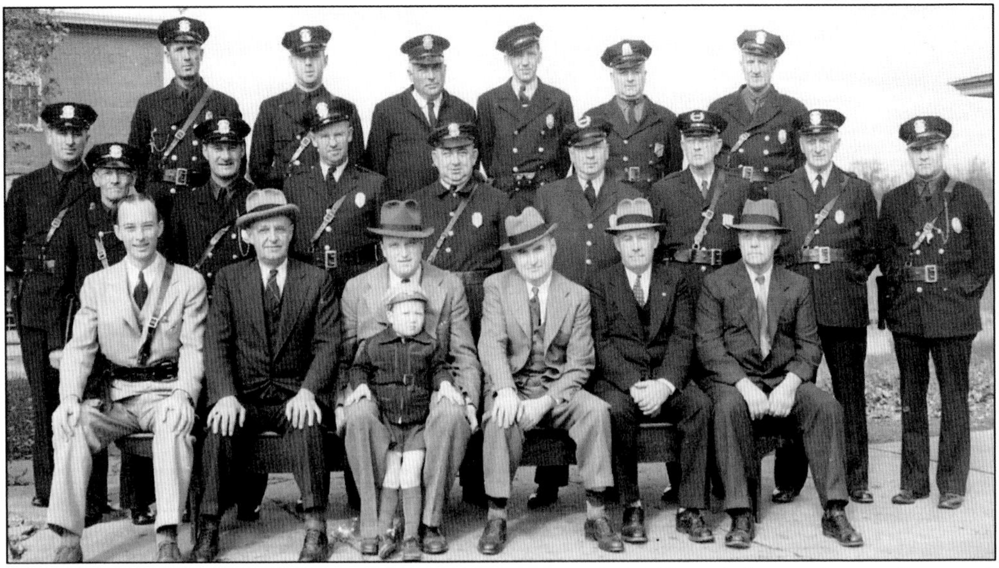

The China Mill security force is in front of Textron in 1944. From left to right are (first row) Robert Lockhart Sr., Joseph Cournoyer, Raymond Fish, Tom Silk, John Lynch, and Mr. Chase; (second row) Ernest Daneault, Alexander Hamel, Chick Souci, Mr. Langford, "Pepsi Cola" Daneault, Buck Bouchard, John Welch, John Kane, and Armand Brisbois; (third row) Arthur Gamache, Arthur Ladurante, Fred Girard, Armand Drolet, Alcide Courtemanche, and Edrouge Lavallee. During World War II, Textron manufactured cloth and other items for the federal government. (Courtesy of Allenstown, New Hampshire, Historical Society.)

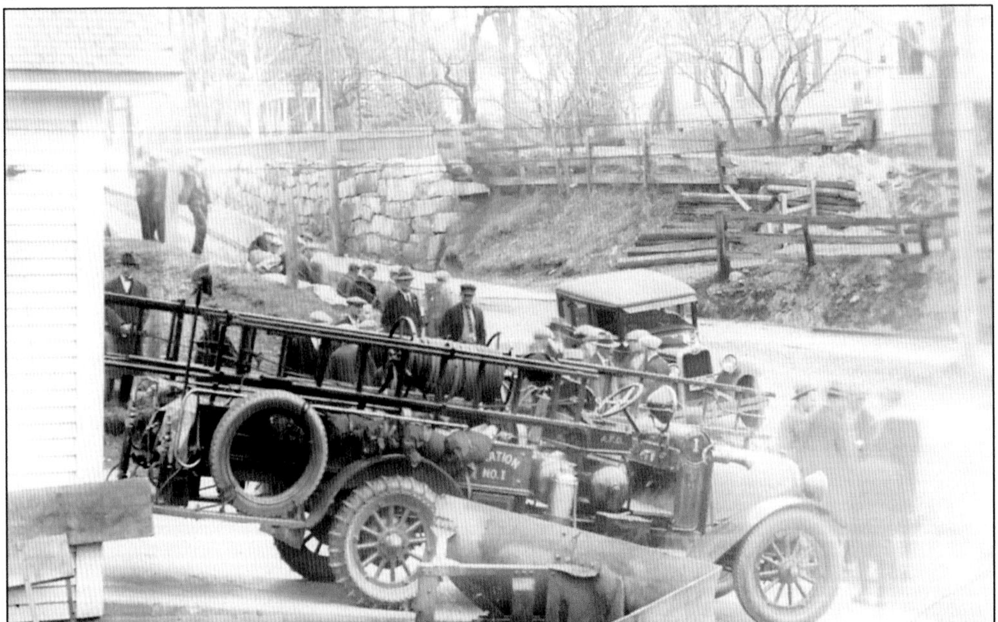

Allenstown's old ladder truck is parked in front of the Ferry Street fire station. The house on the opposite side of the road was the Leblanc residence. Suncook Village services were provided by Pembroke and Allenstown. Each town had its own fire and police department. (Courtesy of Armand and Claudette Verville.)

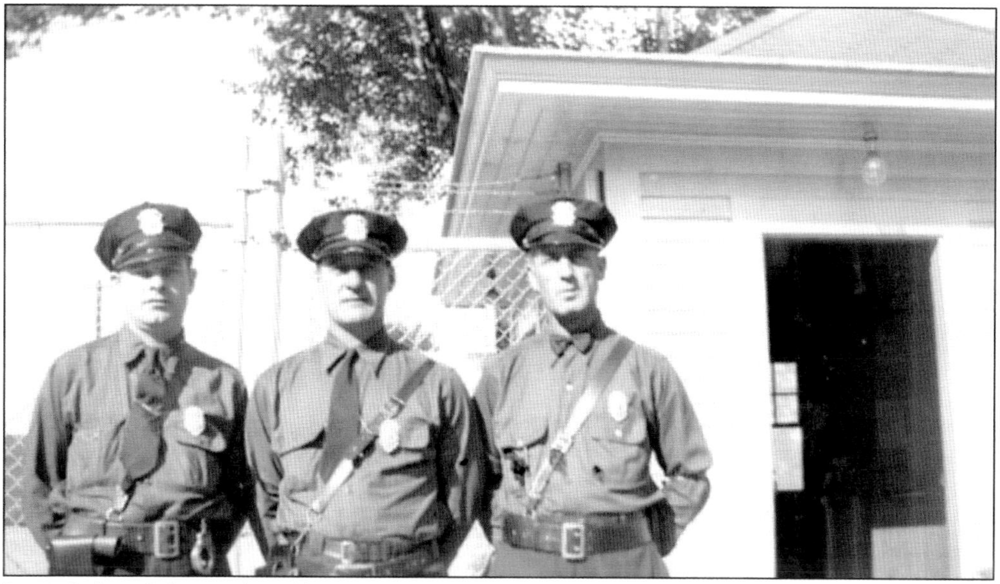

In 1942, from left to right, Allenstown police officers Armand Brisbois, Chick Souci, and Arthur Gamache stand in front of the police station located at the China Mill. The building was converted from a fire hose house to a police station. (Courtesy of Allenstown, New Hampshire, Historical Society.)

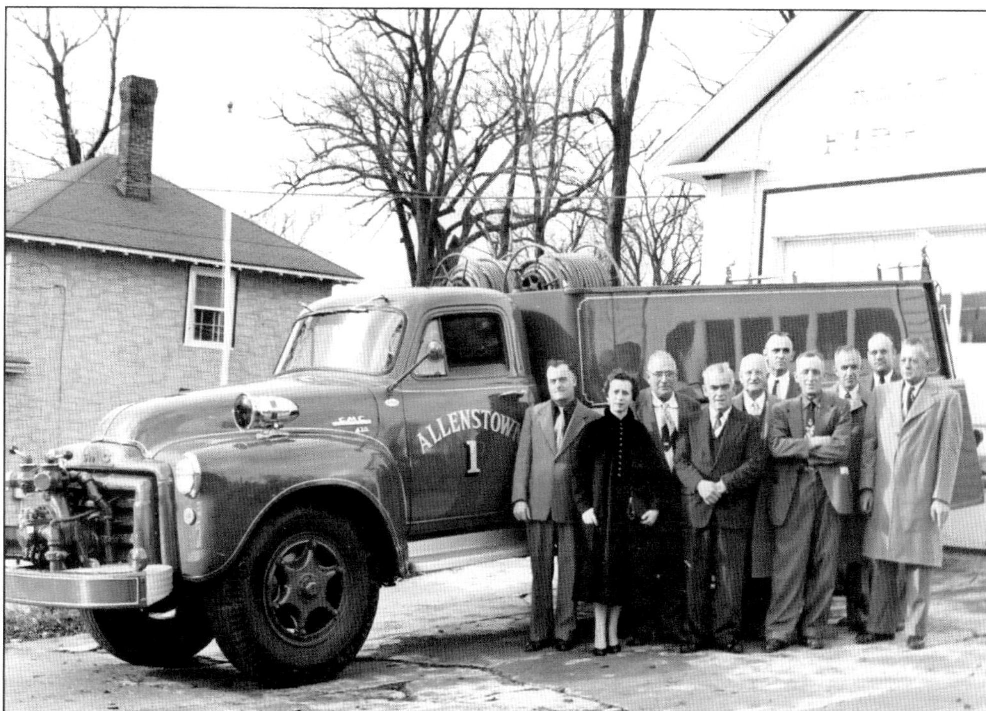

The new Allenstown fire truck is parked in front of the Allenstown Fire Station in 1954. From left to right are Chief Henry Lavoie, Prisilla Baron, Fred Girard, William Baillargeon, Arthur Desmaris, Armand Dupont, Frank Fleury, Doug Peabody, George Michiels, and Louis Gagne. (Courtesy of Allenstown, New Hampshire, Historical Society.)

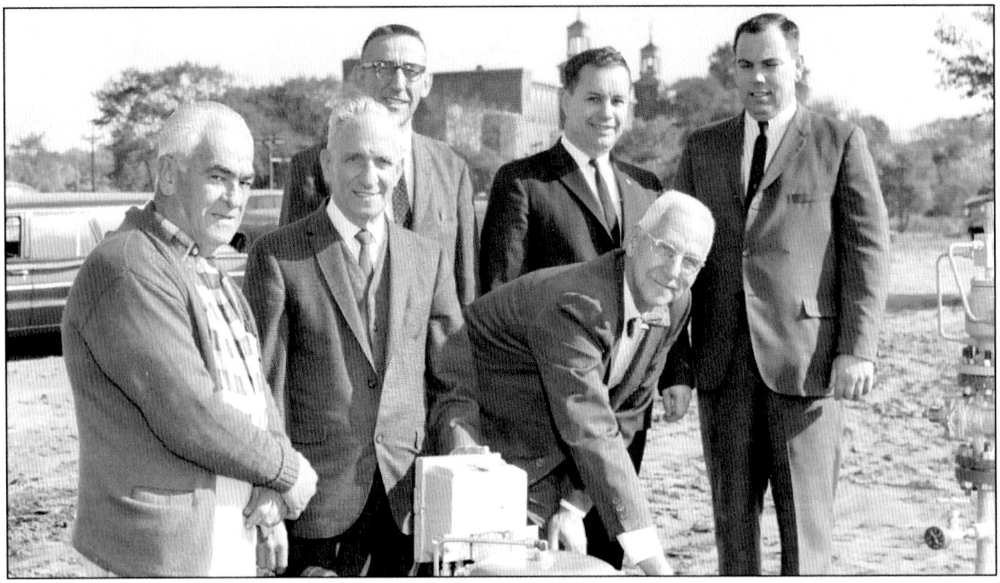

This is Concord Natural Gas Corporation's initial delivery of natural gas to the Suncook Village area. From left to right are (first row) William Baillargeon, Allenstown selectmen; Honore Bonenfant, Pembroke selectmen; and Joseph Robinson, chairman of the Pembroke Board of Selectmen; (second row) Ernest Coulomb, chairman of the Allenstown Board of Selectmen; Cedric Dustin, vice president and general manager of Concord Natural Gas Corporation; and Robert Plourde, Pembroke selectmen. (Courtesy of Allenstown, New Hampshire, Historical Society.)

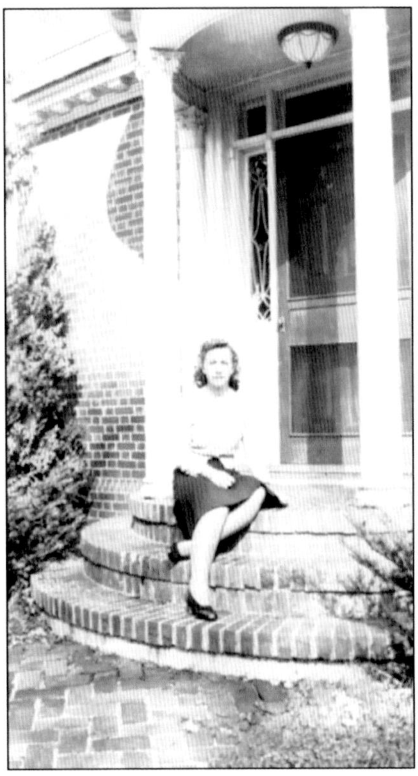

Doris Courchesne is seated on the steps of the new Allenstown Library. Allenstown acquired a 30 percent grant from the federal government and built the library as a Works Progress Administration (WPA) project around 1934. Harold H. Owen of Concord was the architect and the contractor was Osgood Construction of Nashua. The first library opened in Allenstown in 1893. Over the years, Pembroke and Allenstown had several libraries in Suncook Village. (Courtesy of Roland Martel.)

Nine

Assimilation, American Traditions, and Celebrations

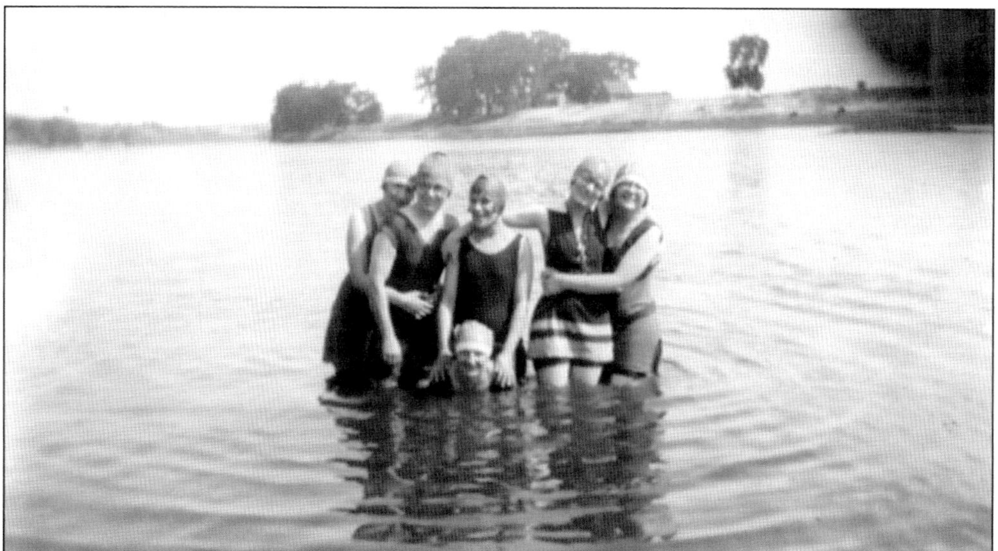

These stylish bathing beauties are enjoying a swim in the Merrimack River around 1910. The Suncook and Merrimack Rivers provided year-round recreational opportunities in the village, particularly fishing, boating, swimming, and ice-skating. The parade grounds and ball field served as a gathering place for civic and patriotic celebrations and as the site for baseball games. Sporting events included ice hockey, bowling, basketball, snowshoe competitions, and log drives. (Courtesy of Roland Martel.)

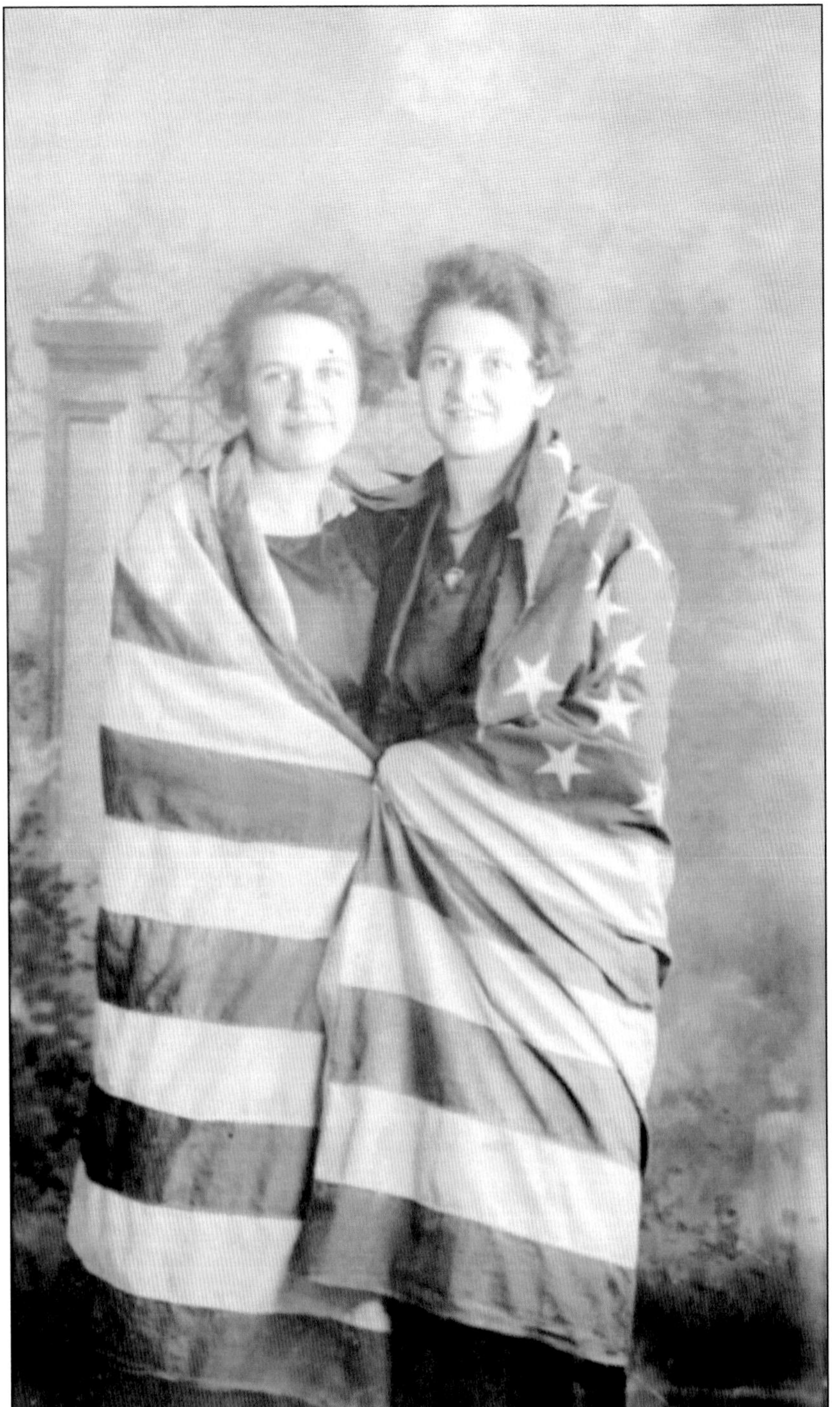

Alice Roy (right) and an unidentified friend pose for this patriotic photograph taken by Comet Photo Company of Manchester during the World War I era. Wrapped in an American flag, the girls are clearly expressing pride for their country, exhibiting patriotic spirit, and their pose symbolizes protection and safety. (Courtesy of Roland Martel.)

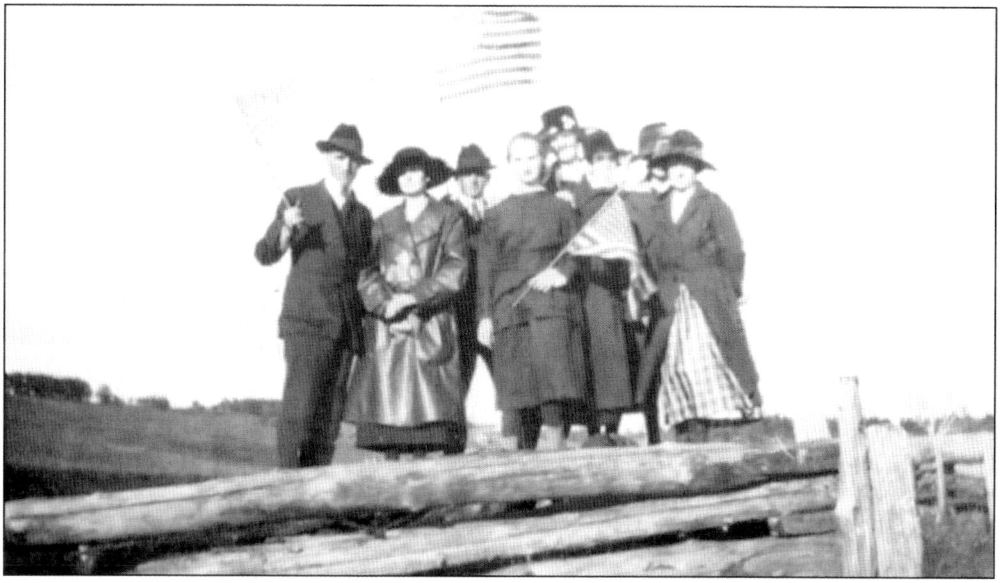

Armistice Day was declared on November 11, 1918, at the end of World War I. Across America, people lined the streets waving flags, paraded in cars displaying flags, used noisemakers, and honked their car horns in celebration. (Courtesy of Roland Martel.)

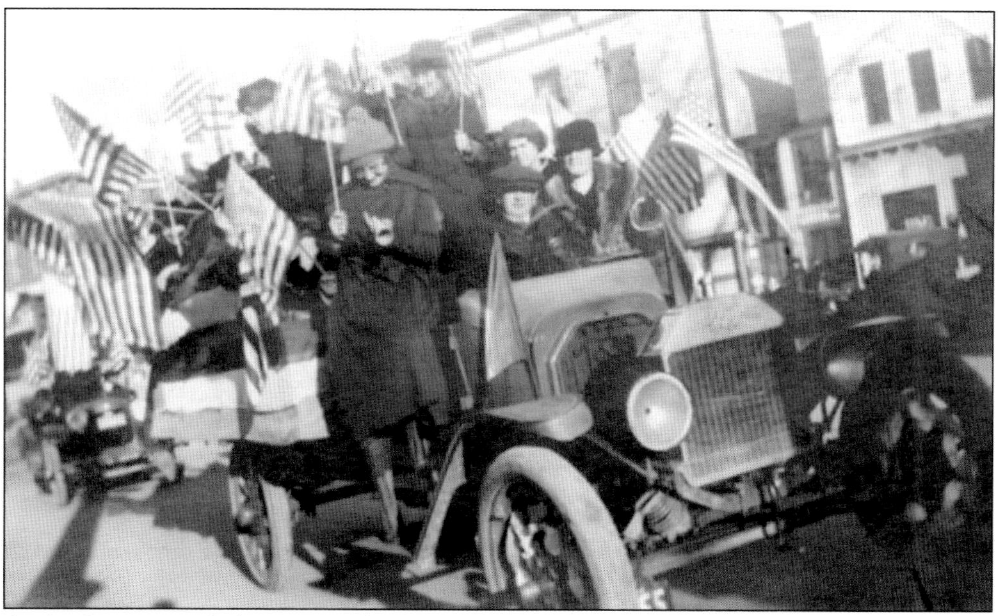

At the first national observance of Armistice Day on November 11, 1919, a moment of silence was observed at 11:00 a.m., and the celebration included parades and public meetings. (Courtesy of Roland Martel.)

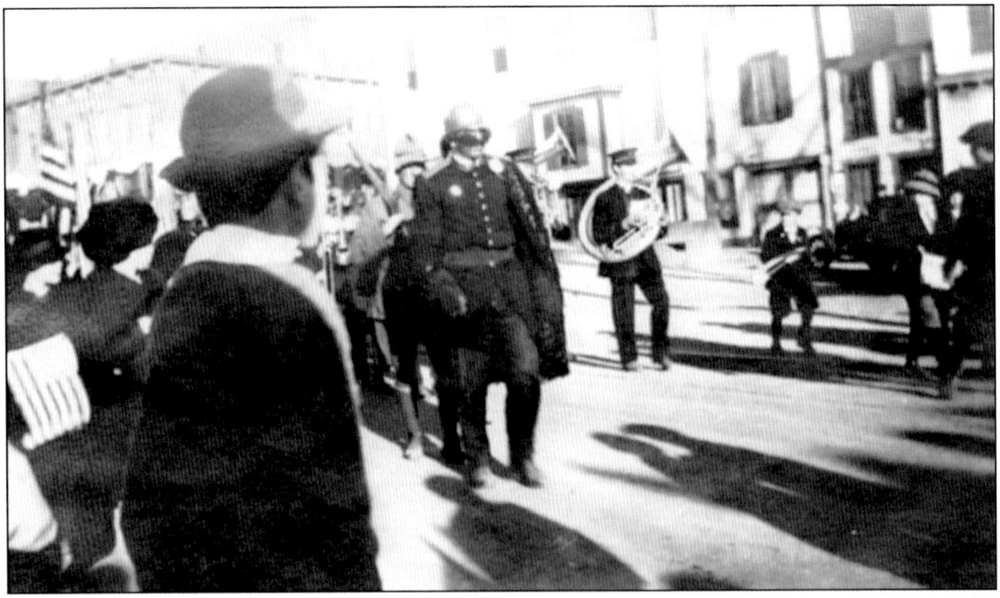

This is a parade at Glass and Main Streets, just before the Main Street bridge around 1919. In the center of the photograph a man is dressed as "Kaiser Bill" of Germany. The man behind him is dressed in a World War I uniform and carries a gun as if capturing Kaiser Bill. The large, wooden structure on the east side of Main Street was purchased by the American Legion in 1922, and by 1929 the legion occupied the entire two-story building. (Courtesy of Roland Martel.)

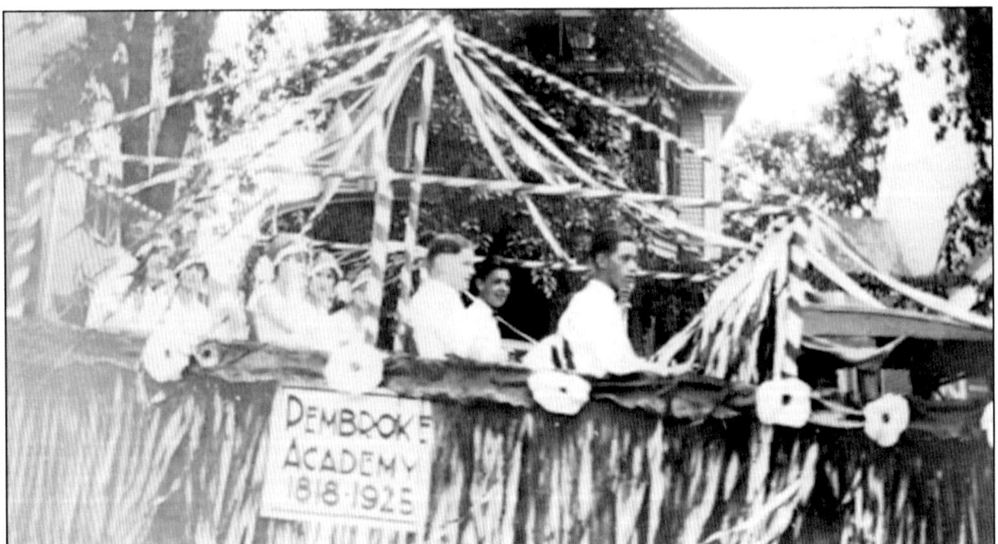

The Pembroke Academy float and some students are pictured at Broadway in 1925. (Courtesy of Pembroke Historical Society.)

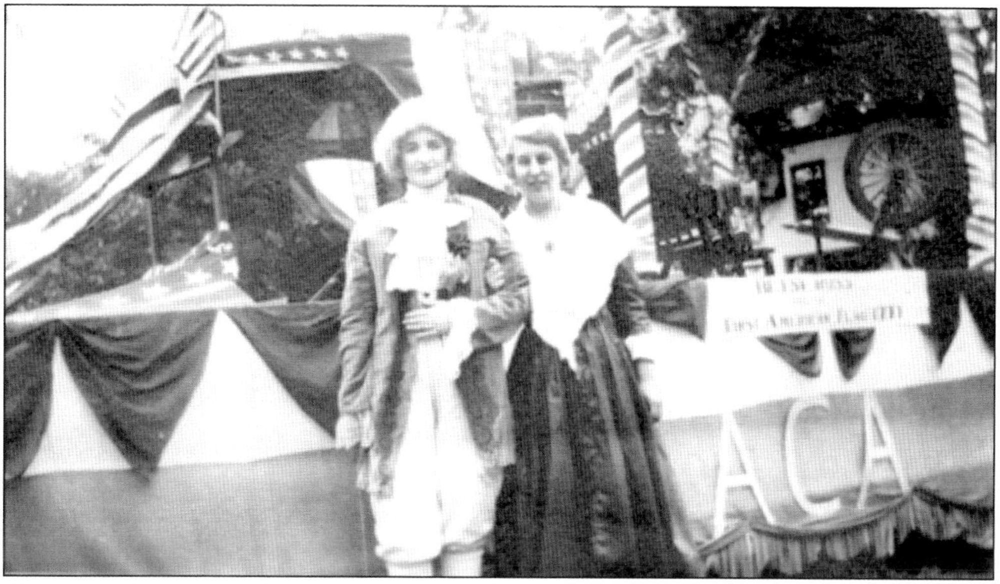

This is the Association Canadian Americans float at a Fourth of July parade during the 1920s. The sign on the side of the float reads, "Betsey Ross First American Flag 1777." Two association members are dressed as Marquis de Lafayette and Betsey Ross in the photograph. The costumes and theme were most likely inspired by Marquis de Lafayette's visit to Caleb Stark's home on Main Street in Suncook Village in 1825. (Courtesy of Roland Martel.)

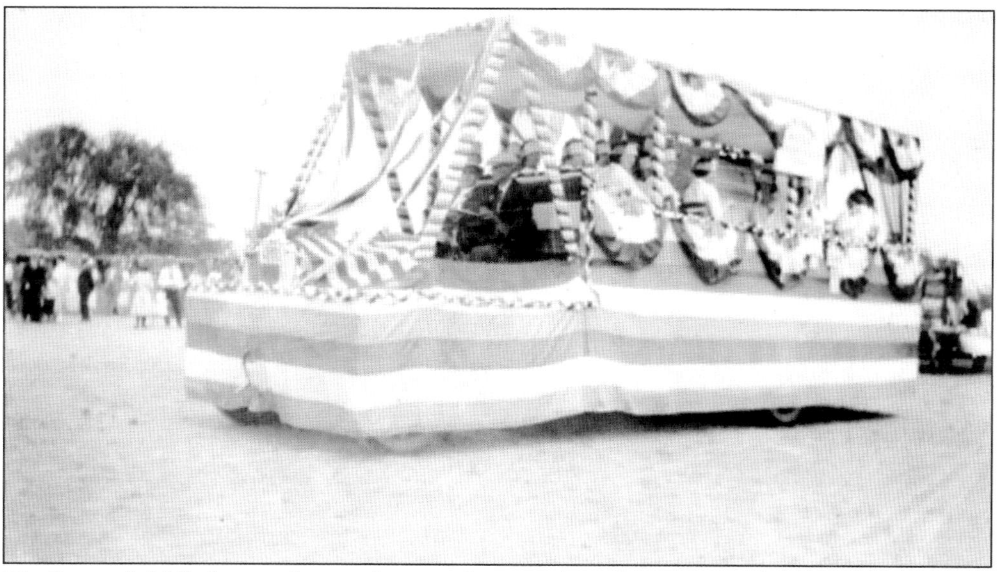

The Suncook Mills float at the parade grounds is seen here during a Fourth of July celebration in the 1920s. Gustave Roy is driving the truck with the float. For many years Suncook Mills agent David Lymen Jewell was at the forefront of organizing elaborate Independence Day celebrations complete with fireworks. (Courtesy of Roland Martel.)

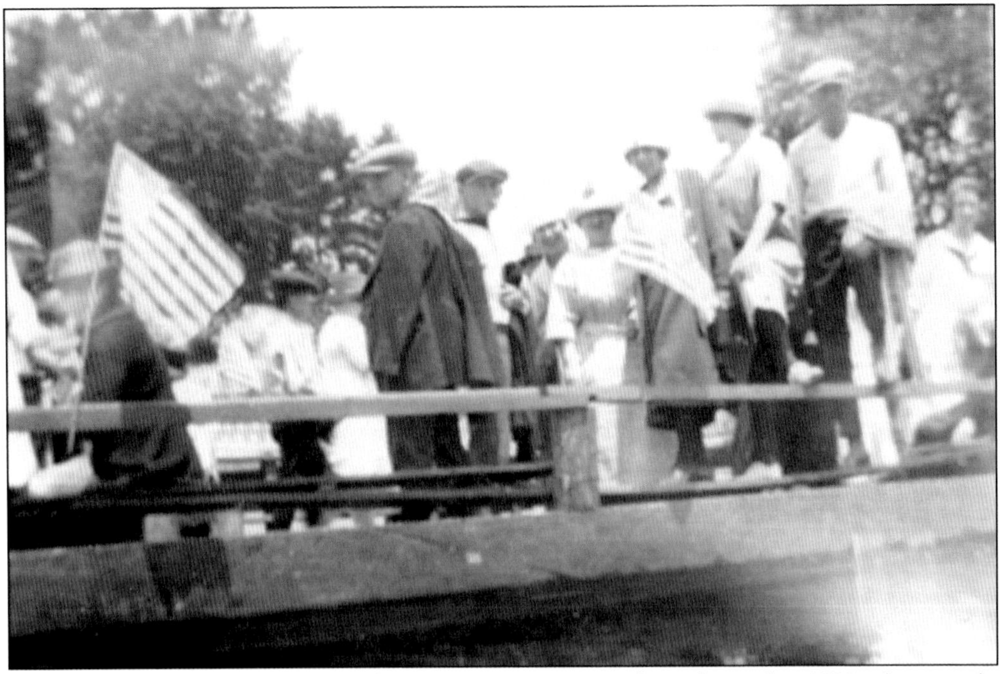

The barge or large ferry appears to have a swinging gate to the right in this 1920s photograph. The passengers were most likely Hooksett or Bow residents who came to enjoy the Fourth of July celebration. (Courtesy of Roland Martel.)

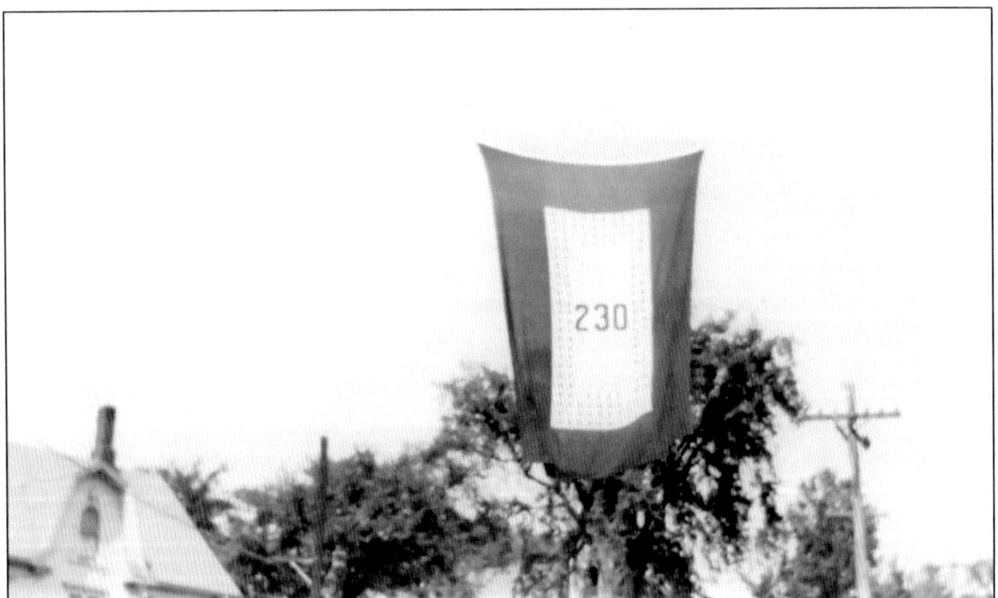

The World War II banner hanging over Main Street in Suncook Village served as a reminder honoring Suncook's service men. The number on the banner represented Suncook men serving in the armed forces during World War II. As the number climbed, the banner was changed. When a life was lost in the war, a large star was added to the banner. (Courtesy of Larry Perron.)

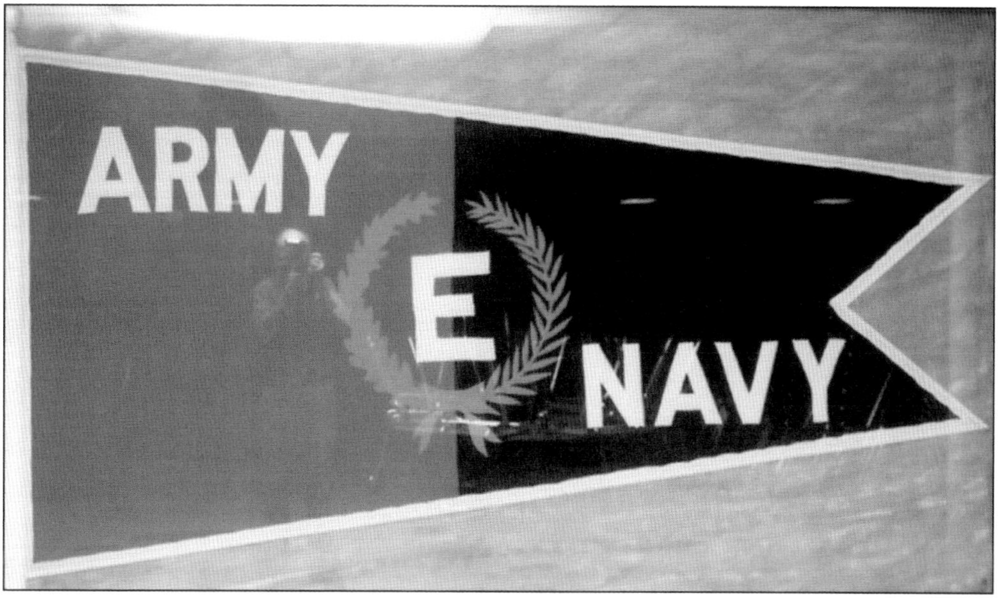

The Army-Navy Award for Excellence in War Production was awarded to the Suncook Mills for their exceptional production of cloth for the armed forces during World War II. The pennant was presented on December 16, 1942, at the China Mill by Lt. Col. J. A. McDonnell of the U.S. Army Air Corps. The Army-Navy E Award was accepted on behalf of the Suncook Mills and employees by Lindsey Weld, the president of the Suncook Mills. (Photograph by Brent Michiels.)

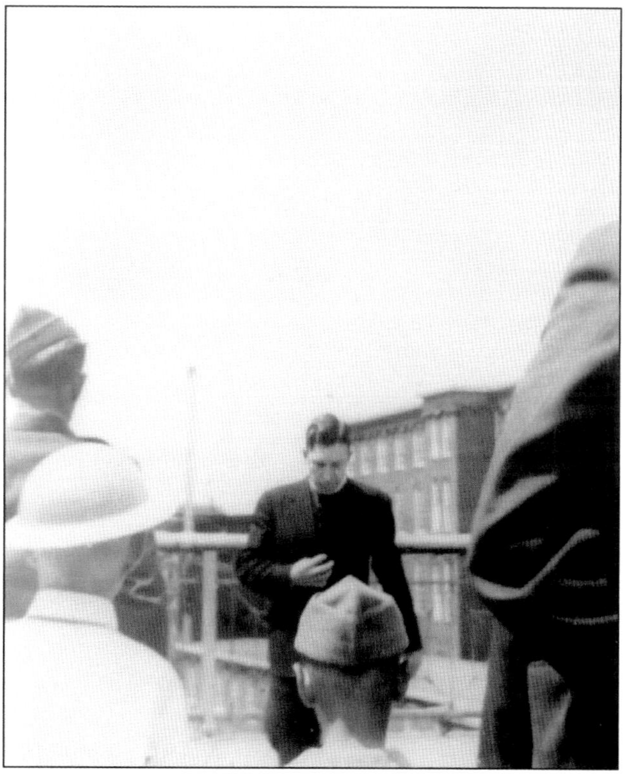

Shown in this photograph from about 1946 is the Memorial Day service on the Main Street Bridge with Fr. Armand Turgeon officiating. A wreath commemorating those in the armed services who were lost at sea during the war was thrown from the Main Street Bridge into the Suncook River as part of the service. (Courtesy of Larry Perron.)

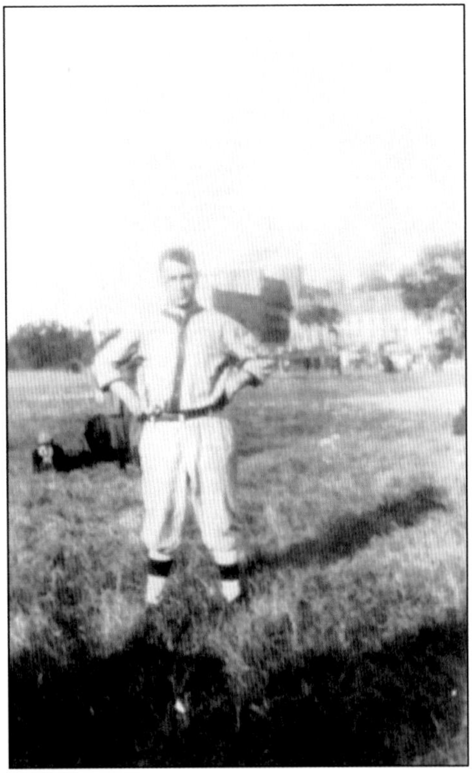

A baseball uniform for one of the Suncook teams is seen here around 1920. The Suncook ball field with the China Mill and tenements are in the background. (Courtesy of Roland Martel.)

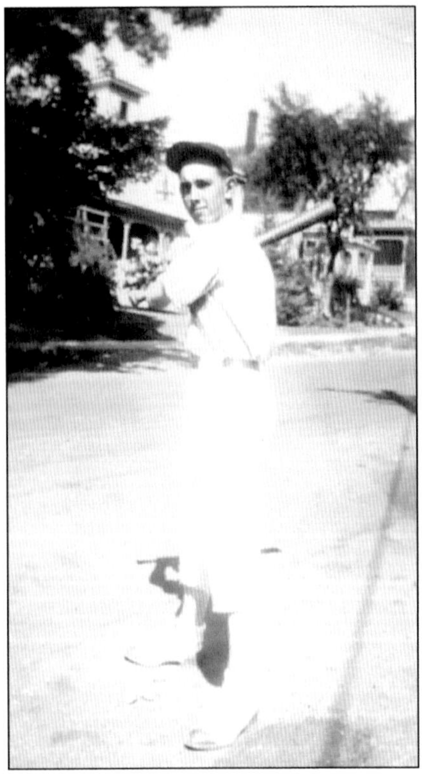

Roland L. Martel played for the Suncook baseball team in 1940. (Courtesy of Roland Martel.)

The Suncook baseball team parades through town on the first day of baseball season. This photograph was taken in 1948 on Main Street with Cass's Hardware in the background. (Courtesy of Leandre Desrochers.)

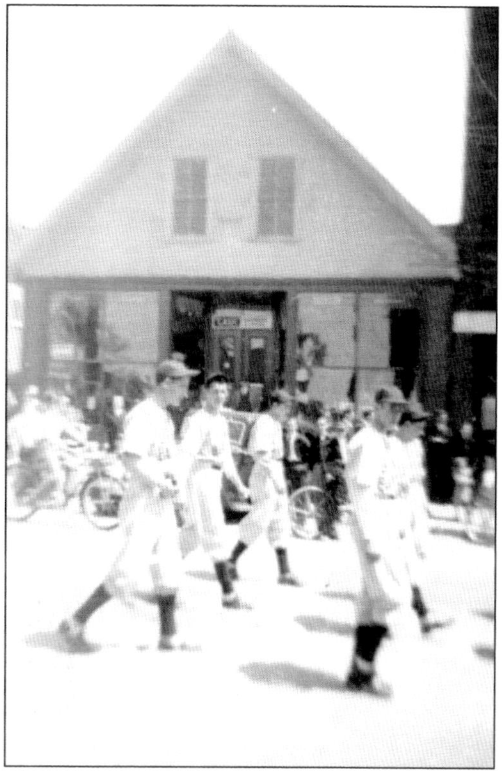

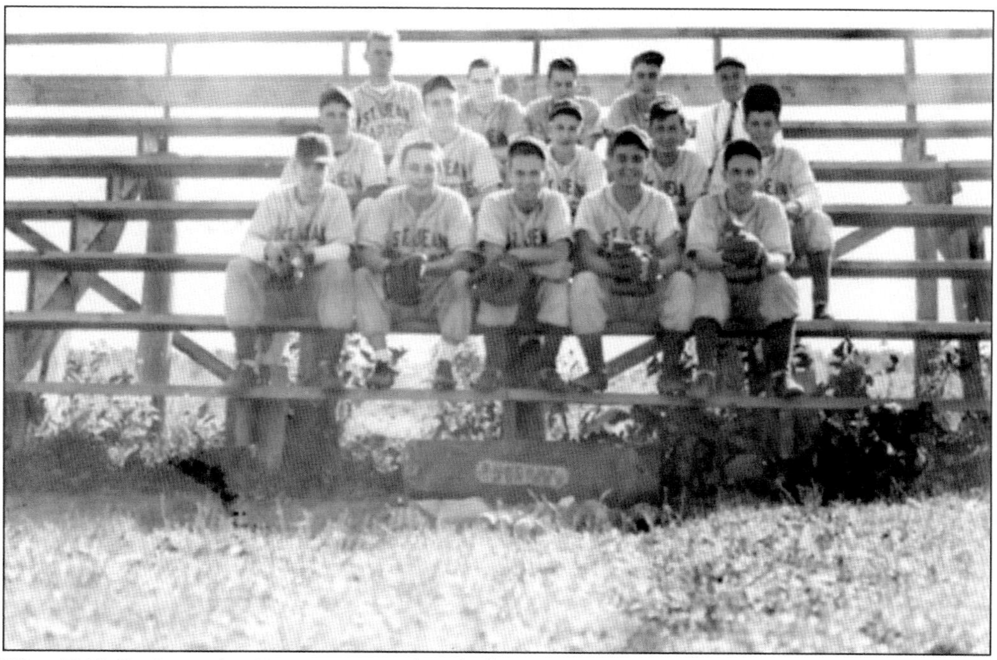

The 1948 St. Jean the Baptist junior baseball team is seen in this photograph. Young boys began playing baseball on the St. John the Baptist team. As they grew older, they joined the Suncook junior baseball team, and afterward joined the Suncook baseball team. (Courtesy of Leandre Desrochers.)

Leandre "Lippy" Desrochers pitches for the Suncook baseball team in 1948. Ferry Street ball field was next to the China Mill. (Courtesy of Leandre Desrochers.)

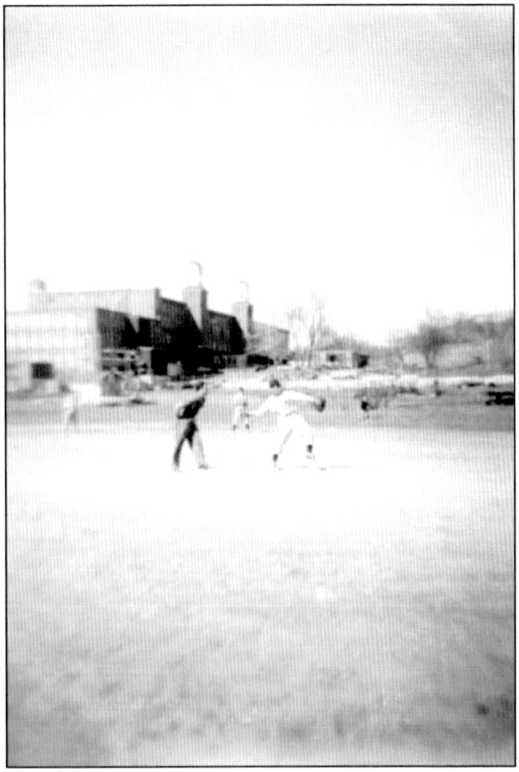

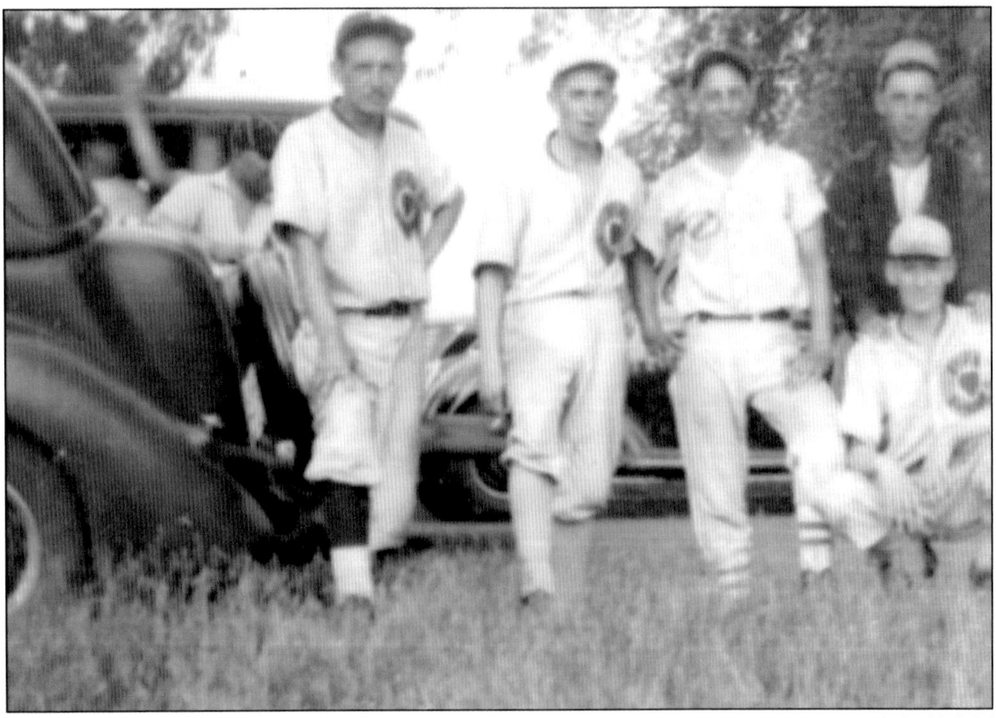

In this photograph, St Jean the Baptist baseball team members are at the Suncook ball field around 1938. (Courtesy of Roland Martel.)

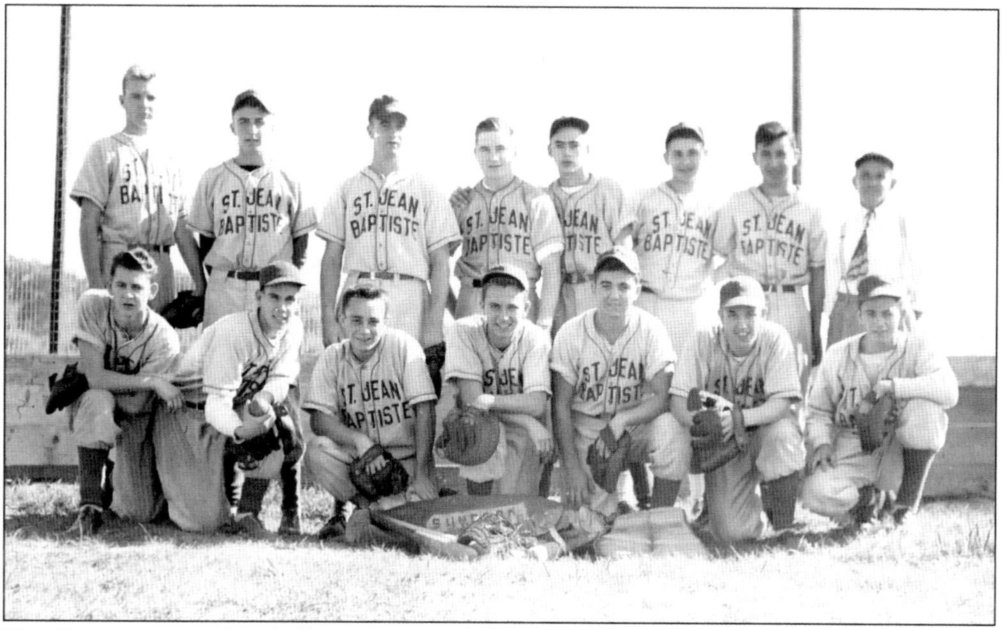

The Suncook junior baseball team was Catholic Youth Organization (CYO) champs in 1948. From left to right are (first row) N. Vezina, R. Plourde, N. Boisvert, H Stokes, L. Desrochers, M. Emond, and G. Proulx; (second row) R. Blackmar, N. Connor, E. Gagne, O. Boisvert, P. Dandurand, R. Campbell, D. Girard, and manager and coach R. Campbell.

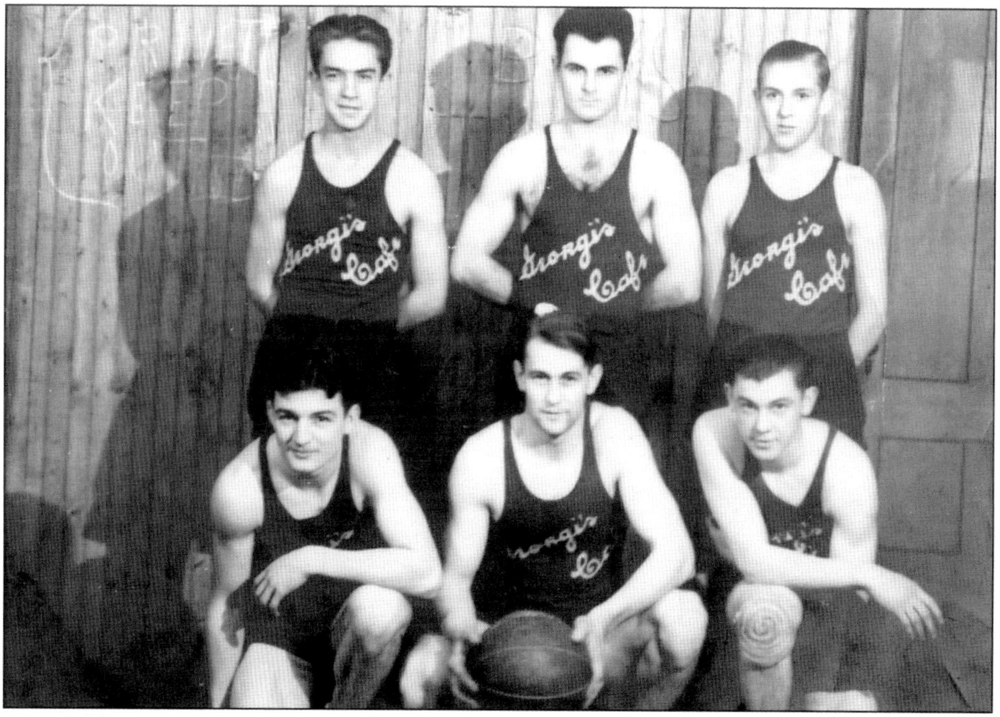

Pictured here is the Georgi's Café basketball team. From left to right are (first row) Lawrence Welch, ? Fowler, and Freddy Gould; (second row) Johnny Gould, Ray Labonte, and Aime Brisbois. (Courtesy of Pembroke Historical Society.)

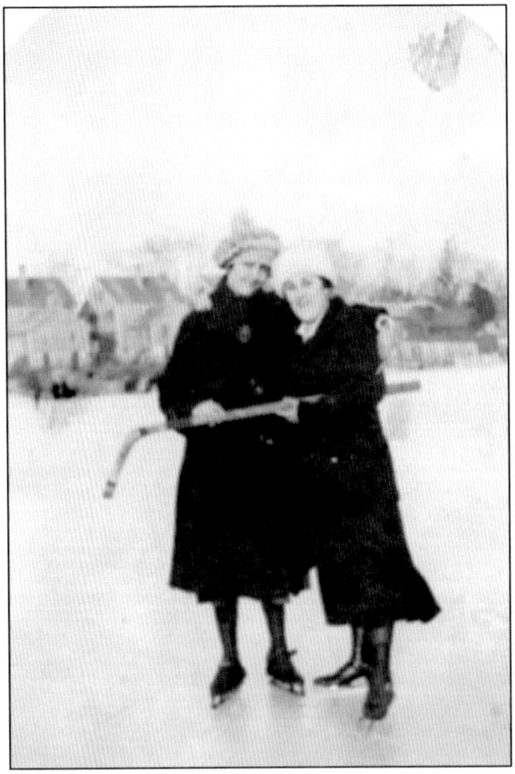

Ice-skaters on the Suncook River pose for this photograph with a hockey stick around 1910. In addition to both rivers, skaters used a man-made skating rink located next to the St. Jean the Baptist Convent and school. (Courtesy of Roland Martel.)

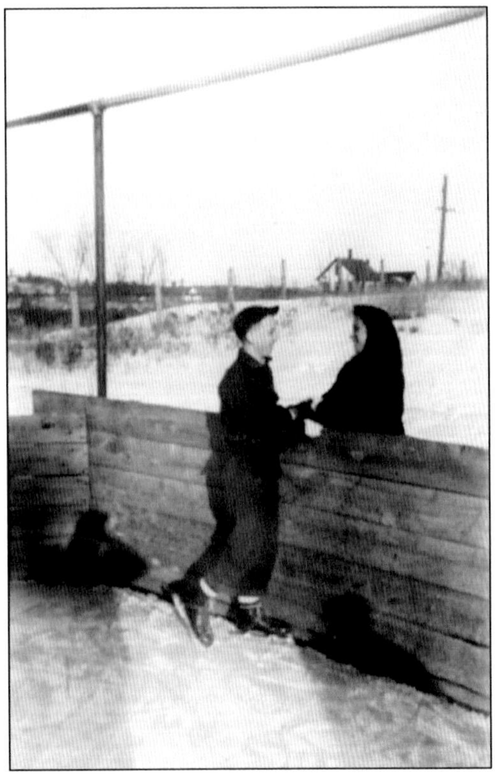

St. Jean the Baptist skating rink, pictured here in the 1930s, was supervised by the parish priests and sisters. The rink was open every night of the week and all day Saturday and Sunday. (Courtesy of Roland Martel.)

Main and Broadway Streets and Loso's field at the top of Broadway were favorite spots for downhill skiing and sledding. Later in the 1940s, a ski tow was installed at Bear Brook State Park, and this, too, became a favorite place for winter sports. (Courtesy of Roland Martel.)

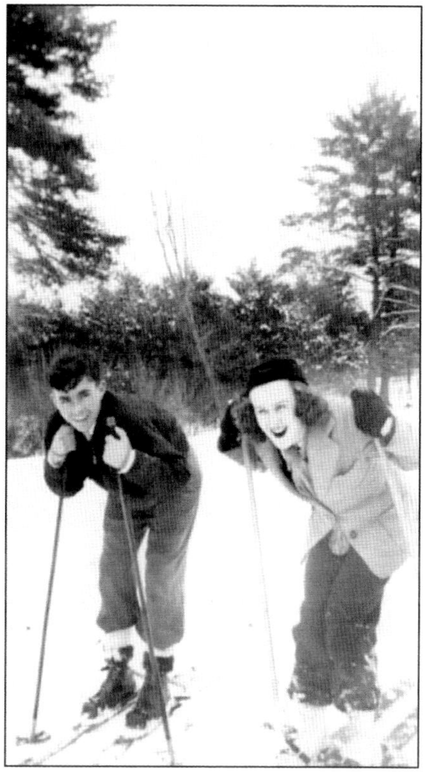

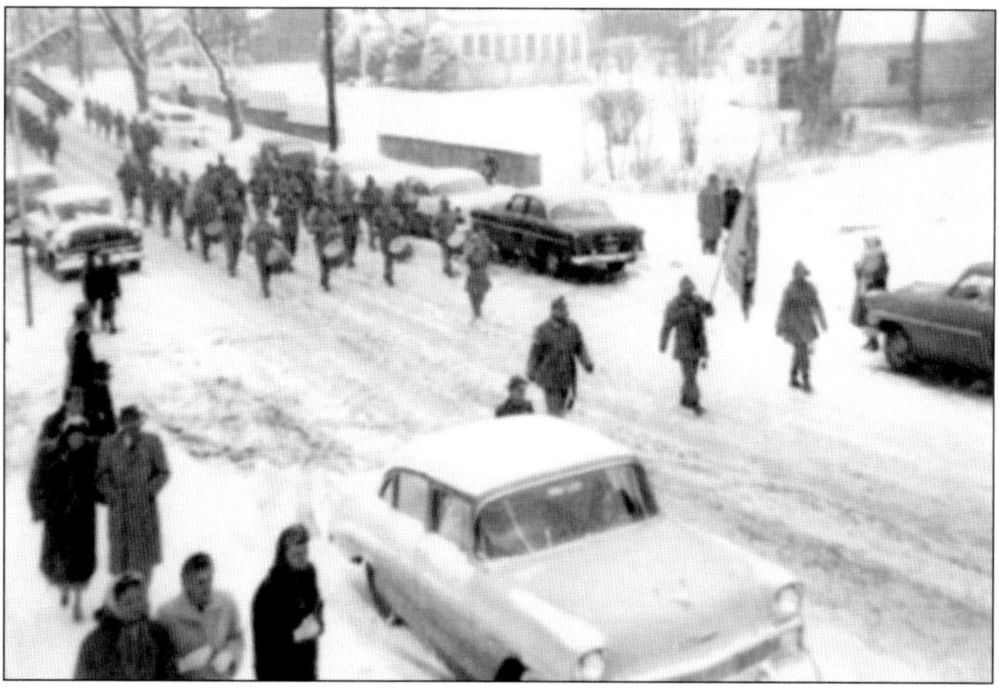

This is the Lion D'Or Snowshoe Club, Drum and Bugle Corp of Suncook parade on Main Street around 1956. Dr. Jean Leblanc's residence and the Allenstown Library are in the background. (Courtesy of Leandre Desrochers.)

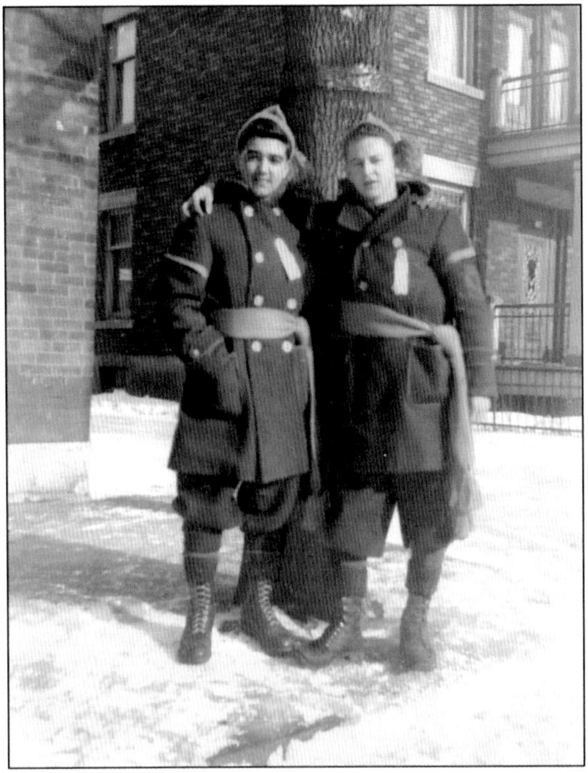

Leandre "Lippy" Desrochers (left) and Norm Vezina are dressed in Lion D'Or Snowshoe Club, Drum and Bugle Corps winter uniforms. This photograph was taken in Montreal in 1949, where they won first prize in the international drum and bugle corps competition. (Courtesy of Leandre Desrochers.)

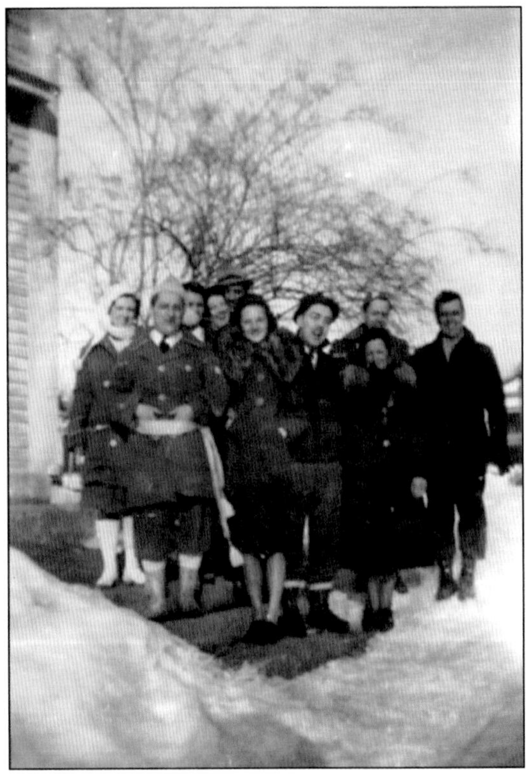

In front of the Roy residence are Lion D'Or Snowshoe Club members and friends after an event in Suncook around 1940. There were many snowshoe clubs in other New England communities and in Canada. It was customary to have competitions and social events with other clubs. (Courtesy of Roland Martel.)

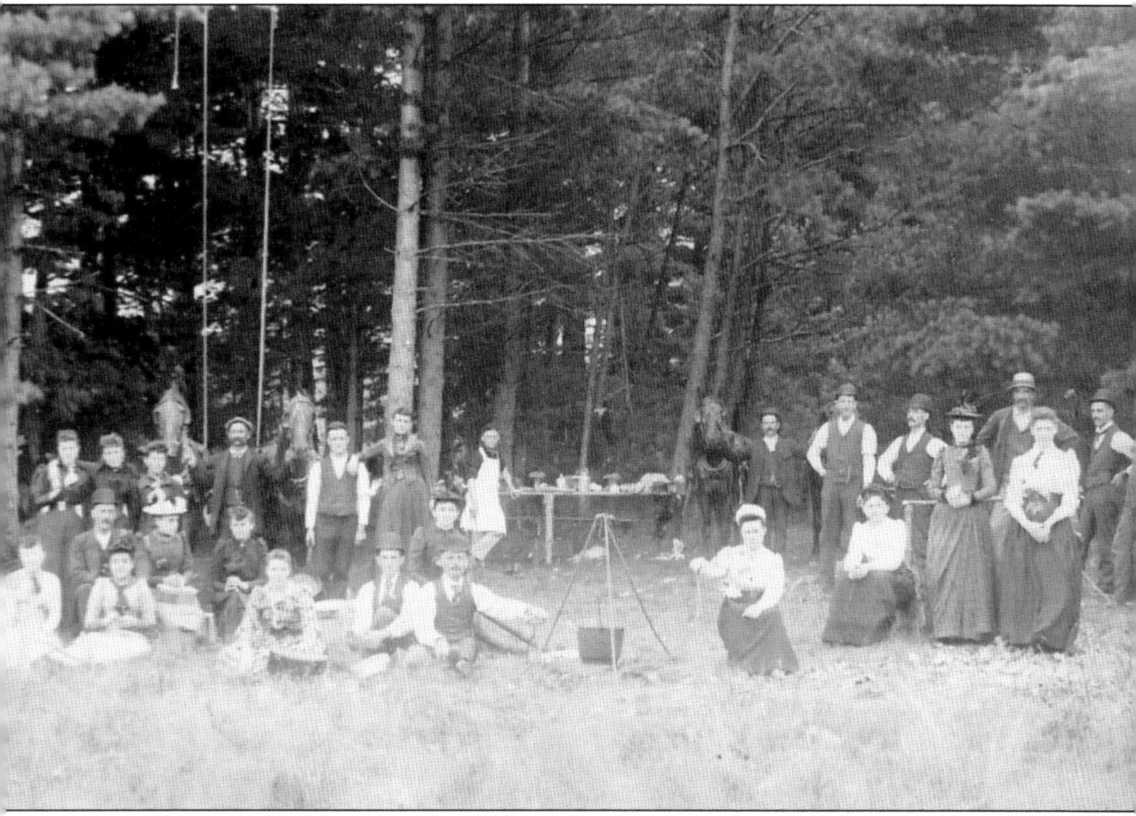

This is the Suncook Mills annual outing around 1900. Teamster Emilien Martel owned a large parcel of land and a camp along the banks of the Suncook River. For many years, the Suncook Mills held their annual outings at this location. Two teamsters with their horses can be seen in the background of this photograph. Wagons transported employees and their families to the picnic grounds for a day of outdoor activities and a catered lunch. Presently this area is known as Clement Road. (Courtesy of Pembroke Historical Society.)

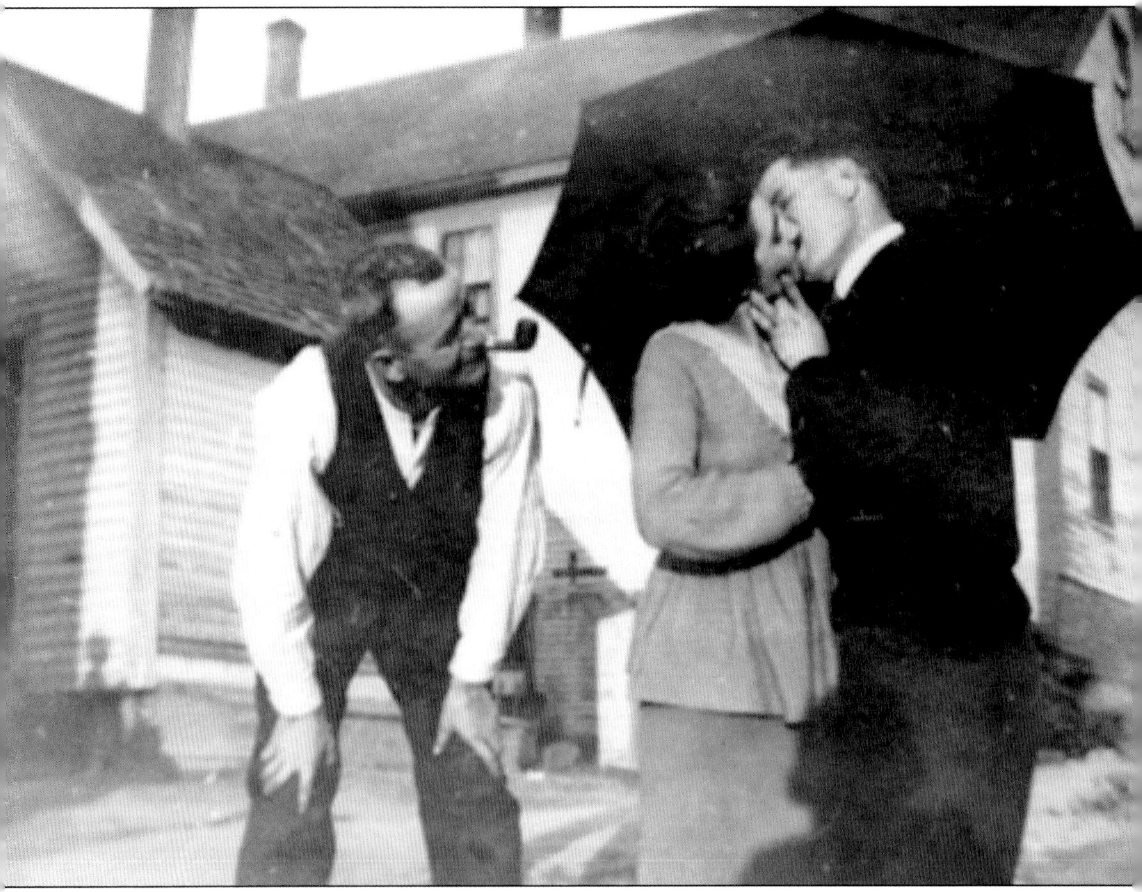

L' amour et `a l'oeil (love and the watchful eye), this humorous photograph was taken during the 1920s. At a glance the image conveys a relaxed lifestyle 60 years after the first French Canadians arrived. The American dream was realized by many who had immigrated to Suncook with hopes for a better life. The assimilation of families new and old in the American tradition transgressed cultural differences and generated the spirit that abounded and created the celebrations of American life in Suncook Village, New Hampshire. (Courtesy of Roland Martel.)

BIBLIOGRAPHY

Aldrich, Frank Levi. "Suncook To-Day." *Granite Monthly* (July 1900). Rumford Press, Concord, NH., July 1900.

Blazon, Gerard. *A Social History Of The French Canadian Community Of Suncook, NH (1870–1920).* University of New Hampshire, Masters Thesis, May 1974. UNH Library.

Carter, Rev. N. F. and Hon T. L. Fowler. *History of Pembroke N.H. 1730-1895.* Concord, NH: Republican Press, 1895.

Dole, Moody. National Register of Historic Places Inventory and Nomination form for the China Mill, 1968.

Garvin, James. Notes on the Methodist Church Building, Suncook Village, NH, Meet Me In Suncook transcript.

Garvn, James. "Pembroke, NH Master Plan." Chapter III, Historic and Cultural Resources, 2004.

Gerber, Bill. "Locks And Canals Of The Merrimack River," Middlesex Canal Association, *Towpath Topics*, Bellerica, MA.

Hamblett, Barbara. "China Mill" By George McConnell, Cooperstown, Graduate Program, 1971.

Martel, Carol A. "Allenstown, NH, Master Plan." Chapter III History and Culture, Town of Allenstown, NH, 2003.

Martel, Carol A. "Suncook Village Walking Tour, Allenstown Script." Transcript from the Meet Me In Suncook Tour, 1998.

Martel, Carol A. *The History of East Allenstown and Bear Brook State Park.* Allenstown, NH: Catamount Publishing, 2003.

McKay, Joyce. "Business Buildings of Suncook Village." Transcript from Meet Me In Suncook, 2007.

Muzzey, Elizabeth. National Register of Historic Places Inventory and Determination of Eligibility form for Suncook Village, 2001. New Hampshire Division of Historical Resources.

Scott, Jeff. "China Mill Tour," 2004. Transcribed by Carol A. Martel.

Suncook Valley Railroad Historical Society. *The Blueberry Express, The History of the Suncook Valley Railroad.* Littleton, MA: Flying Yankee Enterprises, 1985.

Verrette, Fr. Adrien. *The History of The Parish Of Saint John the Baptist, Suncook NH January 3, 1873, From La-Saint Jean-baptiste, Suncook, New Hampshire, compte-Rendue, Manchester, New Hampshire: L'Avenir National, 1940.* Translated by James L. Garvin.

Wilson, Artelia. Old Suncook Village vitalization area architectural survey, 1983.

Wilson, Kenneth M. *New England Glass and Glassmaking.* New York: Thomas Y. Crowell, 1972.

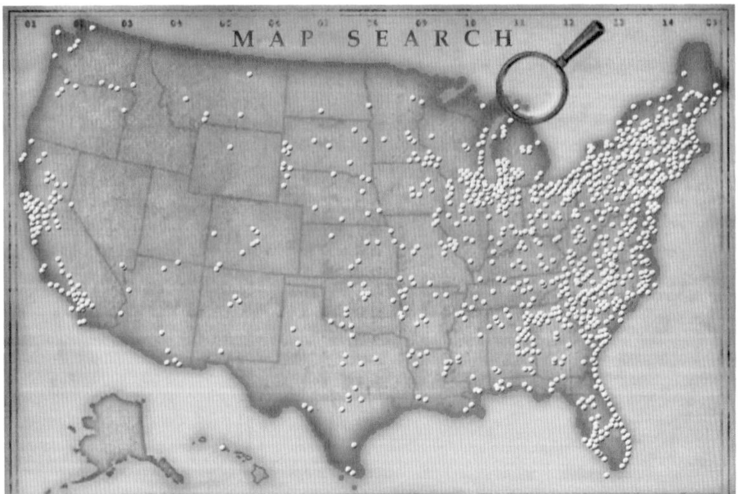
MAP SEARCH